Nelson's Tea

on

FIRST CORINTHIANS

Thomas Nelson Publishers

Portions of this volume (as identified in the Acknowledgements) originally appeared in: *Talk Thru the Bible,* by Bruce Wilkinson and Kenneth Boa, copyright © 1983 by Thomas Nelson Publishers; *Nelson's New Illustrated Bible Manners & Customs,* copyright © 1999 by Howard F. Vos; *Illustrated Bible Handbook,* by Larry Richards, copyright © 1982, 1987 by Word, Inc.; *Nelson's New Illustrated Bible Commentary,* copyright © 1999 by Thomas Nelson Inc.; *Believer's Bible Commentary,* copyright © 1989, 1990, 1992, 1995 by William MacDonald; *With the Word,* copyright © 1991 by Warren W. Wiersbe; *Pathways to Pure Power,* by Gary Curtis and Jack W. Hayford, copyright © 1994 by Jack W. Hayford; *1, 2 Corinthians,* by Kenneth Chafin, copyright © 1985 by Word, Inc.; and *The Word in Life Study Bible,* copyright © 1993, 1996 by Thomas Nelson Inc.

Unless otherwise indicated, all Scripture quotations are from the New King James Version, copyright © 1979, 1980, 1982, 1990 by Thomas Nelson, Inc.

Verses marked "KJV" are taken from the King James Version of the Bible.

The Scripture quotations contained herein from the New Revised Standard Version (NRSV) of the Bible are copyright © 1989 by the Division of Christian Education of the National Council of the Churches of Christ in the U.S.A., and are used by permission. All rights reserved.

Verses marked "RSV" are taken from the Holy Bible: Revised Standard Version, second edition, copyright © 1946, 1952, 1971, 1973 by the Division of Christian Education of the NCCCUSA. Used by permission.

Scripture quotations marked "NIV" are taken from the Holy Bible: New International Version, copyright © 1973, 1978, 1984 by the International Bible Society. Used by permission of Zondervan Publishing House. All rights reserved.

Scripture quotations marked "NEB" are taken from the New English Bible, Copyright © 1961, 1970 by The Delegates of The Oxford University Press and The Syndics of The Cambridge University Press, used by permission.

Nelson's Teacher's Resource on First Corinthians

ISBN 0-7852-4982-6

Printed in the United States of America
1 2 3 4 5 6 7 — 06 05 04 03 02

Contents

Acknowledgments   v

How to Use This Book   vii

1. Introduction to 1 Corinthians   1

2. Outline of 1 Corinthians   11

3. Chapter-by-Chapter Commentary on 1 Corinthians   13

4. Concise Commentary on 1 Corinthians   29

5. Extended Commentary on 1 Corinthians   75

6. Background Studies for Deeper Understanding   185

     A. Biblical Word Studies   185

     B. Historical and Cultural Information   188

     C. Context and Application Articles   193

7. Questions for Personal Reflection and Group Discussion   203

Appendix: Illustrations, Outlines, and Sermon Starters   213

Acknowledgments

Thomas Nelson has been publishing helpful biblical studies resources for many years. We have selected the best of our materials on 1 Corinthians to bring you this *Teacher's Resource* on Paul's first epistle to the church at Corinth. Our thanks to the following authors for their permission to use their work in this handy compilation.

- Bruce Wilkinson and Kenneth Boa, authors of *Talk Thru the Bible*. Excerpts from this volume appear as the Introduction to 1 Corinthians (chapter 1) and as the Outline of 1 Corinthians (chapter 2) in this book.
- Howard Vos, author of *Nelson's New Illustrated Bible Manners & Customs*. Some material from this book appears in the Introduction to 1 Corinthians (chapter 1) and in the Background Studies (chapter 6).
- Larry Richards, author of *Illustrated Bible Handbook*. His material appears in this *Teacher's Resource* as the Chapter-by-Chapter Commentary on 1 Corinthians (chapter 3).
- Earl Radmacher, general editor, and H. Wayne House, New Testament editor of *Nelson's New Illustrated Bible Commentary*. They contributed the Concise Commentary on 1 Corinthians (chapter 4).
- William MacDonald, author of *Believer's Bible Commentary*. His insightful verse-by-verse comments on 1 Corinthians appear as the Extended Commentary in this book (chapter 5).
- Finally, several authors contributed to the background studies, questions, and illustrations which appear at the back of this book. These contributors include Gary Curtis and Jack W. Hayford, authors of

Pathways to Pure Power; Warren Wiersbe, author of *With the Word;* Kenneth Chafin, author of *1, 2, Corinthians* in the Mastering the New Testament series; Howard Vos, author of *Nelson's New Illustrated Bible Manners & Customs;* and the writers and editors of the *Word in Life Study Bible.*

How to Use This Book

Paul's first letter to the Corinthian church is one of the most important books of the New Testament. Among the issues which he explores in this masterful epistle are unity in the church, Christian freedom, church discipline, marriage in God's plan, honoring Christ through observance of the Lord's Supper, spiritual gifts, the appropriate exercise of gifts in the body of Christ, the resurrection of christ and its significance for believers, and the centrality of Christian love. These issues are just as timely and significant for believers today as they were when Paul first wrote 1 Corinthians about A.D. 56.

This *Teacher's Resource on 1 Corinthians* has been created to help you get to know this key New Testament epistle as you have never known it before. It is also designed to help you communicate its Christian truths to others—through teaching, preaching, or informal devotional presentations. Whether you study 1 Corinthians for your own personal edification, present its major truths to others in survey fashion, or teach through it meticulously on a verse-by-verse basis, you will find the help you need in this *Teacher's Resource.*

Matters of general information about 1 Corinthians are covered in chapter 1. This thorough introduction to the book helps you understand the background, setting, and historical factors that led to the emergence of 1 Corinthians from the pen of Paul. Equally helpful as an overview element is the outline of the epistle in chapter 2.

The heart of this *Teacher's Resource on 1 Corinthians* consists of the three different commentaries (chapters 3–5). The Chapter-by-Chapter Commentary works through the epistle in chapter-size strokes. The Concise

Commentary focuses on major themes in groups of verses. And the Extended Commentary uses a thorough, in depth, verse-by-verse approach to exegesis of the content.

You will find helpful information in each of these commentaries. But all three are included in the book to give you a choice in personal learning and presentation styles. If you are looking for a quick overview of the epistle, use the shorter commentaries. For a longer and deeper approach, use the Extended Commentary.

Throughout all these commentaries you will find three different cross-reference icons to the valuable information at the back of the book: background studies (chapter 6), questions (chapter 7), and illustrative and communicative material (the appendix).

This symbol alerts you to helpful questions that you can use as a review for your own personal learning or as discussion starters in a class setting.

Check these items with a cultural historical, or contextual twist to increase your understanding of a theme, a verse, or a group of verses in 1 Corinthians.

This symbol sends you to teaching or communication suggestions that can enhance your presentation of the insights of 1 Corinthians in a group setting.

Blessings upon you as you are confronted by the power of God's truth in 1 Corinthians and as you pass this truth on to others.

1
Introduction to 1 Corinthians

(From *Talk Thru the Bible,* by Bruce Wilkinson and Kenneth Boa)

CORINTH, the most important city in Greece during Paul's day, was a bustling hub of worldwide commerce, degraded culture, and idolatrous religion. There Paul founded a church (Acts 18:1–17), and two of his letters are addressed "To the church of God which is at Corinth."

First Corinthians reveals the problems, pressures, and struggles of a church called out of a pagan society. Paul addresses a variety of problems in the lifestyle of the Corinthian church: factions, lawsuits, immorality, questionable practices, abuse of the Lord's Supper, and spiritual gifts. In addition to words of discipline, Paul shares words of counsel in answer to questions raised by the Corinthian believers.

The oldest recorded title of this epistle is *Pros Korinthious A*, in effect, the "First to the Corinthians." The A was no doubt a later addition to distinguish this book from Second Corinthians.

AUTHORSHIP

Pauline authorship of First Corinthians is almost universally accepted, since Paul is cited twice as its author (1:1, 2; 16:21). Instances of this widely held belief can be found as early as A.D. 95, when Clement of Rome wrote to the Corinthian church and cited this epistle in regard to their continuing problem of factions among themselves.

SETTING

Corinth was a key city in ancient Greece until it was destroyed by the Romans in 146 B.C. Julius Caesar rebuilt it as a Roman colony in 46 B.C. and it grew and prospered, becoming the capital of the province of Achaia. Its official language was Latin, but the common language remained Greek. In Paul's day Corinth was the metropolis of the Peloponnesus (southern or lower Greece) since it was strategically located on a narrow isthmus between the Aegean Sea and the Adriatic Sea that connects the Peloponnesus with northern Greece. Because of its two seaports it became a commercial center, and many small ships were rolled or dragged across the Corinthian isthmus to avoid the dangerous 200-mile voyage around southern Greece. Nero and others attempted to build a canal at the narrowest point, but this was not achieved until 1893. This cosmopolitan center thrived on commerce, entertainment, vice, and corruption; pleasure-seekers came there to spend money on a holiday from morality. Corinth became so notorious for its evils that the term *Korinthiazomai* ("to act like a Corinthian") became a synonym for debauchery and prostitution.

In Paul's day the population of Corinth was approximately 700,000, about two-thirds of whom were slaves. The diverse population produced no philosophers, but Greek philosophy influenced any speculative thought that was there. In spite of these obstacles to the gospel, Paul was able to establish a church in Corinth on his second missionary journey (3:6, 10; 4:15; Acts 18:1–7). Persecution in Macedonia drove him south to Athens, and from there he proceeded to Corinth. He made tents with Aquila and Priscilla and reasoned with the Jews in the synagogue. Silas and Timothy joined him (they evidently

The ruins of Corinth, one of the wealthiest and most immoral of ancient cities (1 Cor. 5:1; 6:9–11) (Photo by Gustav Jeeninga)

brought a gift from Philippi; see 2 Cor. 11:8–9; Phil. 4:15), and Paul began to devote all his time to spreading the gospel. Paul wrote First and Second Thessalonians, moved his ministry from the synagogue to the house of Titius Justus because of opposition, and converted Crispus, the leader of the synagogue. Paul taught the Word of God in Corinth for eighteen months in A.D. 51–52.

PAUL'S MINISTRY IN CORINTH

What sort of place was Corinth when Paul arrived and what sort of ministry did he have in it? Corinth controlled the trade routes between the Peloponnesus and central Greece and across the Isthmus of Corinth. In this connection, she had built a tramway across the Isthmus and was served by ports on the Saronic and Corinthian gulfs. She administered the Isthmian Games, thereby serving as a religious, athletic, and cohesive center in Greece. The city itself lay about a mile and one-half south of the Corinthian Gulf on the north side of its acropolis at an altitude of about 400 feet. The acropolis towered about 1,500 feet over the city to an altitude of 1,886 feet. From its peak on a clear day the Acropolis at Athens can be plainly seen.

A wall over six miles in circumference enclosed the city and its acropolis. Numerous large towers were spaced along this wall. In the north central part of town, about equidistant from the east and west walls (about a mile from each) stood the Agora, nerve center of the metropolis. Outside the walls in the surrounding plain stretched grain fields, olive groves, vineyards, and other agricultural holdings of the city.

As a new city—less than 100 years old when Paul visited it—Corinth had not had time to develop a social structure with an aristocracy possessing illustrious genealogies. Probably the social and economic structure was more fluid than at most other centers in Greece. Many of those possessing wealth were the *nouveaux riches,* with all of the attendant inadequacies of that class. Since Corinth had not had time to develop a native culture, the culture it had was imitative and, as a result of the overweening economic interests of the community, was only a shallow veneer.

Since much of the population was mobile (sailors, businessmen, and government officials), it was cut off from the inhibitions of a settled society. To make matters worse, the Corinthians commonly practiced religious prostitution in connection with the temples of the city. For instance, religious prostitution employed one thousand priestesses of the Temple of Aphrodite on the Acropolis. The social mobility and the evils of religious practices produced a general corruption of society. "Corinthian morals" became a byword even in the pagan Roman world.

It is no wonder that Paul had so much to say about the sacredness of the body in his first Corinthian letter. And if he wrote the epistle to the Romans from Corinth (as is commonly believed), he had plenty of reason for condemning the unmentionable practices alluded to in Romans 1. The conditions which Paul and the Christian gospel faced in Corinth should give pause to the modern preacher who laments the moral corruption of his own day and feels that his task is almost impossible in such a context. Conditions in Corinth were far worse. The message and power of the gospel are the same in the twentieth century as they were in the first.

The Agora. The Agora served as the center of Corinthian life. Located in the north central part of town, it measured about 700 feet east and west and 300 feet north and south. Following the natural configuration of the land, the southern section was about 13 feet higher than the northern part. At the dividing line of the two levels a row of low buildings flanked the rostrum, which served as a speaker's stand for public addresses and a judgment seat for magistrates. Here Gallio heard the case that the Jews presented against Paul (see Acts 18:12–17).

On the east side of the Agora stood a large basilica of the Augustan period known as the Julian Basilica. In this court building many of the cases must have been tried in which believers were going to law before unbelievers (1 Cor. 6:1–8). Alternatively, another court building stood at the south of the Agora, south of the south stoa.

The south stoa stretched across almost the entire south side of the Agora. About 500 feet long, it was probably the largest secular structure in Greece proper and consisted of a double colonnade behind which were thirty-three small shops. All of these except two had a well in them, connected with a water channel, which in turn was connected to the Peirene Fountain. These were apparently wine shops, each with its private cooler. Other perishables were sold there as well.

The stoa also contained shops for the sale of meat. In one of them an inscription "Lucius the butcher" was found. In another an inscription appeared which called the shop a macellum, the Latin equivalent of the Greek *makellon,* used in 1 Corinthians 10:25 and commonly translated "meat market." Paul dealt with the question of meats offered to idols here and in effect tells his readers that they need not be concerned about the source of meats displayed in public markets. If the meats retailed there had been sold by the temples to legitimate businessmen, housewives were not responsible for that fact.

Eating meat or other foods offered to idols involved more than what one bought in the market, however. It was common practice for people who were or were not devotees of a pagan deity to share in the eating of sacrificial meat in the deity's temple grounds. That such a practice existed in Corinth is evident

Ruins of the civil law court known as the Julian Basilica in ancient Corinth. Some of the charges of the Corinthian Christians against one another (1 Cor. 6:1–11) may have been reviewed on this very site. (Photo by Howard Vos)

from the fact that numerous dining rooms have been found on a terrace of the acropolis of Corinth in the sacred grounds of Demeter and Kore. They have appeared elsewhere in Greece as well.

As a matter of fact, Paul specifically referred to eating in a dining room of a temple in Corinth food offered to idols (1 Cor. 8:10). He observed that such an act might not negatively affect the person who did so because he had in his own mind dismissed the reality of the god. But the act of eating might serve as a stumbling block to brothers who were weaker (1 Cor. 8:11–13) or had not yet fully turned to God from idols (1 Thess. 1:9).

This knowing participation in religious feasting is what the Council of Jerusalem must have had primarily in mind when it commanded that Gentiles "abstain from things offered to idols, from blood, from things strangled and from sexual immorality" (Acts 15:29 NKJV). The "sexual immorality" in this context certainly involved abstaining from patronizing the religious prostitutes connected with pagan temples all over the Mediterranean world.

Religious Conditions. Of course Corinth, like all other Greco-Roman cities, was given over to idolatry. Towering above the Agora on the northwest, on a rocky terrace of its own, stood the Temple of Apollo. In the terror of 146 B.C. the Romans did not destroy the temple built during the sixth century B.C. The temple measured 174 feet long by 69 feet wide, and the 38 columns of its peri-style stood almost 24 feet in height. These fluted Doric columns were more impressive than many in Greece because they were made of single blocks of stone instead of being built up with drums of stone.

Cut into the hill just to the northwest of the Agora rose the great theater of Corinth. Its seating capacity was probably over 18,000, but it is impossible to give an accurate estimate for Paul's day. Our interest in the theater centers in the fact that near the stage building is an inscription that concerns Erastus, an aedile (a Roman municipal official) of the city who laid a pavement at his own expense. Paul in writing to the Romans from Corinth sent greetings from a "chamberlain" (Gk., *oikonomos*) or steward by this name (Rom. 16:23). Erastus is also referred to in 2 Timothy 4:20 and Acts 19:22. A Roman aedile and a Greek *oikonomos* would both have been commissioners of streets and public buildings. Perhaps the Erastus of this inscription may be equated with the person of the same name mentioned in the New Testament. Some scholars think so.

The Race and the Isthmian Games. When Paul came across the isthmus to Corinth, he passed the location of the Isthmian Games. The following year, in April and May of A.D. 51, while he was still in Corinth, the biennial games would have been held. Paul probably saw these. And perhaps the opportunity of preaching to the large crowds gathering for the event had led Paul to go to Corinth in the first place. Some scholars think so. In any case, Paul was probably alluding to this important event in the life of the people in 1 Corinthians 9:24–27.

The competitors came chiefly from Corinth, Aegina, Thebes, Athens, and some of the islands of the Aegean, but crowds at the Isthmian Games probably exceeded those at the Olympics. Corinth administered the games. Held in honor of Poseidon, god of the sea, and beginning with a sacrifice to the god, the games included athletic, equestrian, and musical competitions, and perhaps also a boat race. They held separate competitions for men, youths, and boys.

The athletic events included footraces of 200 and 800 yards, races in armor, throwing the discus and javelin, two-horse chariot racing, the Pentathlon (running, jumping, discus and javelin throwing, and wrestling), and the Pankration (a combination of boxing and wrestling). It is difficult to determine exactly what events occurred during the first century A.D. when the great athletic festivals of Greece were in a state of decline.

Greek athletics had become degraded and corrupt during Paul's lifetime—and they were nowhere more degraded than at the Isthmia. Professionalism had taken over, with plenty of quackery in training and dieting. The gymnasia, instead of producing healthy, useful citizens, had become schools of idleness and immorality; from a physical and military point of view the whole nation

The Temple of Apollo at Corinth and the acropolis of the city in the background. (Photo by Howard Vos)

had degenerated. The victor's crown seems to have been withered wild celery during the first century A.D., a corruptible crown indeed (1 Cor. 9:25).

Judging from the available accounts of what went on at the Isthmian Games, one gets the impression that they were more like "old home week" than a serious religious and athletic event. Philosophers parried intellectual blows; their students wrangled. Magicians showed off their stunts. Fortune-tellers preyed on a gullible and superstitious public. Hucksters hawked their wares among the assembled throngs.

The area given over to the Isthmian Games was about six miles from Corinth, just south

Starting blocks at Isthmian Race Track. (Photo by Howard Vos)

of the east end of the present Corinth Canal. In recent years the area has been quite thoroughly investigated and largely excavated. The three main structures at the site are the Temple of Poseidon, the stadium, and the theater. Originally constructed in the seventh century, the temple was ravaged by fire and was rebuilt about 470 B.C. Heavily damaged by fire in 390 B.C., it was restored and stood until the mid-sixth century A.D. Inside stood colossal statues of Poseidon, lord of the sea, and the goddess Amphitrite, joint ruler of the sea. Near the

The theater at Corinth. (Photo by Howard Vos)

temple stood an impressive altar to Poseidon.

From the temple to the stadium, located to the southeast of the sanctuary, stretched an avenue lined with pine trees and statues of victorious athletes. About fifty yards northeast of the sanctuary of Poseidon stood the theater, where musical and dramatic events could be staged. Very likely the Isthmian Games occurred prior to Paul's arraignment before Gallio. After his acquittal he remained in Corinth a little longer.

Paul Before Gallio. One of the governors of Achaia, Gallio, holds special interest for us because of his contact with the apostle Paul (see Acts 18:12–17). He came from a distinguished family and was a brother of the philosopher Seneca. After he was adopted by the orator and senator L. Junius Gallio, he was known by the name Gallio.

The date of his governorship in Corinth is of special interest in fixing the chronology of Paul's missionary activity. An inscription found at Delphi indicates that Gallio probably took office about the beginning of July of A.D. 51. Presumably Paul arrived in Corinth before the procurator took office, perhaps in A.D. 50. The hearing before Gallio probably took place near the beginning of the governor's term of office, after Paul had been there for a year. The edict of Claudius, which expelled the Jews from Rome and sent Aquila and Priscilla to Corinth (Acts 18:2), may be dated in A.D. 49. The Council of Jerusalem (Acts 15) must have taken place in A.D. 48. The first missionary journey, then, probably occurred in A.D. 46–47.

Paul appeared publicly before Gallio-before the judgment seat or bema or rostrum in the agora in Corinth. Any tourist may see the excavated remains of it there today. What the Jews meant to say in their charge ("This fellow persuades men to worship God contrary to the law," Acts 18:13) is not clear. Perhaps they were deliberately ambiguous. Did they mean contrary to Jewish law or to Roman law, which forbade proselytizing of Roman citizens? But there is no evidence here that he had been involved in converting Roman citizens. Judaism was a legally recognized religion in the Roman Empire. Perhaps these Jews were trying to get Gallio to distinguish between Jews and Christians and to declare that Christians were operating outside the Roman law. That would have embroiled Christians in real trouble.

Gallio concluded that he was dealing with a prejudiced group and that the issue was an internal Jewish dispute, a quibbling with "words and names." So he ruled that it was beyond his legal jurisdiction to try the matter and dismissed the hearing—even before Paul had a chance to defend himself. Gallio's action should not be taken to mean that he was indifferent to religion, as Bible expositors often claim, but rather that he refused to be involved in a case over which he had no rightful or clear jurisdiction.

DATE OF WRITING

When Paul was teaching and preaching in Ephesus during his third missionary journey, he was disturbed by reports from the household of Chloe concerning quarrels in the church at Corinth (1:11). The church sent a delegation of three men (16:17), who apparently brought a letter that requested Paul's judgment on certain issues (7:1). Paul wrote this epistle as his response to the problems and questions of the Corinthians (he had already written a previous letter; 5:9). It may be that the men who came from Corinth took this letter back with them. Paul was planning to leave Ephesus (16:5–8), indicating that First Corinthians was written in A.D. 56. The Corinthian church would have been about four years old at that time.

THEMES AND PURPOSE

Though true believers, the Corinthians had a lot of growing up to do. They had to stop following the immoral, selfish, and contentious ways of their pagan neighbors in Corinth. One can sense the disappointment of a hurt father in Paul's stern words for the Corinthians. Yet Paul, like a surgeon, diagnosed the problem and aimed his efforts straight at the source: pride and a lack of true love in the church.

This epistle is extremely practical in its thrust, and it focuses on basic social, moral, and spiritual issues. Unlike Romans, First Corinthians is not rhetorically elegant; it is plain, earnest, and unvarnished. The unusual simplicity and directness of this letter is appropriate to the practical content. The sentences are uncomplicated, and Paul forcefully amplifies his thoughts with abundant literary devices (narrative, sarcasm, appeal, etc.).

THEOLOGICAL CONTRIBUTION OF 1 CORINTHIANS

The problems Paul faced in the church at Corinth were complex and explosive. The correspondence that resulted is rich and profound in theological insight. While addressing the problems in Corinth, the apostle reaches some of the most sublime heights in all New Testament literature.

Corinth, like its neighboring city of Athens, symbolized Greek culture in its desire for wisdom and power. Paul must have been tempted to write to the Greeks as a Christian philosopher (1 Cor. 2:4). He rejected this tendency, however, and relied instead on the irony of the cross, "to the Jews a stumbling block and to the Greeks foolishness" (1 Cor. 1:23). The foolishness of the gospel—indeed, its offensiveness to cultured Greeks—was indication of its power to save. To those who respond, "Christ is the power of God and the wisdom of God" (1 Cor. 1:24). According to Paul, the preaching of the Cross is not a human teaching but a revelation of the Spirit, who makes known the mind of Christ (1 Cor. 2:10–16). The centrality of the Cross overcomes all divisions within the church.

Since many of the problems arising in Corinth concerned behavior and morals, Paul majored on ethical advice in this epistle. The leading principle he uses is that "all things are lawful for me, but not all things are helpful" (1 Cor. 6:12; 10:23). Christians ought to use their freedom not for self-advantage, but for the glory of God and the good of their neighbors. This principle goes beyond legislating simply "dos and don'ts." Instead, it cultivates a mature and responsible faith that will provide guidance for every moral problem.

First Corinthians is also important because of its teaching on the gifts of the Spirit (ch. 12) and the resurrection of the dead (ch. 15). Paul recognized a variety of gifts (12:4–10), but insisted that "one and the same Spirit" gives them. The body consists of different parts, but remains one organism. Likewise, Christ's body of believers consists of members with different gifts, each given by the one Spirit.

First Corinthians 15 is our earliest record of the resurrection in the New Testament. Unless Christ has been resurrected, Paul maintained, the faith of Christians is empty (15:12–19). As death came through Adam, so new life comes through Christ (15:21, 45). The resurrection of Jesus is the "firstfruits" (15:20) of the victory to come. Because of the resurrection the believer can confess, "O death, where is your sting?" (15:55).

2
Outline of 1 Corinthians

(From *Talk Thru the Bible*, by Bruce Wilkinson and Kenneth Boa)

PART ONE:
IN ANSWER TO CHLOE'S REPORT OF DIVISIONS
(1:1–4:21)

I. Introduction (1:1–9)
   A. Greetings of Grace (1:1–3)
   B. Prayer of Thanksgiving (1:4–9)
II. Report of Divisions (1:10–17)
III. Reasons for Divisions (1:18–4:21)
   A. Misunderstanding of the Gospel Message (1:18–3:4)
      1. The Gospel Is Not Earthly Wisdom (1:18–2:5)
      2. The Gospel Is Heavenly Wisdom (2:6–3:4)
   B. Misunderstanding of the Gospel Messenger (3:5–4:5)
      1. Ministers Are Fellow Workers with God (3:5–17)
      2. Ministers Are Accountable to God (3:18–4:5)
   C. Misunderstanding of Paul's Ministry (4:6–21)

PART TWO:
IN ANSWER TO REPORTS OF FORNICATION (5:1–6:20)

I. On Incest (5:1–13)
   A. Deliver the Fornicators for Discipline (5:1–8)
   B. Separate Yourselves from Immoral Believers (5:9–13)
II. Concerning Litigation between Believers (6:1–11)
III. Warning against Sexual Immorality (6:12–20)

PART THREE:
IN ANSWER TO THE LETTER OF QUESTIONS (7:1–16:24)

I. Counsel Concerning Marriage (7:1–40)

A. Principles for Married Life (7:1–9)
B. Principles for the Married Believer (7:10–16)
C. Principle of Abiding in God's Call (7:17–24)
D. Principles for the Unmarried (7:25–38)
E. Principles for Remarriage (7:39–40)
II. Counsel Concerning Things Offered to Idols (8:1–11:1)
A. Principles of Liberty and the Weaker Brother (8:1–13)
B. Illustration of Paul and His Liberty (9:1–27)
1. Paul Lists His Rights as a Minister (9:1–14)
2. Paul Limits His Rights for Ministry (9:15–27)
C. Warning against Forfeiting Liberty (10:1–13)
D. Exhortation to Use Liberty to Glorify God (10:14–11:1)
III. Counsel Concerning Public Worship (11:2–14:40)
A. Principles of Public Prayer (11:2–16)
B. Rebuke of Disorders at the Lord's Supper (11:17–34)
C. Principles of Exercising Spiritual Gifts (12:1–14:40)
1. Test of the Spirit's Control (12:1–3)
2. Diversity of the Gifts (12:4–11)
3. Importance of All Gifts (12:12–31)
4. Exercise Gifts with Love (13:1–13)
5. Superiority of Prophecy (14:1–6)
6. Gift of Tongues (14:7–25)
7. Exercising Gifts in Public Worship (14:26–40)
IV. Counsel Concerning the Resurrection (15:1–58)
A. Fact of Christ's Resurrection (15:1–11)
B. Importance of Christ's Resurrection (15:12–19)
C. Order of the Resurrections (15:20–28)
D. Moral Implications of Christ's Resurrection (15:29–34)
E. Bodies of the Resurrected Dead (15:35–50)
F. Bodies of the Translated Living (15:51–58)
V. Counsel Concerning the Collection for Jerusalem (16:1–4)
VI. Conclusion (16:5–24)

3
Chapter–by–Chapter
Commentary on 1 Corinthians
(From *Illustrated Bible Handbook*, by Larry Richards)

I. THE PROBLEM OF DIVISIONS IN THE CHURCH (CHS. 1–4)

Paul first deals with the nagging problem of cliques and party factions that existed in Corinth. Like some today who identify themselves first by denomination or a favorite preacher, persons in Corinth began to see themselves as "followers of" Paul, or Peter, or another, rather than as Christians. To resolve the problem Paul goes back to basics. He examines the difference between natural and divine wisdom, urging the believers to look at all things from Christ's point of view. If God's wisdom is applied to the problem of divisions, it is clear that human leaders are simply servants of Jesus. Jesus, not a man, is to have our full allegiance.

Chapter 1: Foolish Wisdom

 For a teaching/communication suggestion on chapter 1 of 1 Corinthians, see "Divisions in the Church" on p. 213.

Salutation (1:1–9). The tone is set immediately. These believers have been set aside ("sanctified") in Christ Jesus for a holy life (v. 2). Although they have been enriched by God and "do not lack any spiritual gift" (v. 7), Paul must call the congregation "mere infants in Christ" (3:1). Yet the apostle is sure that God is at work in Corinth and will strengthen His people, because God is faithful (1:9).

 For insight on the meaning of fellowship, see the word study on "Fellowship" on p. 185. For information on the precise location of Corinth and its significance as a trade center, see "The Peloponnesus, Achaea, and the Isthmus of Corinth" on p. 188.

Divisions in the Church (1:10–17). Factions and party divisions harm the unity of the church, so believers are no longer "perfectly united in mind and thought" (v. 10). The error is revealed when one simply asks, "Is Christ divided? Was Paul crucified for you" (v. 13)?

For insight on the Apollos faction at Corinth, see "Who Was Apollos?" on p. 189.

Foolish Wisdom (1:18–25). The cross of Christ has shown God's approach to solving spiritual problems to be at odds with mankind's "wise" ways. Neither the Jew's "do a miracle" approach, or the Gentile's rational philosophical approach, can grasp the power and wisdom which God expressed in the Cross. Thus it is clear that God's wisdom and man's wisdom are completely different—and contradictory.

Superior Wisdom (1:26–31). The superiority of God's wisdom is shown in its success: in Christ we have "righteousness, holiness, and redemption" (v. 30). Clearly then we should seek God's wisdom in approaching any problem and not rely on the foolish "wisdom" of man.

 See discussion questions on issues raised in chapter 1 of 1 Corinthians on p. 203.

Chapter 2: Wisdom from God

 For a teaching/communication suggestion on chapter 2 of 1 Corinthians, see "Wisdom and Power Go Together" on p. 213.

Paul's Preaching (2:1–5). Paul simply presented Jesus, without using oratorical skills. In Paul's day many people were highly trained in the art of persuasion; some of the books on swaying an audience from the time exist today. But Paul relied only on the simple truth to show that God's wisdom and power can be trusted.

Access to Divine Wisdom (2:6–10). Human beings have no way to deduce or discover God's thinking. But His very thoughts have been communicated to us in the words of Scripture by the Spirit.

 For a teaching/communication suggestion on the theme of judgment (1 Cor. 2:15), see "What About Judging All Things?" on p. 214.

Application of Divine Wisdom (2:11–16). The Holy Spirit, living in the believer, serves as interpreter of the written Word. This enables us to make judgments about all things on the basis of God's wisdom. Both the written Word and the Spirit are needed to operate by God's wisdom. But through these two gifts from God, we have access to the very mind of Christ (vv. 15, 16)!

 See discussion questions on issues raised in chapter 2 of 1 Corinthians on p. 203.

Chapter 3: The Place of Human Leaders

 For a teaching/communication suggestion on chapter 3 of 1 Corinthians, see "Maturing, Harvesting, Building, and Glorifying" on p. 214.

Evidence of Unspirituality (3:1–4). The quarrels and bickering over leaders show the Corinthians are not "spiritual" but "worldly." That is, they are not acting on God's wisdom but like "mere men."

The Divine Perspective (3:5–9). God is the source of spiritual birth and growth. Human leaders are "only servants," each performing the task God has assigned. It is God, not human leaders, who are important.

 For a teaching/communication suggestion on cooperation rather than competition in the body of Christ, see "Who Gets the Credit?" on p. 216.

The Divine Foundation (3:10–15). Jesus is the foundation on which every life and ministry must be built. Certainly each person's service is important: it should be performed carefully and will be judged. But the foundation for all is Jesus.

 For a teaching/communication suggestion on unity in the church, see "How to Cure Divisions in the Church" on p. 215.

The judgment mentioned here has nothing to do with salvation. It is to determine rewards which God will graciously provide for those believers who serve Him (cf. 2 Cor. 5:10).

The Divine Priority (3:16, 17). It is not the builders (the leaders) who are important, but the building! God places great value on each individual, because each of us is a living temple—a residence for the Spirit. How foolish to exalt some believers over others when each of us is privileged to be a living temple and dwelling place for God!

 For a teaching/communication suggestion on God's judgment of our works, see "The Ultimate Performance Review" on p. 216.

Focus on Jesus (3:18–23). It is futile and foolish to make distinctions between human leaders and boast about one or another. In Christ all has been given to us—life, death, the present and future, and many different leaders to serve us. All this is ours because of Jesus. He should be the focus of our lives, and be the One of whom we boast.

 For insight on the futility of human wisdom, see the word study on "Futile" on p. 186.

 See discussion questions on issues raised in chapter 3 of 1 Corinthians on p. 204.

Chapter 4: Privileges of Leaders

For a teaching/communication suggestion on chapter 4 of 1 Corinthians, see "The Dimensions of Life" on p. 217.

The Privilege of Faithfulness (4:1–7). Believers should view leaders simply as "servants of Christ" (v. 1). As such, Jesus will evaluate their work when the time comes, and the criteria He will use is simply that of faithfulness (vv. 2–5). God does not evaluate us on the basis of the different gifts or tasks He has given us. We should not boast about these differences either, as if our assignments reflected some personal superiority rather than simply a gift or calling given us by God.

This is encouraging for each of us. We may not have a gift the worldly person views as important. But what counts with God is our faithfulness in using the gifts and abilities we do have to serve others.

The Privilege of Suffering (4:8–13). Rather than build little empires, spiritual leaders abandon all and willingly accept suffering to better serve God and other believers.

The Privilege of Modeling (4:14–17). Leaders model the life they teach. The Corinthians are to adopt the attitude Paul has taken and follow his example in thinking of leaders.

The Privilege of Authority (4:18–21). Paul concludes this section on divisions in the church with a warning. Spiritual leaders do have authority, and this matter of unity is so vital that any who remain arrogant or divisive will be disciplined when Paul next visits.

II. The Problem of Church Discipline (Chs. 5–6)

The second problem area dealt with by Paul involves discipline. How are Christians to react when a fellow believer persists in sinning? What happens when disputes between Christians can't be resolved? The pattern Paul sets out is clear, simple, and powerful.

 See discussion questions on issues raised in chapter 4 of 1 Corinthians on p. 204.

Chapter 5: Immorality

 For a teaching/communication suggestion on chapter 5 of 1 Corinthians, see "Separation, Celebration, and Isolation" on p. 218.

Open Immorality (5:1–8). Corinth was known throughout the Roman Empire for its loose sexual standards. But one of the Christians was now involved in a sexual relationship that even the pagans abhorred! Paul has "already passed judgment" on this individual and demands that he be "put out of your fellowship" (vv. 2, 3).

In such a case, passing judgment simply involves agreeing with God that a practice, identified in Scripture as sin, is sin. Discipline relates specifically and only to such sin.

When Paul speaks of handing the man over to Satan, he expresses the conviction that persistent sin will lead to physical death. Satan can have his handful of dust in the dead body. If the individual is a believer, God will take his spirit (v. 5)!

 For a teaching/communication suggestion on discipline in the body of Christ, see "Guidelines for Redemptive Church Discipline" on p. 218.

Paul is greatly concerned because of the indifference of the Corinthians to sin in their fellowship (vv. 6–8). The whole community is called to be holy. Undisciplined, sin will spread, as yeast does in dough, to corrupt the whole congregation.

 For insight on the problem of blatant immorality in the Corinthian church, see "The Problem with Cover-Ups" on p. 193.

Immoral Nonbelievers (5:9–13). Christians are not to withdraw from immoral non-Christians. That would mean isolation in our society. We are not called to judge nonbelievers, but to share Jesus. We are called to judge those who call themselves "brother" and yet practice sin. Purity and holiness are to mark each community of God's people.

 See discussion questions on issues raised in chapter 5 of 1 Corinthians on p. 204.

Chapter 6: Lawsuits

 For a teaching/communication suggestion on chapter 6 of 1 Corinthians, see "Basic Truths of the Christian Life" on p. 204.

Civil Disputes (6:1–8). Believers embroiled in lawsuits against one another are told to let committees of believers settle the disputes, rather than pagan courts. "Even men of little account" who are in the church could settle such "trivial cases" fairly (vv. 1–5).

What disturbed Paul was the fact of the suits in the first place. They showed that believers were actually trying to cheat and wrong one another! It would be better to be cheated than to be a cheater (vv. 6–8)!

 For insight on the problem of lawsuits at Corinth, see "Lawsuits Among Believers" on p. 194.

God's Kingdom (6:9–11). God's kingdom is more than a place or time. It is a relationship with God, in which He is free to act in and through us. Paul says flatly that no one who habitually practices sin can enter into this experience. But Christ has cleansed us from what we were, to live new lives as citizens of His kingdom.

For a teaching/communication suggestion on authentic Christian freedom, see "What Controls You?" on p. 220.

Immorality (6:12–20). Paul now restates a principle developed in Romans 6:15–27. A believer *can* do anything. But our body is designed to serve and glorify God. Thus we choose to serve righteousness, not sin.

Sexual immorality is particularly abhorrent to Paul. Jesus lives within each believer. Our body is a temple of God, won at the price of Christ's own blood, and must be committed to uses which honor God. No wonder Paul was so troubled when sexual sins were simply ignored by the members of the Corinthian fellowship!

 For insight on the meaning of the body as God' temple, see the word study on "Temple" on p. 185.

 See discussion questions on issues raised in chapter 6 of 1 Corinthians on p. 205.

III. PROBLEMS RELATING TO MARRIAGE (CH. 7)

Background. In the immoral society of Corinth, warped attitudes toward sex were reflected in the church. One extreme is seen in chapter 5, in the open immorality practiced by a believer. Another extreme provides the background for this chapter.

Some people in Corinth felt that Paul's condemnation of immorality was a condemnation of sex. They either sought divorces or insisted on celibate marriage. Some there felt that when Paul's Christian teaching lifted women to the place of personhood (rather than simply being sex objects), that the physical side of the man-woman relationships was ruled out.

Divorce also caused problems. The believers remembered that Jesus had called for a permanent marriage relationship. But often conversion meant that a person's non-Christian spouse deserted or divorced him or her. What about divorce? And what about remarriage for those who had been deserted?

All of these issues provide the background against which Paul gives his brief but pointed instruction concerning marital relationships.

 For a teaching/communication suggestion on chapter 7 of 1 Corinthians, see "The Meanings of Marriage" on p. 220.

Sexuality (7:1–7). Paul begins by quoting a position taken by one group at Corinth. Yes, he says, it is "good for a man not to marry." But he immediately corrects the impression that marriage and sex are wrong. Both men and women have sexual needs: spouses belong to each other physically as well as in other ways. To those who have taught that Christian marriage should be

CHAPTER-BY-CHAPTER COMMENTARY

sexless, Paul says that sexual relations can be abstained from only when three conditions are met: it is by mutual consent, for a short time only, and for the purpose of devoting oneself to prayer (vv. 1–5).

 For insight on the meaning of marriage, see "Practical Lessons on Marriage" on p. 194.

It is important here to note that Paul speaks of the wife possessing the husband as well as the husband possessing the wife (v. 4). Christian women are persons, not playthings, and their needs are to be given as much consideration as the needs of men.

 For insight on sexuality in marriage, see "A New View of Sexuality" on p. 195.

Paul himself prefers the unmarried state and knows that not everyone is called to be married. Each person must seek his own calling, to marriage or singleness, and view it as a gift from God.

Marriage Not Wrong (7:8, 9). Those who are presently unmarried are free to marry and should do so if their sexual drive is strong.

 For insight on Paul's personal experience with marriage, see "Paul's Marital Status" on p. 195.

Divorce Problems (7:10–16). Some believers had left non-Christian spouses, misapplying Paul's teaching that one should marry only those belonging to the Lord (cf. 7:39). Other Corinthians had been deserted by their spouses and now tormented themselves with guilt because Christ taught marriage should be permanent. How can these problems be resolved? Paul lays down principles to cover several of the situations common in Corinth.

- Christians who divorce in spite of Paul's instructions to the contrary should remain unmarried and seek a reconciliation (vv. 10–11).
- The Christian is not to initiate a divorce, even if the spouse is an unbeliever (vv. 12–13). The presence of the believer is an important factor is setting aside any children for faith in the Lord (v. 14).
- A believer abandoned by an unbelieving spouse who refuses to live with him or her is to consider himself unbound. The implication is the person is free to remarry; the reason given is that "God has called us to live in peace." There is no need to wait forever, just in case the spouse should return (vv. 15–16).

The passage is not intended to cover every possible marital situation. But there is a strong emphasis on faithfulness and grace. When one person's faithfulness is rejected and a spouse is abandoned, release is given for remarriage.

Opportunity to Serve (7:17–24). Both married and unmarried states are equally "spiritual," because God calls individuals to each. Each gives us opportunities to serve. Neither state is superior to the other.

 For insight on the nature of Christian vocation, see "Living Out God's Call Where We Are" on p. 196.

Advice for the Unmarried (7:25–35). Paul is careful to note that he is not passing on a divine command when he observes that there are advantages to being unmarried. The married person must, rightly, think of how to please his or her spouse. The single person can concentrate on pleasing the Lord. To Paul the single state seems better. But again he makes it clear that God will guide each individual into his or her own calling.

 For insight on marital roles in Paul's time, see "Women and Work in the Ancient World" on p. 190.

Free to Remarry (7:36–40). Paul says those who are widowed and unmarried are free to marry another believer. Couples should marry if not doing so would harm or hurt one of them (v. 36). But Paul cannot resist expressing again his feelings that there are great advantages in not being married.

IV. CONFLICTS OVER DOCTRINE (CHS. 8–10)

In first-century cities, animals were offered as sacrifices at pagan temples. Part of the meat was burned; much of it was sold in the temple meat market. Some Christians in Corinth regularly bought this meat, convinced that the idols had no real existence except as lumps of rock or metal. Other Corinthians associated idol worship with demonic powers and were convinced that to eat meat sacrificed to idols was to associate with demons. Each side rested its case on doctrine. Idols are not real, said one. Evil spiritual powers are real, answered the other. Each side argued strongly that its doctrine, and thus practices, were correct.

In dealing with this doctrinal dispute, Paul goes back again to basic principles. He shows first how doctrinal disputes are to be dealt with by Christians. Then he shows which doctrinal position in the dispute is right.

 See discussion questions on issues raised in chapter 7 of 1 Corinthians on p. 206.

Chapter 8: Food Sacrificed to Idols

 For a teaching/communication suggestion on chapter 8 of 1 Corinthians, see "Life, Conscience, and Knowledge" on p. 221.

Knowledge or Love? (8:1–3). Paul argues first that we must approach such disputes from the perspective of love, rather than asking "Who is right?" The attitude that we know tends to puff up and create pride. This is foolish, for while we all have some knowledge, no one has complete or perfect knowledge. We must then hold our doctrines humbly, confessing imperfect knowledge. On the other hand, the attitude that we *will love* builds others up—and opens everyone up to the Lord.

Paul's point is important. Whenever there are doctrinal disputes each party must give love for the other high priority.

The Problem According to Knowledge (8:4–8). Paul agrees that "we know an idol is nothing at all in the world, and that there is no God but one." Strictly speaking this position is doctrinally correct.

 For insight on the responsible use of Christian freedom, see "Dealing with Gray Areas" on p. 196.

The Problem According to Love (8:9–13). But being "right" is not the only issue. Some who do not see this truth are being harmed by those buying from the temple market! When the practice of a correct doctrine seems to justify wounding a brother, it is sin.

 See discussion questions on issues raised in chapter 8 of 1 Corinthians on p. 206.

Chapter 9: Love vs. "Rights" Illustrated in Paul

 For a teaching/communication suggestion on chapter 9 of 1 Corinthians, see "Giving Up Our Rights" on p. 221.

Paul admitted that the doctrinal foundation on which the meat-eating party based its practice is correct. This implies that these people have a right to purchase from the temple market (8:4–8).

But then Paul shows that love should lead these Corinthians to surrender their "right" for the sake of their weaker brothers (8:9–13).

Paul also shows that he himself has chosen to surrender many of his own "rights"—which he might have demanded on biblical grounds—for the sake of others. He has given up the right to marriage (9:3–5). He has given up the right to be supported financially by those he ministers to (9:6–14). He has even given up his right to freedom from the Mosaic Law when he is with Jews, so as not to offend them (9:20–23). He has done this, to "make myself a slave to everyone, to win as many as possible" (9:15–19).

 For insight on the meaning of genuine freedom, see the word study on "Liberty" on p. 186; for insight on support of the ministry, see "Paying Vocational Christian Workers" on p. 197.

Paul concludes by pointing out that only by setting a goal and working toward it can an athlete win the prize. As a Christian, Paul has the goal of ministry; he will sacrifice everything to achieve it.

 For insight on athletic metaphors used by Paul, see "Paul and the Greek Games" on p. 190.

Paul was not just preaching self-sacrifice to the Corinthians. He lived a self-sacrificial life for their sake.

 See discussion questions on issues raised in chapter 9 of 1 Corinthians on p. 207.

Chapter 10: Idolatry Reexamined

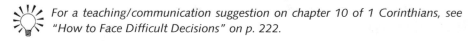 *For a teaching/communication suggestion on chapter 10 of 1 Corinthians, see "How to Face Difficult Decisions" on p. 222.*

Earlier Paul admitted that "an idol is nothing at all in the world" (8:4). But he also said that our knowledge is incomplete (8:2). Now he raises issues that those who frequented temple markets, and some who even went to feasts dedicated to idols, had not considered.

Israel's Errors Repeated? (10:1–22). Israel also enjoyed many spiritual privileges, but most did not please God. They turned to idolatry and the immorality associated with it (vv. 1–8). In Corinth, too, idolatry is associated with immorality. Israel's experience provides a warning for Christians. It is unwise to test God by associating with that which stands for evil, and which is likely to stimulate and to tempt us as well (vv. 9–13).

 For teaching/communication suggestions on facing temptations, see "Dealing with Trials and Temptations" on p. 222 and "How to Deal with Temptation" on p. 223.

As sensible people the Corinthians should flee idolatry. The idol may be nothing. But there are demonic powers behind paganism. The Lord's Supper and feasts for idols simply do not mix (vv. 14–22).

For insight on worship of false gods, see the word study on "Idolatry" on p. 186.

Freedom to Be Used Constructively (10:23–11:1). Paul now returns to his basic theme. Freedom is to be used for the benefit of others (10:24). Meat is irrelevant and can be eaten with a clear conscience. But if for instance an unbeliever announces the meat was offered to an idol, it should not be eaten for that person's sake (10:28, 29).

In his summary, Paul suggests that "rights" are really irrelevant. God has called each of us to live for His glory. God gains no glory by our being right. He is glorified when we do not seek our own good but the good of others (10:31–33). In choosing the way of love, we will be following the path in which Paul walked—and he tried only to follow close behind Jesus our Lord (11:1).

 See discussion questions on issues raised in chapter 10 of 1 Corinthians on p. 207.

V. PROBLEMS OVER WORSHIP CUSTOMS (CH. 11)

Two issues related to worship practices caused divisions in Corinth. One involved the Lord's Supper, and the other gives us insight into what was perhaps the first "women's lib" movement stimulated by Christian teaching.

 For a teaching/communication suggestion on chapter 11 of 1 Corinthians, see "Questions to Ask About Worship" on p. 225.

Women at Worship (11:2–16)

Background. In the first-century culture, a veil covering was a symbol of respectable womanhood: something a wife might wear to affirm herself as a woman of dignity. The Corinthian women, thrilled at Paul's teaching that in Christ they were equal to men in worth and value (cf. Gal. 3:26–28), wanted to symbolize this status by removing their veils in church meetings. Paul does not put down their aspirations: he praises them for affirming their value (v. 2). But he does want to show them why removal of the veil is an inappropriate symbol of equality and shows a misunderstanding of the meaning of equality.

 For insight on why Paul exhorted female believers to keep their heads covered at church, see "Head Coverings" on p. 191.

Denial of Identity (11:3–10). Paul returns to creation to point out that God has made men and women different. The order of creation shows the difference. The charge to men to function as "head" shows the difference. Note that "head" here does not connote superiority or suppression. In the context, Christ's headship implies the exaltation of mankind as the "image and glory" of God. Thus to say man is head implies the exaltation of women as the glory of man (v. 7). Women then can take pride in their identity as women.

 For insight on the meaning of man as the "head," see "What Is Headship?" on p. 198.

In fact, what wearing a veil as a "sign of authority" really symbolizes, to men and to angels, is that in Christ it is no shame to be a woman. Each time these Corinthians participate as *women* in the life and ministry of the church, they affirm their own worth and value as women. No woman has to be "like a man" to be equal.

True Interdependence (11:11, 12). Paul does not want anyone to think his argument from creation implies that men are "better" than women. "Woman came from man," he says, but "so also man is born of woman." Neither sex is adequate or whole without the other, and so neither can be more important than the other.

A Cultural Illustration (11:13–16). In the first century, long hair was regarded as feminine. No Corinthian woman would think of cutting off her hair and appearing in public. She would be ashamed and in some significant way would deny her identity as a woman. Paul wants the Corinthian women to think of taking off their veil in church not as a symbol of equality, but as a denial of their worth and value as women. How unnecessary to be ashamed of being a woman! In Christ women have been lifted up, to once again be the glory of humankind.

The Lord's Supper (11:17–34)

The Corinthians had turned the Lord's Supper into a feast at which the rich ate like gluttons and the poor went without. Paul restates his simple instructions for this great sacrament of remembrance and warns those who engage in it casually that because they have failed to take communion as an opportunity for self-examination and turning from sin, many experience God's judgments and some have died.

 For a teaching/communication suggestion on the Lord's Supper, see "The Meaning of the Lord's Supper" on p. 225.

 See discussion questions on issues raised in chapter 11 of 1 Corinthians on p. 207.

VI. THE PROBLEM OF MISUSE OF SPIRITUAL GIFTS (CHS. 12–14)

In the first century, it was universally accepted that trances, ecstatic speech, and bizzare behavior indicated a special closeness to the gods. It's easy to understand why epilepsy was named the "divine disease." In view of this cultural notion, it is not surprising to find many Christians at Corinth viewed those who spoke in tongues as especially spiritual. This assumption led to problems, and it led Paul to include a long section in this letter instructing the church about true spirituality. In the process Paul puts all spiritual gifts in perspective, helping us all to understand the nature of true spirituality and how to recognize spiritual maturity.

Chapter 12: Spiritual Gifts

 For a teaching/communication suggestion on chapter 12 of 1 Corinthians, see "Some Truths About Spiritual Gifts" on p. 227.

Spirituality (12:1–3). The word *gifts* is not in the Greek text of verse 1. Paul is writing of spirituality and countering the pagan notion (v. 2) that anyone making an ecstatic utterance is "speaking by the Spirit of God" (v. 3). Apparently some Corinthians even viewed such utterances as having more authority than Scripture. In chapters 12–14 Paul will thoroughly discuss all aspects of spiritual giftedness, of spiritual maturity, and of ministry.

Spiritual Gifts (12:4–11). Paul teaches that each believer has a gift which involves the Spirit working through him to serve and build up others. Since the same Spirit is at work through every gift, no gift should be singled out as "special."

One Body and Its Members (12:12–31). God the Spirit unites every believer with Jesus and one another to form a single, living body (vv. 12, 13). The members of the body are interdependent, and the whole needs what each part contributes (vv. 14–19). The teaching has two applications: in the body every member and his gift is indispensable. Thus all should be honored "so that there should be no division in the body" (vv. 21–26). And, since gifts are distributed, everyone should not expect to have the same gift (vv. 27–30). Against the background of the Corinthian preoccupation with tongues, and the desire of many for this more spectacular gift, this last reminder was important.

 For insight on Paul's comparison of the church to parts of the body, see "Lessons from the Human Body" on p. 199; for insight on the importance of every member of the body of Christ, see "Are Some Jobs More Important Than Others?" on p. 199.

Paul's final statement is to the Corinthian church as a whole and not to individuals, and is an exhortation to them to give their attention to the "greater gifts" (see ch. 14).

See discussion questions on issues raised in chapter 12 of 1 Corinthians on p. 208.

Chapter 13: Love

 For teaching/communication suggestions on chapter 13 of 1 Corinthians, see "The Centrality of Love" on p. 227 and "Characteristics of Genuine Love" on p. 227.

This brief chapter presents the priority of love in understanding spirituality. No gifts benefit the users if they are not motivated by love (vv. 1–3). Love is not shown in the use of a gift, but in the patience, kindness, selflessness, and forgiveness which infuse a person's character (vv. 4–7). Spiritual maturity is revealed by love, and maturity comes through loving. This, rather than the childish approach of the Corinthians and their focus on gifts, is the "more excellent way" (12:31) to gauge and to grow in true spirituality.

 For insight on the nature of Christian love, see "The Meaning of Love" on p. 192; "Agape: Self-Giving Love" on p. 200; and "Sounding Brass or a Clanging Cymbal" on p. 191.

 See discussion questions on issues raised in chapter 13 of 1 Corinthians on p. 209.

Chapter 14: The Place of Tongues

 For a teaching/communication suggestion on chapter 14 of 1 Corinthians, see "Why Go to Church?" on p. 229.

More Important Gifts (14:1–5). Paul compares the gift of tongues with the gift of prophecy (teaching God's Word authoritatively). As the purpose of gifts is to build up the body (1 Cor. 12), Paul would "rather that you prophesy," because this edifies the church. The Corinthians have been majoring on a minor gift!

Limitations on Tongues (14:6–19). Paul does not forbid the expression of tongues. It is a valid spiritual gift. But he does insist that unintelligible speech in church must be interpreted for the edification of the congregation (cf. vv. 14–17).

Purpose of Tongues (14:20–25). This debated passage is best understood in the context of the Greek culture where ecstatic utterances were taken as signs of divine presence. Unbelievers may take tongues as such signs, even though believers are not to (v. 22). So an outsider might come to a Christian meeting through hearing of such a miraculous event. But if everyone at the meeting is shouting out in tongues, the impression given is likely to be, "What a madhouse!" (v. 23). If an unbeliever comes to a meeting and hears the Word in plain speech, he will be convinced by the Spirit and converted (vv. 24, 25).

Conclusions about Tongues (14:26–33a). Paul concludes by describing what happens at a typical gathering of the New Testament congregation. Many participate, and one or two—at most three—may contribute in a tongue, if an interpreter is present. No one should excuse bursting out in a tongue by saying he "couldn't help it," for this is just not true (vv. 32, 33). In general, Paul affirms the validity of tongues as a spiritual gift, restricts their use in public meetings, and helps the Corinthians see that this is not a particularly significant gift.

 For insight on the spiritual gift of speaking in tongues, see the word study on "Tongues" on p. 187.

Women Remain Silent? (14:33b–40). This comment is hard to understand, particularly as Paul in 11:5 instructs women how to pray and prophesy in the church. As no Old Testament law suggests women should not speak in religious meetings, the word here may refer to some civil law or to a custom of the Greeks or Romans about women and public speaking. It is also possible that the early women's liberation movement, noted in chapter 11, was particularly vocal, and these instructions, in the context of Paul's emphasis on orderly worship (v. 32), were to correct abuse. Surely our interpretation must be in harmony with the voice of the New Testament as a whole on this question.

 See discussion questions on issues raised in chapter 14 of 1 Corinthians on p. 209.

VII. UNCERTAINTIES RELATING TO RESURRECTION (CH. 15)

 For a teaching/communication suggestion on chapter 15 of 1 Corinthians, see "Three Great Possessions of Believers" on p. 230.

Some people at Corinth continued in the typical Greek attitude toward the idea of resurrection: disbelief. Paul firmly presents resurrection as a doctrinal keystone of Christian faith.

 For insight on and a handy review of the central truths of the resurrection presented in chapter 15 of 1 Corinthians, see "Facts About the Resurrection" on p. 200.

Resurrection Basic to the Gospel (15:1–11). Jesus' resurrection is critical to the gospel message and well attested by witnesses.

Our Resurrection Attested by His (15:12–19). Jesus' resurrection was literal, and ours will be also. Otherwise Christian faith is an empty shell.

 For insight and information on the resurrection of Christ and believers, see the word study on "Resurrection" on p. 187.

God's Plan Hinges on Resurrection (15:20–28). It is in the resurrection that

God's plan to defeat the powers of death and sin will be carried out. In God's time the end will come, and with it victory.

Impact on Daily Life (15:29–34). Paul's willingness to endanger his own life for the gospel makes sense only in view of resurrection. Even those who practice baptism on behalf of the dead (something that Paul does not endorse, and speaks of as "their" practice) show that belief in resurrection influences present behavior.

Nature of Resurrected Bodies? (15:35–49). While few analogies exist, Paul points for illustration to a dry, dead-looking seed which, planted in the ground, reappears vital and green. There will be relationship or similarity between our mortal and resurrection bodies, but there will also be transformation. Then we will not be like Adam, but "we shall bear the likeness of the man from heaven" (v. 49).

 For insight on the new bodies that believers will receive at the resurrection, see the word study on "Life-Giving Spirit" on p. 188.

Transformation Ahead (15:50–58). Paul is caught up in a vision of the glory coming, and the great moment when all that is mortal in us is transmuted to immortality. Then we will experience fully the victory won for us through Jesus. Until then, we are to commit ourselves to the work of the Lord, knowing that our labor in Him is not in vain.

 See discussion questions on issues raised in chapter 15 of 1 Corinthians on p. 210.

VIII. PARTING INSTRUCTIONS (CH. 16)

 For teaching/communication suggestions on chapter 16 of 1 Corinthians, see "Expressions of Christian Love" on p. 230; "From Enemies to Family and Friends" on p. 231; and "Putting Money to Work" on p. 231.

Paul closes this letter with a reminder to continue collecting funds for the relief of other believers (vv. 1–4; cf. 2 Cor. 8; 9). He mentions his plans and the friends he hopes to send to the Corinthians soon (vv. 5–18). And he conveys the greeting of the churches of Asia.

 For insight on Paul's relationship to three early Christian leaders, see "Who Was Timothy?" on p. 192 and "Who Were Aquila and Priscilla?" on p. 192.

 See discussion questions on issues raised in chapter 16 of 1 Corinthians on p. 211.

4

Concise Commentary on 1 Corinthians

(From *Nelson's New Illustrated Bible Commentary*, ed. by Earl Radmacher and H. Wayne House)

CHAPTER 1

1:1–3. Paul's words of introduction are more than simple words of greeting. The first few verses introduce the themes of his letter. Thus in his greeting, Paul introduces his apostolic authority (9:1–27), the sanctification of his readers (5:1), and the unity of all believers (1:10–17), all major themes of the letter and concerns for the Corinthian believers.

 For information on the precise location of Corinth and its significance as a trade center, see "The Peloponnesus, Achaea, and the Isthmus of Corinth" on p. 188.

 For a teaching/communication suggestion on chapter 1 of 1 Corinthians, see "Divisions in the Church" on p. 213.

1:1. through the will of God: The Corinthian church greatly valued human wisdom. This misplaced emphasis had caused some in the church to challenge Paul's authority (v. 12; 9:1, 2). They forgot that Jesus Christ Himself had called him to his ministry as an apostle **of Jesus Christ** (Paul uses the same title in 2 Cor. 1:1).

1:2, 3. A local **church of God** is a group of people who identify themselves with God and gather together to worship and serve Him. **sanctified in Christ Jesus:** The Corinthians' holiness came from their position in Christ, not from their own goodness. The tense of the verb *sanctified* indicates that God had sanctified the Corinthians at a specific time in the past, producing a condition that they still enjoyed in the present.

called to be saints: The work of Jesus Christ makes a believer holy forever in God's eyes. But in everyday living, sanctification involves small, daily changes (Heb. 10:14). This is why Paul could call the Corinthian believers to become saints, even though the problems in their church testified that they were far from the goal of holiness. **In every place** is most likely a reference to local churches throughout the Roman Empire (1 Tim. 2:8).

1:4–9. The thanksgiving Paul offers to God for the Corinthians seems odd, considering the many problems the church was experiencing. However, Paul focuses his praise not on the troubled Corinthians but on the eternally faithful God. Paul does not praise the Corinthians for their good works as he does some other churches (Eph. 1:15); instead, he praises God who works in them. When we focus on people's faults, hope soon wanes and discouragement follows. But when we concentrate on the Lord, even the darkest hours can be filled with praise.

1:5, 6. Enriched means that the Corinthians had been spiritually destitute but had become abundantly prosperous through God's grace.

1:7. Gift here is probably a reference to the spiritual gifts described in chapters 12–14. Despite the boasting of the Corinthians, their many gifts had come from God (12:11, 18, 28). They were richly blessed with spiritual gifts because God was giving them everything they needed to do His will (12:14–27).

1:8, 9. Because God is faithful to His word, Paul was confident that even the sin-plagued Corinthians would stand **blameless** before Him. This blamelessness does not refer to the Corinthians' works, but to their standing in Christ, their justification (3:14, 15).

 For insight on the meaning of fellowship, see the word study on "Fellowship" on p. 185.

1:10–17. Paul began his response to the disturbing report concerning the Corinthian church by attacking the worldly wisdom that had divided the church.

1:10. Paul pleaded for an outward expression that comes from an inward spirit. Not only did Paul encourage the Corinthians to **speak the same thing** and have external unity; he also urged them to be **joined together in** a unity of hearts and minds that expresses the unity of the one body of Christ.

1:11. Paul avoided dealing in rumors or secrecy; he openly named his sources: **Chloe's household.** We know little of this woman and her household except what this verse implies. Chloe lived in Corinth or Ephesus, and the Corinthians respected her word.

1:12, 13. The Corinthian church was divided into at least four factions, following four prominent leaders.

 For insight on the Apollos faction at Corinth, see "Who Was Apollos?" on p. 189.

1:14–16. Paul said **I thank God that I baptized none of you,** because the Corinthians had taken to identifying with their spiritual mentors rather than Christ. **Crispus** was the ruler of the synagogue in Corinth when Paul began to preach there (Acts 18:8). He was instrumental in the conversion of many other Corinthians. **Gaius** may be the same person who hosted Paul and the entire church (Rom. 16:23). **Stephanas** was one of Paul's first converts in Achaia, the region of which Corinth was capital. Paul praised him and his household for their devotion to the ministry and for their assistance (16:15). Stephanas was one of the couriers who took correspondence to and from Corinth.

1:17. Paul's primary ministry was **to preach the gospel.** Baptism naturally followed conversion but was secondary in importance. With the phrase **not with wisdom of words,** Paul addressed the Corinthians' tendency to place undue emphasis on human wisdom. The immature Corinthians were so impressed by clever oratory and learned debate that many of them ignored the relatively "simple" message of **the cross.**

1:18–25. In this section, Paul emphasizes that salvation is in the message of Christ, not in human philosophies. The powerful simplicity of Christ over human wisdom negates any cause for people to boast. Many people stumble over this simplicity because the religions of the world make the source of salvation something we do rather than a **message** we believe.

1:18. The message of the cross is the gospel, the Good News about Christ's death and resurrection for our sins. The gospel penetrates to the core of self-centeredness. For those who exalt self, the message sounds absurd. But for those who bow humbly in faith, it becomes the power that is able to snatch them from death and impart eternal life. No wonder Paul put such confidence in this message (Rom. 1:16).

1:19. In Isaiah 29:14, the Lord rebuked Old Testament Israel for their hypocritical worship and their human rules for salvation (Is. 29:13). He declared He would confound their carnal wisdom. Paul used this quote to illustrate his point that God has voided any human attempts to find favor with God.

1:20, 21. The wise is probably a reference to Greek philosophers. The scribe is a technical term for a Jewish scholar trained to handle details of the Law. **The disputer** refers to a Greek person, especially one trained in rhetoric. These professionals tried to solve every problem with logic and debate. The point of this passage is that all human efforts to find favor with God fall woefully short (Rom. 3:9–28). Only through faith in Christ can we be saved from our sins.

1:22, 23. The **Jews** sought miraculous signs from the Messiah to signal the beginning of the deliverance God had promised (Mark 8:11; John 6:30). The

Greeks, especially the philosophers, sought to use wisdom to answer their questions about God and life. To the Jews, who expected a political savior, Jesus was **a stumbling block.** To the Greeks, whose self-centered wisdom could not make sense of the cross, to believe in Jesus was **foolishness.**

1:24, 25. Paul uses a paradox to say that the most insignificant thought or work of God is greater than the most extraordinary achievement of humans.

1:26. Wise refers to the Greek philosophers. Mighty refers to influential, politically powerful people. **Noble** includes all the aristocratic upper classes. Most of the Corinthians came from the lower classes.

1:26–31. Although the Corinthians thought highly of themselves, Paul challenged them to survey their own congregation and realize that most of them came not from the upper classes, but from the lowly of the world. Paul attacked the pride that had caused schisms by comparing humans to God (1:20–25), then by comparing the church to the world around them (1:26–31). Both arguments display the greatness of God's wisdom in saving the insignificant of the world so that none have a basis for boasting.

1:27. God's plan of salvation does not conform to the world's priorities. In fact, it seems **foolish.** Yet in reality, eternal salvation is more valuable than all the fame, wealth, and success pursued by the world.

1:28. base . . . despised: Paul's use of these two terms for the slave class would capture the attention of his readers in Corinth, where many slaves lived. **the things which are not:** No doubt many of the Corinthian believers were people who did not count in the eyes of the world but had found grace in God's eyes.

1:29–31. God uses what is considered foolish and despised in this world to reveal His truth, so that He alone will receive the glory. Otherwise, the powerful would boast that they had found the truth. Instead, God sent His Son to become a humble carpenter and to die in the most despicable way, on a cross. Jesus' life and death reveals God and His **wisdom.** Since Christ not only imparts wisdom but also righteousness, the Christian cannot boast, except in **the Lord.**

 *See discussion questions on issues raised in chapter 1 of 1 Corinthians on p. 203.*

CHAPTER 2

2:1–5. Paul continued his illustration of the futility of human wisdom by using his own ministry in Corinth as an example. Paul's preaching, by human standards, was unimpressive (2:1), but it was the vehicle of God's Spirit to save the Corinthians. Paul's obvious weakness had moved his readers to trust not in Paul, but in God.

For a teaching/communication suggestion on chapter 2 of 1 Corinthians, see "Wisdom and Power Go Together" on p. 213.

2:1, 2. excellence of speech or of wisdom: Paul did not rely on his eloquence or on Greek wisdom to convince his listeners. Instead, he gave **the testimony of God** which had not been explained before, but which was being revealed by the Holy Spirit (vv. 10–14). The focal point of Paul's preaching was **Jesus Christ.**

2:3–5. Whereas the Corinthians gloried in their strength, their wealth, and their gifts, Christ was glorified in His humility and death. Paul wanted to model Christ's humility by presenting his "weaknesses." Then the "strength" of the gospel message could be clearly seen. **My speech** probably refers to the way Paul spoke; **my preaching** probably refers to the content of his message. **not with persuasive words . . . but in demonstration of the Spirit:** Even though Paul had many strengths of his own (Phil. 3:4–9), he wanted to be counted among those who relied on God's strength. Rather than using the rhetoric of the day to win converts, he gave a straightforward message. **power of God:** Miraculous signs had sometimes accompanied Paul's preaching (2 Cor. 12:12; 1 Thess. 1:5; Heb. 2:3, 4). Such signs were intended to magnify God, not the human speaker.

2:6. among those who are mature: After having heard eloquent addresses by men like Apollos, the Corinthians may have viewed Paul's message as elementary or unpolished. Paul assured the Corinthians that he was imparting **wisdom**—instruction that mature Christians would appreciate. **rulers of this age:** In some passages Paul used the word rulers to refer to spiritual beings (Eph. 6:12; Col. 2:15); here he referred to earthly rulers, the Roman and Jewish leaders who presided over Jesus' Crucifixion. If these rulers had been among the wise, they would have worshiped the Lord instead of crucifying Him. **coming to nothing:** People look at beauty, wealth, and power as greatly desirable. But all earthly splendor will be rendered meaningless and worthless by death and the coming of God's judgment (Luke 16:19–29; 2 Pet. 3:10–13).

2:7. The **mystery** that Paul referred to here is defined in Romans 16:25, 26 as "revelation . . . kept secret since the world began, but that now has been made manifest." The message was **hidden,** known only to God, until He chose to reveal it (Eph. 3:1–11). This is in contrast to the teachings of the Gnostics, a group of false religious teachers who would infiltrate the early church (1 John 2:18–27). They claimed that there existed a body of secret knowledge that was only available to those initiated into an inner circle of spiritual teachers.

2:8. Lord of glory: Though Jesus emptied Himself of His majesty when He became human, He remained fully equal with the Father.

2:9–12. through His Spirit: Only the Holy Spirit could reveal the truths of God (2 Pet. 1:19–21). **knows . . . know:** The first verb refers to innate knowledge; the second refers to experiential knowledge. We could never have discovered the mysteries of God or the benefits of Christ's death by ourselves. But we can know them by experience because they have been **freely given** to us by God.

2:13. the Holy Spirit teaches: Paul emphasized that the intellectuals of this world could not teach the knowledge he was giving to the Corinthian believers. Note that the Spirit did not simply dictate words to Paul and the other apostles; He taught them. The apostles related with their own vocabulary and style what they had learned from the Spirit. **comparing spiritual things with spiritual:** These words are difficult to translate and interpret. The Greek term translated comparing may also mean "to combine" or "to interpret." The two references to spiritual may mean interpreting spiritual truths to spiritual persons, or else combining spiritual truths with spiritual words. The latter seems better. In other words, the phrase teaches that the spiritual truths of God are combined with the spiritual vocabulary of the apostles (2 Pet. 1:20, 21; 2 Tim. 3:16).

 For a teaching/communication suggestion on the theme of judgment (1 Cor. 2:15), see "What About Judging All Things?" on p. 214.

2:14–16. natural man: The natural person does not have the Spirit of God, in contrast to the Christian who does have the Spirit (15:44–46). **Receive** here means "to welcome." This verb does not pertain to discovering the meaning of a passage, but *applying* the meaning to life.

See discussion questions on issues raised in chapter 2 of 1 Corinthians on p. 203.

CHAPTER 3

3:1. Paul says he cannot speak to them as **spiritual** but **as to carnal.** How can a person be spiritual and yet carnal? Observe that the specific terms *carnal* and *natural* do not speak to the same truth. The natural person (2:14) is devoid of the Spirit of God. The carnal person is not equated with the natural person but with a babe *in Christ.* The person has not attained spiritual maturity but is considered in union with Christ. The carnal person is spiritual in the sense of having the Spirit of God but is not living consistently or maturely. This is often the experience with Christians today, but it was equally the problem of many Christians in the first century (Heb. 5:11–14).

For a teaching/communication suggestion on chapter 3 of 1 Corinthians, see "Maturing, Harvesting, Building, and Glorifying" on p. 214.

3:2. fed . . . milk: Paul did not expect the Corinthians to be mature in Christ at the time of their conversion. By placing their faith in Christ, they had been justified. They had been united with Him and his death on the cross (Rom. 6:3–5), and the Spirit of God had come to live in them (2:12; Rom. 8:9). They were considered righteous before God because of Jesus' righteousness. Thus, when Paul first established the church at Corinth he taught them as new converts, as those justified. Yet he expected them to grow in their faith—that is, become sanctified. The behavior of the Christians in Corinth should have begun to line up with their righteous position in Christ.

3:3, 4. for you are still carnal: An immature Christian naturally lacks many Christian traits, but no one should expect this condition to last. Paul was surprised that the Corinthians had not yet grown into spiritual maturity or become able to distinguish between good and evil (Heb. 5:14).

3:5–10. Paul had **planted,** or started, the church in Corinth; Apollos had **watered** it—had a significant ministry there after Paul left. But both men were only servants through whom God worked. The ones who plant and water have nothing to boast about because God gives **the increase:** Only God draws unbelievers to Himself. It is our responsibility to do our job no matter what the results, for God will reward us for our efforts and the quality of our work (9:24–27). We are like tools in the hands of the craftsman. As long as we are usable, God will use us. When we cease this function, we could be put on the shelf or disqualified (1 Cor. 9:27).

 For a teaching/communication suggestion on cooperation rather than competition in the body of Christ, see "Who Gets the Credit?" on p. 216.

Paul develops four conclusions from his observation in verse 6: (1) We are God's servants, helpers of Christ who do our assigned tasks. Without Him we can do nothing (John 15:5). Even the faith of those who believe through us is a gift from God. (2) The servants in their diverse tasks are really one. They are not competing with one another. They are all doing the work of God who gives the increase. (3) Even though the servants are one, each person's reward will be based on the quality of work done. The kind of material used will determine the kind of reward one gets. (4) Paul concludes that the church is **God's building** to be worked on by God's **fellow workers** (that is, Paul, Apollos, and other ministers, v. 9).

For a teaching/communication suggestion on unity in the church, see "How to Cure Divisions in the Church" on p. 215.

3:11–15. Paul had established the church at Corinth on the **foundation** of Christ. **gold, silver, precious stones, wood, hay, straw:** These building materials refer to the quality of work done by the Corinthians, and possibly also to their motivations or the kinds of doctrines they taught. **The Day** speaks of the time when Christ will judge the merits of His servants' work (2 Cor. 5:10), not whether they receive forgiveness of sin. Likewise, **fire** does not refer to the "eternal fire" of damnation (Rev. 20:10) but to the evaluation of believers' works (Rev. 2:18, 19; 3:18; 22:12). Fire proves the quality of gold, but it consumes wood, hay, and stubble. Some "good work" is actually self-centered aggrandizement. The true value of such "service" will become obvious to all in the day of God's judgment (Rev. 3:17, 18).

 For a teaching/communication suggestion on God's judgment of our works, see "The Ultimate Performance Review" on p. 216.

3:16, 17. Do you not know: This phrase, found in nine other places in 1 Corinthians (5:6; 6:2, 3, 9, 15, 16, 19; 9:13, 24), always introduces an indisputable statement. **temple:** There are two words translated *temple* in the New Testament. One refers to the temple building and all its courts; the other refers strictly to the Most Holy Place where no one but the high priest could go. Paul uses the latter term to describe the local church, in whom **God dwells.** Unlike 6:19, where the word *temple* refers to the individual believer, and Ephesians 2:21, where the word speaks of the church universal, these verses speak of the local church as God's temple. God takes very seriously our actions in the church. **destroy:** Any person who disrupts and destroys the church by divisions, malice, and other harmful acts invites God's discipline (11:30–32).

3:18–23. The wisdom of this world does not coincide with God's wisdom, the foolishness of Christ crucified (1:18–25). Paul quotes from Job 5:13 and Psalm 94:11 to urge the members of the Corinthian church to humble themselves. **all things are yours:** The Stoic literature of the time, which the Corinthians would have known, often spoke of the wise man as possessing everything. Everything God has done in the church, and in the entire universe, benefits all believers. There is no place for foolish boasting or competition among Christians.

 For insight on the futility of human wisdom, see the word study on "Futile" on p. 186.

3:21–23. let no one boast in men: This is the conclusion of chapter 3. The Corinthians had seriously limited themselves by boasting in different teachers, when Christ is the source of **all things.** Earthly teachers are simply God's servants for the benefit of His people (v. 5). **Life** and **death** belong to the Christian who lives and dies victoriously by the power of Christ (15:55–57). In Him we have nothing to fear from **things present** or **things to come.**

 See discussion questions on issues raised in chapter 3 of 1 Corinthians on p. 204.

CHAPTER 4

4:1–21. These verses escalate the discussion of workers as servants of Christ. First Corinthians 4:1–5 states that those called servants of Christ are also accounted as stewards or managers who have been committed a trust. Thus, we should not compare ourselves with other servants. Our accountability is to Christ.

For a teaching/communication suggestion on chapter 4 of 1 Corinthians, see "The Dimensions of Life" on p. 217.

4:1. Servants had no unique position, but **stewards** did. A steward was a slave who administered all the affairs of his master's household, though he himself owned nothing (compare the testimony of the early church in Acts 4:32). Joseph held such a position in the house of Potiphar (Gen. 39:2–19). As stewards, believers manage the message and ministry God has entrusted to them.

4:2–5. each one's praise will come from God: A steward was not to worry about the evaluations of those around him or even his own self-assessment; he needed only to please his master. Similarly, while believers can benefit from the constructive evaluations of fellow believers, their ultimate judge is the Lord Himself. Since God is the judge, we should be careful not to make any premature evaluations of others.

4:6–13. Paul upbraided the Corinthians for their immense pride (v. 6). He reminded them that they boasted of gifts which God had graciously distributed (vv. 7, 8). Then, almost in a sarcastic manner, he contrasted their "greatness" with the servant attitude of Apollos and himself (vv. 9–13). The very men they exalted to the point of causing schisms in the church (1:11–17) viewed themselves as destitute servants of God (vv. 10–13).

4:6, 7. The Greek term translated **learn** is related to the word translated "disciple" in Matthew 28:19. It implies the use of a skill and not just knowledge. The Corinthians knew about humility, so Paul called on them to become humble. Greeks considered humility to be a fault, a characteristic of slaves. To the Christian, however, it exemplifies the attitude of Christ (Phil. 2:5–8). **in us:** Paul presented himself and Apollos as models to follow (v. 16; 11:1). **what is written:** This word is often used to introduce a quotation of the Old Testament (Rom. 14:11). Paul was exhorting the Corinthians not to go beyond the teachings of Scripture. Then they would avoid the pride and divisions that were fracturing their church. A true minister of God's Word will use Scripture to unify and strengthen the church. Only those who want to exalt themselves will misuse Scripture and thus weaken and divide the church.

4:8. The Corinthians thought Christians were to be **full, rich,** and to **reign** in the present. But Paul knew that we must go through trials now if we are to reign when Christ returns. **I could wish:** That you were indeed involved in the **reign** of Christ and that we might be united in His true kingdom.

4:9, 10. Spectacle alludes to the public executions carried out by the Romans. In these executions condemned men were brought into the coliseum, where they were tormented and killed by wild animals as cheering crowds looked on. Paul pointed out that the whole world and the angels were witnesses to the humiliation of God's servants. With biting sarcasm Paul contrasted the Corinthians' lofty evaluation of themselves with the world's evaluation of him. Paul knew that true strength is found in understanding our weakness and Christ's sufficiency (2 Cor. 12:7–10; Phil. 4:11–13).

4:11–13. Paul lists the hardships he had suffered in Christ's ministry, both physical challenges and verbal abuse (2 Cor. 11:22–30).

4:14. Although the Corinthians should have been ashamed of their conduct, Paul's aim in writing was to warn them of the serious consequences of their actions. **As my beloved children** emphasizes the responsibility of parents to practice tough love in appropriate discipline.

4:15. instructors . . . fathers: Paul used these two terms to differentiate between his role and the role of the Corinthian teachers, slaves who took care of their masters' children. Paul was the Corinthians' spiritual father. He had final responsibility for them and the right to command them to follow his example.

4:16. Paul urged his readers to **imitate** him as he followed Christ (11:1). The word refers to the way a student would follow a teacher or the way an actor would play a role (11:1).

4:17. For some reason Paul could not come immediately to Corinth, but he had confidence in Timothy to teach the Corinthians properly. Timothy was already doing what Paul hoped his readers would begin to practice: following Paul's good example.

4:18–20. Some people in Corinth, probably the instructors who had caused divisions (v. 15), acted as though Paul would never return to hold them accountable for their actions. **puffed up:** These people were conceited and prone to boasting. **The kingdom of God** here does not refer to the future reign of Christ, but to Christ's present rule in the hearts of His people. This reality guaranteed that Paul would have the power to expose and discipline those who afflicted the Corinthian church.

4:21. Paul uses the same Greek word for **rod** here that Luke uses to describe the instrument that was used to beat Paul and Silas (Acts 16:22–24). The term also is used figuratively of Christ's authority to judge (Rev. 19:15). God had given Paul authority to punish the agitators in Corinth, although he preferred not to use that power.

 See discussion questions on issues raised in chapter 4 of 1 Corinthians on p. 204.

Chapter 5

5:1–13. Paul has just concluded a lengthy segment dealing with the divisions within the Corinthian church (1:10–4:21). Now he moves into the problem of incest in the church and the failure of the Corinthians to deal with it.

 For a teaching/communication suggestion on chapter 5 of 1 Corinthians, see "Separation, Celebration, and Isolation" on p. 218.

5:1. The **sexual immorality** of incest was forbidden by Old Testament law (Lev. 18:8; Deut. 22:30) and by Roman law. Paul used the phrase **his father's wife** instead of "his mother" probably to indicate that the woman was the offender's stepmother. The omission of discipline for the woman implies that she was not a believer. The church is responsible for disciplining only its members, not unbelievers.

5:2. puffed up: The Corinthians had a twisted view of grace that caused them to be proud of their tolerance of the sexual offender. They believed that because God's grace is limitless, the freedom that every Christian enjoys is also limitless.

5:3–5. Paul displays the apostolic power he spoke of earlier (4:20, 21). He had already judged the sin and gave the church his authoritative command to remove the man from the congregation. When a person is living in sin, he or she is open game for Satan.

5:5. Destruction of the flesh may refer to God's turning the sexual offender over to **Satan** for physical affliction or even physical death. After being separated from the spiritual protection of the church, ideally the offender would recognize his sin, repent, and return to the church. All church discipline has restoration as its ultimate goal.

 For a teaching/communication suggestion on discipline in the body of Christ, see "Guidelines for Redemptive Church Discipline" on p. 218.

5:6–8. The backdrop for this passage is the Passover (Ex. 12), when the Israelites removed yeast from their homes in preparation for the feast. The removal of leaven was a reminder of the Israelites' quick departure from Egypt. They did not have time to wait for leavened bread to rise. The point here is that a little leaven has tremendous impact or influence on whatever it is in. The Corinthian church was tolerating sexual sin. This leaven of sin, though small in size, was dangerous, because it could spread through the church. Like cancer, sin demands drastic surgery.

5:6. Like a tiny pinch of **leaven** spreading through a loaf of bread, unchallenged sin can soon contaminate the whole church. The sexual offender was guilty of sin, but the whole congregation was also guilty of ignoring the man's disobedience and failing to hold him accountable. Left unchecked, this sin could have caused many new believers to commit sexual immorality.

 For insight on the problem of blatant immorality in the Corinthian church, see "The Problem with Cover-Ups" on p. 193.

5:7. Jewish people were required to sweep all leaven out of their houses in preparation for the Passover (Ex. 12:15). The *leaven* here symbolizes the powerful influence of sin.

5:8. The feast is a figure of speech for Christ. As Israel was to remove all leaven from the celebration of the Passover, so the Corinthians were not to contaminate their relationship with Christ with any **malice** or **wickedness.**

5:9–13. Paul here corrects a misunderstanding arising out of his previous letter (v. 9). He had commanded the Corinthians to withdraw themselves from sexually immoral people. In this letter, Paul explains that he was not speaking of the pagan culture around them. If they withdrew totally they would be unable to function in the world. Instead, he was talking about the immorality in their midst. They should judge the sin among themselves, while still reaching out to the lost in Corinth.

5:9. My epistle refers to an earlier letter from Paul to the Corinthians that no longer survives.

5:10. out of the world: Christians are called to influence the world, not run away from it (Matt. 5:13–16). They are agents of God to carry the light of Jesus Christ into a dark world (Phil. 2:14–16; 1 Pet. 2:11, 12).

5:11. not even to eat with such a person: Eating together is a key part of fellowship and closeness with others. The Corinthians were not to have fellowship with those who claimed to be Christians but whose lives were dominated by sin.

5:12, 13. do you not judge . . . God judges: The church's responsibility is to discipline its members while trusting the Lord to judge the world (Matt. 13:30).

 See discussion questions on issues raised in chapter 5 of 1 Corinthians on p. 204.

CHAPTER 6

6:1–11. In these verses, Paul instructs the Corinthians to stop taking their personal disputes into the pagan courts. The Corinthians had been carrying their conflicts to the Roman courts and thus were making a mockery of Christianity by feuding in public. Their inability to settle personal disputes illustrated the sharp divisions in the church (1:10–17). Paul wanted to bring home several important ideas to these Corinthians: Public litigation is a disgrace to a Christian congregation (v. 1). Personal disputes should be settled within the church (vv. 2–6). The presence of contentions indicates spiritual defeat (vv. 7, 8). All unrighteousness, such as the disputes, should have been vanquished when the Corinthians became believers (vv. 9–11).

 For a teaching/communication suggestion on chapter 6 of 1 Corinthians, see "Basic Truths of the Christian Life" on p. 204.

6:2. do you not know: Paul uses this phrase six times in this chapter (vv. 3, 9, 15, 16, 19) to introduce truths that the Corinthians should have known. This phrase must have deflated the pride of a church infatuated by its own knowledge and wisdom.

6:3. Believers will participate in judging fallen **angels** (Rev. 19:19, 20; 20:10). Paul suggested that if the Corinthians were going to be judging with Christ in His future kingdom (Matt. 19:28), then surely they had the means to settle their own personal differences.

6:4–6. Those who are least esteemed refers to judges in civil courts. The Corinthians, though they had the ability to judge the issues themselves, took their disputes to pagan court for the judges there to decide.

6:7, 8. cheated . . . cheat: In all of their bickering, the Corinthians made frivolous and even dishonest charges against one another. Paul suggested that it was better to be cheated by one of these dishonest people than to dishonor one's Christian witness before pagans.

For insight on the problem of lawsuits at Corinth, see "Lawsuits Among Believers" on p.194.

6:9, 10. The kingdom of God here seems to refer to a future time when God will rule the earth in righteousness (Matt. 6:10; Luke 11:2). **do not be deceived:** Tragically, Christians sometimes deceive themselves into thinking that God does not require them to live righteously. Paul emphasizes that the kinds of people listed in these verses will not **inherit** or possess the kingdom of God.

6:11. In this verse, Paul uses three terms to describe the conversion of the Corinthians. The tense of all three verbs indicates an action in the past that is complete. **Washed** means spiritually cleansed by God. **Sanctified** means set apart as God's people. **Justified** means declared righteous by God because of Christ's work on the Cross.

6:12–20. Paul moves from his discussion of the relationship of the Corinthians to the law courts to personal integrity in body and spirit. Paul tackled the issue of Christian liberty by addressing three Corinthian slogans that reflected their attitudes toward sexual sins (vv. 12, 13, 18). In the process he presented a greatly elevated concept of the human body as created by God the Father, redeemed at great price and service to Christ the Son, and made the temple of God by the indwelling Spirit. Thus, the triune God is involved in what we do with our bodies. We call the room where the church meets the "sanctuary." Actually, *we* are God's sanctuary—His temple. What a difference it would make if we lived with that realization. Our bodies are not garbage dumps. They are temples!

For a teaching/communication suggestion on authentic Christian freedom, see "What Controls You?" on p. 220.

6:12. All things are lawful for me was a slogan the Corinthians had coined to justify their immoral behavior. Paul reminded the Corinthians that freedom from the ceremonial laws of Moses did not give them license to sin or indulge their own selfishness. This would only enslave them in the sin from which Jesus had freed them. **under the power of any:** The only power that should control us is the Holy Spirit. Sin should never dominate our lives because the Spirit empowers us to fight temptation.

6:13, 14. Foods for the stomach and the stomach for foods was another phrase the Corinthians used to justify their sinful lifestyles (v. 12). Food was gratifying and essential for life. When the Corinthians became hungry, they ate. Following the same logic, whenever the Corinthians craved sex, they indulged themselves. In their opinion any physical activity should not affect one's spiritual life, just as digesting food did not affect one's spirituality.

The Corinthians' reasoning had two faults: (1) The stomach and the digestive process are in a sense no more than earthly and without function in eternity. But the body, through the resurrection power of Christ, is eternal. It has been sanctified by God to bring Him glory (v. 20). (2) While the stomach's purpose is to digest food, it is not the purpose of the body to commit immorality. Furthermore, by design God put restrictions on both eating and sexual activity. Eating to the point of gluttony and having wanton sex outside of marriage violate God's intent and are therefore sinful.

6:15–17. Believers' lives are greatly changed when they are joined to Christ. The union affects both the believer and Christ. When a believer commits immorality, he or she is dragging the union with Christ into the illicit relationship. By quoting Genesis 2:24, that **the two . . . shall become one flesh,** Paul illustrates the seriousness of sexual sin.

6:18. Every sin that a man does is outside the body was another slogan used by the Corinthians to justify their immorality (vv. 12, 13). Paul pointed out that the opposite is true: sexual sin is done **against** the body, not outside of it. Paul exhorted the Corinthians to **flee** any temptation to indulge in sexual sin (Gen. 39:1–12).

6:19. The **temple** (3:16, 17) was the congregation of believers. The temple was recognized as the sacred dwelling place of God. The Shekinah glory of Yahweh filled the tabernacle (Ex. 40:34) and the temple (1 Kin. 8:10, 11). Now, the glory of God in the person of the Holy Spirit dwells within every believer (John 14:16, 17) and thus inhabits the entire church. The Old Testament priests took great pains to maintain a pure sanctuary for God's presence. Every Christian ought also to care diligently for his body, the temple of the Holy Spirit, in order to honor God and the church.

 For insight on the meaning of the body as God' temple, see the word study on "Temple" on p. 185.

6:20. Bought at a price alludes to someone purchasing a slave at a slave auction. With His death Jesus Christ paid the cost to redeem us from our slavery to sin (Eph. 1:7; 1 Pet. 1:18, 19). While it is true that this is applicable to all people, even those who deny the Lord (2 Pet. 2:1), it has a very unique and special significance for the believer (compare 1 Pet. 2:9; 1 Tim. 4:10). Paul concludes with the imperative **therefore, glorify God in your body.** In other words, use your bodies in order that other people may see that you belong to God.

See discussion questions on issues raised in chapter 6 of 1 Corinthians on p. 205.

CHAPTER 7

7:1. things of which you wrote to me: After addressing the problems reported by the people of Chloe's household (1:11), Paul began to answer questions that had been sent to him (7:1–14:40). **It is good for a man not to touch a woman:** There were two extreme positions in the Corinthian church. Both groups falsely separated the physical and the spiritual, believing that neither affected the other. One group was hedonistic. This group claimed that sin only had to do with the physical body, and that believers could sin in their body without any consequence to their spiritual lives. Paul corrects this misunderstanding in chapter 6. The other group believed that all things spiritual are good, and all things physical are bad, and that in order to be truly spiritual a person has to suppress every physical desire. Proponents of this view claimed that celibacy is the only proper lifestyle. Paul corrects their misunderstanding here and explains that while sexual relationships in marriage are good, he chose celibacy in his own personal situation.

 For a teaching/communication suggestion on chapter 7 of 1 Corinthians, see "The Meanings of Marriage" on p. 220.

7:2. Because of the rampant **immorality** in Corinth, Paul encouraged those who might be tempted to commit sexual sin to marry. It is better to develop a permanent relationship with a wife or husband than to lapse into sexual sin.

 For insight on the meaning of marriage, see "Practical Lessons on Marriage" on p. 194.

7:3–5. affection: Husbands and wives have a duty to maintain sexual relations with each other so that neither will be tempted by **Satan** to have sex outside of marriage.

 For insight on sexuality in marriage, see "A New View of Sexuality" on p. 195.

7:6–9. I say this as a concession, not as a commandment: This brief clause reveals for us an important understanding of Paul's method of argument and also what we believers must consider as mandate over against option. If Paul had indicated this teaching was a commandment, we would have been under an obligation. The apostle Paul at times gave direct commands or spoke so directly to an issue that it is the teaching of the Lord. For example, 1 Corinthians 11:28–34 provides commands of how things should be conducted at the Lord's Table. His teachings on gifts in 1 Corinthians 12–14 are not mere opinion but apostolic truth. In verse 7 he stated his preference that the unmarried **remain even as** he is but recognized that God has different purposes and capabilities for His people.

 For insight on Paul's personal experience with marriage, see "Paul's Marital Status" on p. 195.

good: To ones who were married but now are widows, it is a good thing to be like Paul because this gives greater opportunity to work for Christ. On the other hand, he recognizes that few have the gift of **self-control** to refrain from sexual relationships. The *good* of verse 8 must be balanced with the teaching of Genesis 2:18 where God said it was "not good" for man to be alone. **it is better to marry than to burn:** Those who burn with passion should go ahead and marry rather than struggle with sexual passion.

7:10–16. Paul turns from the concerns of celibate persons to those who are married. He speaks of the commands that Christ gave on the subject while on earth, along with insight that he has as an apostle of the Lord.

7:10, 11. not I but the Lord: When Christ was on earth, He told us not to *divorce* a spouse; instead of *divorce,* Paul uses the word translated **depart,** which refers to wives leaving their husbands. The idea is the same: a believing husband and wife should not leave each other. The further statement that if the couple divorced they were to remain **unmarried** is consistent with Jesus' teaching (Mark 10:9–12).

7:12, 13. I, not the Lord, say: Paul now presents a problem that was not addressed by Jesus. Sometimes a husband or wife would become a Christian, but the spouse would not. Paul exhorts the believer to remain married if the unbelieving spouse does not want to divorce.

7:14. Sanctified primarily means "set apart." Here the term refers to the special situation an unbelieving husband or wife enjoys when his or her spouse is a believer, being exposed to God's teachings. **Unclean** here probably means the opposite of *sanctified.* Children with one believing parent may learn about God and come to Christ.

7:15. If an unbeliever seeks to divorce a believing spouse, the Christian is **not under bondage** or obligation to continue the marriage. There is no conflict here between Paul's advice and that of our Lord in Matthew 5:32. The point is that the divine standard cannot be imposed upon the unregenerate. There is nothing the believer can do but submit to the divorce. The overriding principle is that **God has called us to peace.**

7:16. how do you know: The Greek grammar suggests that Paul asked the question expecting a negative answer. The promise given in 1 Peter 3:1–6, however, reminds us that consistent obedience to God can make a skeptical spouse into a believing one.

7:17–24. so let him walk: This section develops the theme of faithfulness to the Christian calling rather than to social status. Whether you are **slave** or **free**—upper class or lower, powerful or powerless, married or single—is irrelevant; what matters is your calling from God (Col. 3:11).

 For insight on the nature of Christian vocation, see "Living Out God's Call Where We Are" on p. 196.

7:25–40. I have no commandment from the Lord: Paul clearly distinguishes his words as an apostle from the words of Christ. **virgins:** This classification of the unmarried in the church is probably smaller than the one mentioned in verse 8, which included widows and those who had been married before. Though Paul is concerned with both celibate men and women, the attention here is on the women. Although the Greek term used in verse 25 could refer to either men or women, the other instances in this passage refer to women (vv. 28, 34, 36, 37). By the second century, the church had developed important offices for virgins, widows, and deaconesses. Since they were unencumbered with the duties of a wife, they could assist the pastors and deacons in baptizing, ministering to the sick, and other works of mercy.

7:26, 27. present distress: Paul saw turbulent days ahead for married Christians because in times of persecution, consideration for family can make it difficult to live out Christian convictions to the fullest extent. A virgin would have lesser family responsibilities and would not be deterred by the possibility of repercussions affecting her husband or children.

7:28–35. Paul does not want to be understood as prohibiting the marriage of virgins. Again, this is his preference, not an apostolic command. If the virgin or unmarried person should marry, they have not sinned. Even if they should marry, however, they should consider themselves similar to those who are unmarried as far as their dedication to God's work. He admonishes them not to get caught up in the world around them because it is only temporary.

 For insight on marital roles in Paul's time, see "Women and Work in the Ancient World" on p. 190.

7:36–38. One interpretation of this passage is that **any man** refers to the father of an unmarried **virgin. She is past the flower of youth** indicates that the virgin is approaching an age at which marriage would be unlikely. Under these circumstances, it would be perfectly acceptable for the father to give **her in marriage.** A second interpretation suggests that the *any man* of verse 36 refers to a fiance who is maintaining a celibate state with a *virgin* but is having difficulty doing so. In this view, the Greek term otherwise translated "she is past the flower of youth" is translated "he has strong passions." If the man has difficulty in controlling his sex drive, he should **marry** (v. 9). On the other hand, if he can control himself **(has power over his own will),** he should maintain his celibacy (v. 8). **having no necessity:** If the man can control himself and keep himself from immoral action, he should stay single. On the other hand, if the man's will is weak, he should go ahead and marry.

7:39, 40. bound by law: This passage is similar to Romans 7:2, where Paul used marriage to illustrate obligation to the law. Here he emphasizes that marriage should be lifelong. In a case where a marriage partner has died, the only restriction concerning remarriage is for the person to marry a fellow Christian. Even though remarriage is permitted, Paul still believes that it is wiser to remain unmarried (v. 8). **I also have the Spirit of God:** The Holy Spirit enabled Paul not only to speak with apostolic authority, but also with spiritual wisdom.

 See discussion questions on issues raised in chapter 7 of 1 Corinthians on p. 206.

CHAPTER 8

8:1–13. Chapter 8 answers the question of the Corinthians on Christian liberties that goes through 11:1, with the first subject being meat sacrificed to idols. In ancient Corinth, when a person went to the marketplace to buy food, among the meat for sale was some which had been offered to a pagan god. Supposedly, a portion of a sacrifice would be taken by the god with the remainder to be eaten by the priests. What they did not eat would be taken to the marketplace. A Christian buying meat might inadvertently be eating meat offered to a false god. Two schools of thought developed at Corinth on this question. The first perspective was that such meat was tainted by the pagan worship, while the other view held that this meat could be eaten by believers.

 For a teaching/communication suggestion on chapter 8 of 1 Corinthians, see "Life, Conscience, and Knowledge" on p. 221.

8:1. We know that we all have knowledge appears to have been a slogan used by certain Corinthian believers as an arrogant statement against weaker Christians. The weaker Christians believed that eating food offered to idols was a sin. Other Corinthian believers thought that such concerns were ridiculous. They argued that if the idols were worthless, then the meat offered to them was fine to eat. Paul agreed that food offered to idols was not contaminated, but he wanted the knowledgeable Christians not to flaunt their enlightened point of view. **Knowledge puffs up, but love edifies:** This is one of Paul's five attacks on the arrogance of some of the church members at Corinth (4:6, 18, 19; 5:2). These people belittled their weaker brothers and sisters with their knowledge. They had missed the point. They should have been using their knowledge to help other believers in the church.

 For insight on the responsible use of Christian freedom, see "Dealing with Gray Areas" on p. 196.

8:2. We know nothing about God as we **ought** unless our knowledge leads us to love others.

8:3–6. The Corinthian believers who claimed to have knowledge readily admitted that **an idol is nothing** (Is. 37:19; Jer. 16:20; Gal. 4:8) and that there is only one God (Deut. 6:4). But Paul did not dismiss the idea of idols altogether because though these gods are not real, they exist in the minds of those who worship them (10:20).

8:7–13. The knowledgeable believers were correct in their view of **idols,** but it did not matter. If the weaker brothers and sisters saw other believers eating **food** offered to idols, they might also eat, in violation of their own conscience. To go against the conscience was in fact sinning. By their knowledge the stronger believers were causing the weaker believers to stumble. Paul exhorted the strong believers to show love to the weaker ones by refraining from offending them.

 See discussion questions on issues raised in chapter 8 of 1 Corinthians on p. 206.

CHAPTER 9

9:1, 2. **Am I not an apostle:** Paul substantiated his apostleship with two arguments: (1) he had seen the resurrected **Lord** (Acts 1:21, 22), and (2) the church at Corinth was his work in the Lord, a **seal** of his **apostleship.**

 For a teaching/communication suggestion on chapter 9 of 1 Corinthians, see "Giving Up Our Rights" on p. 221.

9:3–18. Paul had the **right to eat and drink** whatever he wanted, to have a **wife,** and to receive wages for his ministry. But he did not exercise these rights. **Is it oxen God is concerned about:** God requires that ministers should be paid for their work just as He requires beasts of burden to be compensated for theirs. **those who preach the gospel should live from the gospel:** To support ministers of the gospel is commanded by God. Even as the priests in Israel were supported for their work, New Testament ministers were to be provided for as well (1 Tim. 5:17, 18).

For insight on support of the ministry, see "Paying Vocational Christian Workers" on p. 197.

9:19–23. I have made myself a servant to all, that I might win the more: Paul put his ministry of the gospel above his personal desires. He was willing to conform to the customs of other people, whether Jew or Gentile, in order to bring them to Christ. For example, in order to relate to the Jews in Jerusalem he made a Nazirite vow in the temple (Acts 21:23, 24). Around those who were under the Law—the Jews—Paul obeyed the Law. Around those who were outside the Law—the Gentiles—Paul did not observe Jewish custom. Paul clarified this, however, lest anyone misunderstand his actions. He obeyed God's law through obedience **toward Christ** (v. 21). This was a broader law than the Mosaic legislation; this was the fulfillment of Christ's will (11:1; Rom. 13:8; Gal. 6:2).

For insight on the meaning of genuine freedom, see the word study on "Liberty" on p. 186.

9:24–26. Paul had a passion to fulfill his ministry at all costs. This was similar to the kind of commitment that goes into preparing for athletic competition. **I run thus: not with uncertainty:** Paul had a clearly defined goal and knew that perseverance was needed to achieve it. In order to prepare properly for the race or the boxing match, he knew he had to force himself to maintain the strenuous, consistent practice needed for success.

For insight on athletic metaphors used by Paul, see "Paul and the Greek Games" on p. 190.

9:27. I myself should become disqualified: The Greek word for *disqualified* means "disapproved after testing." Although some have cited this verse as evidence that Christians can lose their salvation, this clause most likely does not refer to salvation. A careful distinction should be made between the *prize* and the *gift*. The free gift of justification cannot be the result of good works

(Rom. 4:1–8). However, the prize or crown is the reward for endurance and suffering for the cause of Christ (Phil. 1:29; 2 Tim. 2:12).

 See discussion questions on issues raised in chapter 9 of 1 Corinthians on p. 207.

CHAPTER 10

10:1–5. Paul places the story of Israel's unfaithfulness to God after his exhortation to the Corinthians to persevere in God's work. He emphasizes the blessings the Israelites enjoyed in the desert. They all had the protection and guidance of God. They all experienced God's miraculous deliverance. They all identified with their spiritual head, Moses. They all enjoyed the bread from heaven. Finally they all drank the water God provided. Paul's key point is that although all of the Israelites received these wonderful blessings from God, most failed to please Him.

For a teaching/communication suggestion on chapter 10 of 1 Corinthians, see "How to Face Difficult Decisions" on p. 222.

10:1. For the ancient Israelites **under the cloud** in the wilderness, the *cloud* served two functions: (1) It provided protection (Ex. 14:19, 20), fire by night in the cold desert, and shade by day from the blistering sun. (2) It guided the people through the desert (Ex. 13:21). **all passed through the sea:** Every Israelite who left Egypt in the Exodus experienced the deliverance of God at the Red Sea.

10:2. all were baptized into Moses: The acts of God **in the cloud and in the sea** joined the people with their spiritual head, Moses.

10:3–5. the same spiritual food . . . the same spiritual drink: They all followed the same God and the same laws (John 4:13, 14; 6:32–35).

10:6–10. our examples: The discipline of God exercised against the disobedient Israelites should serve notice to Christians that God will punish His people's sin.

10:6. The first failure of the ancient Israelites was that they **lusted,** or "craved." They were not satisfied with God's provision but looked back to the provision that they had in Egypt (Num. 11:4–34).

10:7, 8. The ancient Israelites were notorious **idolaters.** Even though the true God had brought them out of Egypt, they insisted on worshiping lifeless idols. Furthermore, the ancient Israelites engaged in **sexual immorality,** a sin that also plagued the Corinthians (5:1; 6:18). **twenty–three thousand:** The account in Numbers gives the figure twenty–four thousand (Num. 25:6–9).

There are several possible reasons for the difference. Some have suggested that Paul's number reflects the number that died **in one day,** while the Numbers account may be a record of all who died in the plague. Another explanation may be that the Numbers account includes the death of the leaders (Num. 25:4) while Paul's figures do not.

10:9. tempt Christ: Apparently this phrase relates to the Israelites' questioning of the plan and purpose of God while on their way to Canaan (Num. 21:4–6).

10:10. The ancient Israelites **complained** against their God-given leaders so much that many **were destroyed,** or put to death (Num. 16:41–49).

10:11. as examples: Paul emphasizes again that the things that happened to Israel are not merely historical events to be read but warnings to heed. This is especially true, in Paul's view, since the **ends of the ages have come.** God's plans were reaching culmination. The God bringing about the end of all things is the same God who brought judgment on the Israelites by killing them; he might do so again (compare 11:30; Rom. 11:22).

10:12. lest he fall: The Corinthians may have had the attitude that since they were justified by God, nothing could happen to them. The discipline of God, however, is not to be taken lightly. No one can sin with impunity (Gal. 6:7, 8).

10:13. Paul provides the Corinthians with a word of comfort. The various temptations they were experiencing were normal; all believers throughout the ages have had to resist temptation. God is so good that He will not let believers experience anything for which He has not prepared them. He will give every believer the grace and power to endure. Furthermore, endurance will bring its own reward (9:24–27).

 For teaching/communication suggestions on facing temptations, see "Dealing with Trials and Temptations" on p. 222 and "How to Deal with Temptation" on p. 223.

10:14–11:1. In this section the apostle Paul addresses the problem of idolatry in the Corinthian church. Worship of various gods was totally ingrained in Greek culture. In the ancient Greek world, there were idols on street corners and in houses. Various civic societies paid homage to their favorite gods. Cities adopted certain gods as their special protectors. The pagan temples were frequented often, especially in Corinth with its temple prostitution. Most of the food in the marketplace had been offered in worship to different gods. Paul first addresses the demonic nature of idol worship and then expounds on the nature of Christian liberty, especially concerning food offered to idols.

10:14–22. flee from idolatry: Pagan worship is a violation of the believer's union with Christ (v. 21). The idols themselves are not a threat (v. 19); the danger lies in the **demons** (v. 20) who, unknown to the worshipers, are the real objects of idol worship.

For insight on worship of false gods, see the word study on "Idolatry" on p. 186.

10:21. You cannot drink: Paul reminded the Corinthians of the fellowship and unity they had in their participation in the Lord's Supper. Participation in idol worship is a violation of that unity.

10:22–24. All things are lawful for me: Though we have freedom, we also have a responsibility to help others in their Christian growth. Our first duty is to others, not ourselves.

10:25, 26. Eat whatever is sold: Paul himself did not ask whether meat was sacrificed in the temple, because pagan worship could not contaminate what God had made clean (Ps. 24:1; Acts 10:15).

10:27–30. These verses present a scenario of a knowledgeable Christian being invited to a private home for dinner. If no one makes an issue of meat offered at the temple, the believer should not make a point of it; this strong believer accepts the truths enunciated in verse 26. On the other hand, if a weak or unknowledgeable believer is present and brings to the strong Christian's attention that the meat is from idol worship, the knowledgeable Christian should refrain from eating out of consideration for the weaker Christian.

10:31–11:1. Doing **all to the glory of God** involves encouraging fellow Christians and spreading the good news about Christ. Paul accomplished this by refusing to offend **Jews, Greeks,** or **the church of God,** even if it meant restricting his freedom. Like **Christ,** Paul did not seek his own way or do things for his own pleasure; instead, he desired to help others (v. 24). This should be our desire as well.

See discussion questions on issues raised in chapter 10 of 1 Corinthians on p. 207.

CHAPTER 11

11:2–34. These verses follow a lengthy section about the improper way the Corinthians had taken advantage of their freedom in Christ. After a series of gentle rebukes (1:10, 11; 3:1; 4:7–13, 18; 5:1–3; 6:1–6; 7:1–5; 8:9–12; 10:1–14) the apostle begins this section with praise because they were following certain traditions he had taught them.

For a teaching/communication suggestion on chapter 11 of 1 Corinthians, see "Questions to Ask About Worship" on p. 225.

11:2. Now I praise you reflects genuine appreciation on Paul's part. The Corinthians had made many mistakes, but they were not totally corrupt. The Corinthians had followed the apostle's instructions in certain areas.

11:3. But introduces an exception to the praise Paul had given the Corinthians in verse 2. He wanted to instruct the Corinthians on another point of confusion. **Head** primarily means "authority" when used in the context of human relationships. Some have said that *head* can also mean "source" or "origin," a claim now rejected by Greek lexical authorities. **the head of woman is man:** The relationship between men and women does not involve inferiority, because, in the parallel clause, **Christ** is not inferior to **God** the Father. Submission does not indicate inferiority, but subordination. Just as Christ and God are equally divine, men and women are equal beings. But just as Jesus and God the Father have different roles in God's plan of salvation, so men and women are given different roles.

 For insight on the meaning of man as the "head," see "What Is Headship?" on p. 198.

11:4. Praying or prophesying may refer specifically to intercessory prayer similar to that of Old Testament prophets (Gen. 20:7; 1 Sam. 12:23; Jer. 27:18), or Anna (Luke 2:36–38), or to the combination of tongues and prayer (14:13–16; Acts 2:4; 10:46). **Having his head covered** probably refers to the wearing up of hair on a man's head. **dishonors his head:** It is impossible to decide whether *head* here refers to the man's physical head or to Christ, the man's authoritative head (v. 3). Either interpretation is possible; Paul may even have meant the word to have a double meaning.

11:5, 6. every woman who prays or prophesies: Women were obviously allowed to pray and prophesy in the Christian assembly because it would have been meaningless for Paul to give instructions for something they were not permitted to do. **Dishonors her head** refers either to the woman's own physical head or to her husband as her head, or possibly both (v. 4). For a woman not to cover her head with her own hair was as shameful as having a **shaved** head, a sign of public disgrace.

11:7–9. man is not from woman, but woman from man: The woman was taken from the side of the man (Gen. 2:21). **Woman for the man** is Paul's way of stating the concept of the "helper" in Genesis 2:20. This does not mean the woman is inferior to the man; it refers only to the purposes of God for man and woman in the creative order.

11:10. Women were to wear a covering on their head **because of the angels.** Evidently God's angels are present at the meeting of the church and actually learn of God's work of grace through the lives and worship of God's people (Eph. 3:10). **symbol of authority:** This might be a symbol of the woman's authority to prophesy in the new church age, which was inaugurated with the giving of the Holy Spirit at Pentecost (v. 5). It also might refer to a symbol of the man's authority over the woman (v. 3).

For insight on why Paul exhorted female believers to keep their heads covered at church, see "Head Coverings" on p. 191.

11:11, 12. neither . . . independent: Men and women need each other, and as creatures of God, both depend on Him. Neither man nor woman can have any claim to special status other than what God has purposed for them as their Creator.

11:13–15. Nature seems to refer, in Paul's usage, to how things naturally ought to be (compare Rom. 1:26; 2:14, 27; also read 11:21, 24; Gal. 2:15; 4:8). To Paul, it is natural for men and women to be different. Women are able to manifest this by wearing their hair longer than men.

11:16. no such custom: Paul's question presupposes his pointed question in verse 13 and his view of what is natural in verse 14. To the question, "Is it proper for a woman to pray to God with her head uncovered?" one must answer a resounding, "Certainly not!"—that is, if one is to make any sense of Paul's discussion to this point. The Christians at Corinth should observe this universal custom. No other church allowed a woman to prophesy without covering her head, and the Corinthian church should not let this occur in their assembly.

11:17–34. This passage concerns the improper activities that were occurring when the church met to participate in the celebration of the Eucharist or Lord's Supper.

11:17. I do not praise you: In contrast to Paul's praise in verse 2, that the Corinthians had followed many of his teachings, here he expressed concern for their sinful practices at worship. **Come together** is a technical term for the meeting of the church and is used three times in this passage (vv. 18, 20).

11:18. divisions: It is tempting to equate the divisions here with the problems occurring in chapter 1, but the divisions in this verse seem to relate to events happening when the church met for the Lord's Supper. Possibly the difficulties were over class distinctions of rich and poor, or Jew and Gentile. When the church meets, all the parties should come together as equals, but such was apparently not the case at Corinth. Instead of the unity urged by Paul in 11:17 and emphasized again in chapters 12–14, there was fractionalism among the believers.

11:19. those who are approved: One of the positive results of division or factions in the church is that it becomes obvious who the genuine Christians are in the congregation.

11:20–22. The Lord's Supper was the centerpiece of early Christian worship. Gathered around one table, fellow believers met with the Lord and with each other in unity. Christ had expressed this type of humility and unity when He instituted the Supper (Matt. 26:26–30; Mark 14:22–26; Luke 22:14–23). Corinthian believers were taking their **own supper ahead of others,** violating the spirit and purpose of the meal. In acting this way, they showed contempt for **the church of God** and shamed those who had **nothing.**

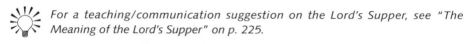 *For a teaching/communication suggestion on the Lord's Supper, see "The Meaning of the Lord's Supper" on p. 225.*

11:21. For in eating . . . one is hungry, and another is drunk: In the early church, the Lord's Supper was commonly preceded by a fellowship meal, later known as the agape feast. Eventually, so many problems accompanied these feasts that at the Council of Carthage (A.D. 397), they were strictly forbidden. And such was the case at Corinth. In their coming together, they were not eating together; hence it could not be called communion, and their behavior was so dishonoring to the Lord, it could hardly be called the Lord's Supper. Some were actually getting drunk.

11:22–25. I received speaks of Paul's revelation from Christ, which he had **delivered** to the people. Paul explained it again.

11:24, 25. Take, eat . . . broken, are all omitted in the best manuscripts. **this is My body:** Certainly not literally, but figuratively. He was there in the midst participating with the disciples in the element of the bread which signifies His Incarnation. **which is . . . for you:** This signifies the sacrificial and vicarious character of the death of Christ. Christ is memorialized at this table, not as a great example, or teacher, or even prophet, but as the Lamb of God who takes away the sin of the world. **do this in remembrance of me:** In contrast to the often thoughtless and reckless gathering of Corinthian believers at their so-called love feast, Jesus asked of His disciples, "Remember me."

11:26. you proclaim the Lord's death till He comes: The Lord's Supper looks back to Christ's death and forward to His Second Coming (Matt. 26:29; Mark 14:25; Luke 22:18).

11:27–29. In an unworthy manner refers to the way in which a person eats the Lord's Supper. The Corinthians had been making the meal a time of overeating and getting drunk rather than a time of reflecting on the death and resurrection of the Lord Jesus Christ.

11:30. Sleep here refers to the death of Christians (15:18; 1 Thess. 4:15, 16). In this passage, it refers to untimely death, a punishment suffered by some Christians who failed to examine themselves at the Lord's Supper (v. 28).

11:31, 32. If we would judge ourselves, God would not need to correct us. But when Christians are unwilling to do this self-examination, God Himself will chasten them.

11:33, 34. wait for one another: Paul concludes his discussion of the Lord's Supper with a practical exhortation that the Corinthian believers show proper concern for one another. He implies his disapprobation of the common love feast in the words **eat at home.** And he demonstrates again pastoral concern when he expresses the thought **lest you come together for judgment:** Paul takes no delight in the chastening hand of the Lord. **I will set in order** (Gk., *diatasso*) refers to outward practical arrangement (compare Matt. 11:1; 1 Cor. 9:14; 16:1; Gal. 3:19). Any other details pertaining to the Lord's Supper, Paul will clarify upon his visit to the city.

 See discussion questions on issues raised in chapter 11 of 1 Corinthians on p. 207.

CHAPTER 12

12:1–14:40. Paul continues his discussion of proper order in the church with the subject of the exercise of spiritual gifts in the church. He presents the proper inter-relationship between unity of the body, yet diversity of gifts, the proper function of gifts, and the primacy of love in the operation of spiritual gifts.

 For a teaching/communication suggestion on chapter 12 of 1 Corinthians, see "Some Truths About Spiritual Gifts" on p. 227.

12:1. Now concerning: The apostle is responding to another question in the letter from the Corinthians (7:1, 25; 8:1). **spiritual gifts:** The Greek text does not contain the word *gifts* but merely reads "spirituals" *(pneumatikon),* which may refer to spiritual things or to spiritual persons. Many have assumed it refers to the **gifts** *(charismata)* of 12:4–11 (Matt. 7:7–11; Luke 11:9–13), but this is probably not the case, in view of how the term is used in chapters 12–14, specifically 12:1–3; 14:1–3; and 14:37.

12:2. Gentiles were looked upon as barbarian or unlearned which Paul uses to emphasize their state of ignorance. Unfortunately, people who are ignorant don't like to admit it, so Paul has to drive it home. Because of their ignorance, they have been **carried away** or swept off their feet. Paul considers demonic forces behind idol worship (10:20) so this personal action of being captivated forcefully may be behind his expression. The term reflects the eroticism of much pagan religion in which the participant was taken by ecstasy and did not use self-control characteristic of the work of the Spirit as taught by the apostle in chapter 14. **Dumb idols** is an expression that would be immediately recognized by the Corinthians familiar with the Old Testament idolatry (compare 1 Kin. 18:26–29; Ps. 65:4–8; Is. 46:7). Bruce suggests that Paul is contrasting the silence of the idols with the noisy (demon-inspired) outcry of their worshipers.

12:3. calls Jesus accursed . . . say that Jesus is Lord: A person truly speaking by means of the Holy Spirit will never curse (i.e., demean or defame) Jesus, and all who genuinely proclaim the lordship of Christ do so by the Spirit's enabling.

12:4–6. gifts: The first use of the word for gifts stands in contrast to *pneumatikon* of 12:1. *Charismata* refers to "grace-gifts" of God on the individual Christian through which He may strengthen His people. **diversities . . . differences . . . diversities** (same Greek word): Note the diversity in the work of the Trinity. In verse 4 the Spirit distributes each one to the believer (12:11). In verse 5 the Son of God assigns the believer the particular way the gift is manifested in the body (12:12–27). In verse 6, the Father provides the energy to the believer in exercising the gift (12:28). God works His will through His people in many ways. Not everyone is intended to be the same or perform the same function in the body. **same Spirit . . . same Lord . . . same God:** Though people are gifted differently by God, God and His work is unified. Regardless of which gifts various persons have or do not have, the one **God . . . works all in all.**

12:7–11. To each one for the profit of all expresses Paul's main teaching on the work of the Spirit. God works in believers to benefit the entire body, not simply the individual Christian (vv. 25, 26). The Christian is a vehicle through which God works toward the upbuilding and unity of the entire body, not the end of God's work. **For to one . . . to another:** The two Greek words *(allos . . . heteros)* point up the diversity and begin a list of *charismata* that are distributed by God throughout His body. No one is given every gift nor are all given one gift, like tongues. Rather, the various *charismata*, or grace gifts, are distributed so as to bring diversity among the unified body. The various gifts of **wisdom . . . knowledge . . . faith . . . gifts of healings . . . working of miracles . . . prophecy . . . discerning of spirits . . . kinds of tongues . . . interpretation of tongues** were probably very understandable to the Corinthians, but their exact nature is difficult for us to know two thousand years later.

Word of knowledge appears to be the ability to discourse on doctrine; not the knowledge itself but the skill of discourse. *Word of wisdom* is quite the opposite of word of knowledge and refers to practical or ethical outworkings of the knowledge, similar to what one observes in the Proverbs. This gift helps solve the problem of the distribution of food in Acts 6. *Faith* appears to be the capacity to believe God for extraordinary deeds. *Miracles* would probably be the ability to do deeds similar to Moses, the prophets, or maybe some nature miracles one observes in the Gospels. Notice that God particularly used these gifts to confirm truth spoken through the early apostles (Heb. 2:3, 4).

Prophecy is the forthtelling or foretelling of the revelation of God, either "new" revelation or divine elucidation of what is already known. More than merely teaching or preaching, this action results from the empowering but not inspiration of the Spirit. Peter demonstrated this gift at Pentecost. *Discerning of spirits* may refer to the ability to distinguish the works of God from demonic activity in the church. *Kinds of tongues* probably refers to the ability to speak various languages that one has not studied. *Interpretation of tongues* is the ability to explain or translate the tongues spoken in the congregation so that the entire group of believers might benefit from the prayer spoken (14:16) by the tongues-speaker (14:13, 28). **As He wills,** not as *we* will. Whether or not Christians are to seek for any of the gifts of the Spirit is discussed at 12:31.

12:12–31. Paul attempts to help the carnal Corinthian Christians to turn from selfish desires and to seek for the unity of the body and to serve with the gifts God has given (vv. 7, 25, 26).

12:12–14. For ... For ... For: Note the development of thought as the Spirit of God continues to give Christ the glory (John 16:12–14; 1 Cor. 12:3).

12:12, 13. so also is Christ: The analogy of the human body illustrates the need for unity in diversity in the body of Christ.

12:13. one ... one ... one: The apostle continues to emphasize unity: one **Spirit,** one **body,** one **Spirit;** Paul denies that the Spirit is partitioned into the groups mentioned in chapters 3 and 4. All believers (v. 3) are infused by the same God. **by one Spirit we were all baptized:** The verse might be better translated "in one Spirit we were all baptized into one body." Christ, the exalted and ascended head of the body, is the active agent who places the new member of the body in the sphere of the Holy Spirit for His care and safekeeping. All believers are baptized into the body in the sphere of the Holy Spirit and thereby made part of the body of Christ, whether **Jews or Greeks, slaves or free.** No one has it over another in Christ's church; everyone enters the same way: by faith into the promise of Abraham (Gal. 3:26–29). Each of us has equal share in the same Spirit of God: we **have all been made to drink into one Spirit.**

Some of the Corinthians—probably the *pneumatikon* (v. 1)—believed that only certain gifted individuals were especially in tune with the Spirit, but Paul puts every believer on an equal footing in the Spirit. It is unlikely that "drinking" refers to common participation in the cup of the Lord's Supper. The Spirit not only surrounds us in baptism; but since we have drunk of the Spirit He also dwells within us.

12:14–27. These verses emphasize one major idea: the body is a magnificent picture of both unity and diversity at one and the same time (vv. 14–19, unity in diversity; vv. 20–27, diversity in unity). None should exalt themselves because of the gift given to them, nor should any think themselves less because they receive a gift some view as less significant.

 For insight on Paul's comparison of the church to parts of the body, see "Lessons from the Human Body" on p. 199.

12:25–27. That introduces the main purpose, namely, **no schism in the body.** The phrase **should have the same care for one another** emphasizes the purpose of the gifts as stated in verse 7—"for the profit of all." Rather than bickering with other Christians and being jealous about other people's positions or gifts, our task is to give of ourselves to others so that if any part of the body is having difficulty or is hurting, we seek to minister and heal that part.

12:28–30. God has appointed continues to emphasize sovereign appointment of gifts by the Spirit (v. 11), Son (v. 18), and Father (v. 28). The gifts are not by our choice. The persons of **apostles, prophets, and teachers** are listed first and with ordinal numbers, probably because they are foundational for the body of Christ, although the Corinthians had valued them less than the spectacular gifts, such as tongues. Sometimes "apostles," used in a general sense, approximates "missionary" (compare 15:7; 2 Cor. 11:5; 12:11; Gal. 1:17, 19; Rom. 16:7); used more specifically, it refers to a small group who witnessed the resurrected Christ and were specially appointed by Him as His representatives (the Twelve and Paul; 15:5 and 9:1; 15:8).

The apostle speaks of Old Testament prophets elsewhere (Rom. 1:2; 3:21; 9:3; 1 Thess. 2:15), but in 1 Corinthians and Ephesians 2:20 he may use the term for only New Testament prophets, whose activity is referred to in chapter 14. As in Old Testament prophecy, the chief job of prophets was not foretelling but forthtelling. New Testament prophets guided the church in its infancy, along with the apostles. Teachers expound the truth of the written revelation of God, as indicated in Galatians 6:6 and 2 Timothy 2:2.

After these three major positions, the apostle Paul mentions a variety of other helpful gifts, listing tongues, their favorite, last. The concluding questions—Should we expect all to be apostles, or prophets, or teachers, or workers of miracles? Do all have the various gifts like healings, or tongues, or interpretation?—expect the answer no! What kind of body would it be that was one big hand, or toe, or tongue? This body would not be functional. It would be grotesque!

 For insight on the importance of every member of the body of Christ, see "Are Some Jobs More Important Than Others?" on p. 199.

12:31. The translation of **earnestly desire** presents a problem: Should it be translated as the NKJV does, as an imperative, or as an indicative, a statement of fact: "You are desiring the sensational gifts"? The Greek word *zeloo,* normally a negative term, allows either. The imperative is chosen by most interpreters, but the indicative is possible and would fit with the correction at which chapters 12–14 aim. In contrast to such unprofitable desire, Paul directs them to **a more excellent way** in chapter 13, the way of exercising any and all gifts only in love.

 See discussion questions on issues raised in chapter 12 of 1 Corinthians on p. 208.

CHAPTER 13

13:1–13. The love chapter is divided into three sections: (1) the futility of gifts without the fruit of the Spirit, love; (2) the nature of love; and (3) the permanence of love in contrast to the temporality of the gifts.

 For insight on the nature of Christian love, see "The Meaning of Love" on p. 192 and "Agape: Self-Giving Love" on p. 200.

13:1. tongues of men and of angels: The miraculous gift of "speaking in tongues" *(glossolalia)* involved human languages, self–evident by the wording here (tongues of men) and also in other passages (Acts 2:4, 6, 8, 11; 10:46). But were the tongues in the Corinthian church angelic languages or humanly unintelligible languages from God? The tongues-speakers may have thought so, but Paul may be using hyperbole: "even if I were to speak in some heavenly language." Either way, without love such a gift would be worthless. **Sounding brass or a clanging cymbal** were standard instruments used in pagan worship. The exercise of the grace gifts apart from Christian love would differ little from the activities of various pagan and mystery religions.

 For insight on the meaning of the phrase "sounding brass or a clanging cymbal," see the article with this title on p. 191.

13:2. gift of prophecy . . . all mysteries and all knowledge . . . all faith: All three are listed in chapter 12. All these gifts, employed without love, amount to nothing.

13:3. Bestow all my goods: People can do works of charity without the proper motivation (4:5). **Body to be burned:** With this ultimate gift, Paul has extended each gift to the nth degree in hyperbole to show their worthlessness apart from love. They are "wood, hay, and stubble" (3:12–15) at the judgment seat of Christ.

 For a teaching/communication suggestion on chapter 13 of 1 Corinthians, see "The Centrality of Love" on p. 227.

13:4–7. Paul now advances from the superiority of the fruit of the Spirit, love, to the important traits of love. Love **suffers long,** or puts up with people that it is easy to give up on. Love is **kind,** namely, treats well people who have treated us poorly. Love doesn't **envy** (Gk., *zeloo*) nor **parade itself** and is **not puffed up.** Self-promotion plagued Corinth and challenges us today. **Behave rudely** means to act in an unfair or unseemly manner, as Paul discussed in 7:36. **seek** (Gk., *zeteo*) **its own:** A person who loves is willing to set aside his or her own plans or entitlements for another's good. **Not provoked** speaks of not being irritated or over-sensitive to others, easily angered. **thinks no evil:** When we love someone we do not immediately assume evil on their part. Furthermore, if we understand "think" *(logizomai),* or "consider," as an accounting term, the text would mean that we do not keep a record or account of evils done to us.

 For a teaching/communication suggestion on the traits of Christian love, see "Characteristics of Genuine Love" on p. 227.

does not rejoice in iniquity . . . rejoices in the truth: Love does not delight in evil in any form, including the fall of a brother or sister. Instead, love delights in all that expresses the gospel, both in word and deed. **bears . . . believes . . . hopes . . . endures all things:** The word for *bears* literally means to "support." Love is the foundation for all acts that please God. Love believes all things in that love never gives up and never loses hope. Love endures any hardship or rejection, revealing its superior strength. In the face of confrontation, love simply continues. To love is the great commandment (compare John 13:34, 35) and no other force promotes righteousness more.

13:8–10. This third section of chapter 13 moves from the nature of love to its permanence. **Love never fails:** This uncompromising affirmation contrasts with grace-gifts, which are transitory at best. One day *all* the gifts will be needed no longer, but love will continue forever. **prophecies . . . tongues . . . knowledge:** Paul focuses on three of the sixteen gifts to demonstrate the temporariness of them all. **prophecies . . . will fail:** The word translated "fail" (*katageo*) is in the passive voice. Literally the translation is "prophecies will be stopped." **tongues . . . will cease . . . knowledge . . . will vanish away [be stopped]:** Prophecy and knowledge (which are among the twelve body gifts for edification) are **in part** (Gk., *ek merous*). They, with all the gifts of chapter 12, serve the body of Christ, but only for now.

we know in part, **we prophesy** in part. These "in part" *(ek merous)* gifts will continue until **that which is perfect** (Gk., *teleios,* complete) **has come** (v. 10). The perfection in view here has been interpreted quite differently: (1) the end of the apostolic era, by which time the core doctrines of the church had been revealed and taught; (2) the completion of the canon of Scripture, which secured the inspired and authoritative source of all true Christian doctrine; and (3) the second coming of Christ, at which point the role and relationship of all believers and the church will be transformed, and the "partial" will no longer be needed. This time of completion (whichever view is embraced) supercedes and replaces all the "only for now," "in part" gifts. Unlike these, love endures forever.

13:11, 12. Child is used five times in verse 11. Paul uses the growth from childhood to adulthood as an illustration to explain his comments in verses 8–10 about movement to completion. It is normal and expected for a child to act and think like a child. But when a person becomes an adult, the acts and toys of childhood need to stop. **now** (used twice) **we see in a mirror dimly:** The mirror is likely the revelation of God, which, while incomplete, is accompanied by these three gifts. **But then** (used twice in balance with "now") refers to the "perfect" when we shall **know . . . as . . . known.** Thus there will be no further need for the body gifts.

13:13. greatest is love: Faith, hope, and love are permanent Christian virtues, yet love clearly stands over the other two. Faith is the foundation (Heb. 11:6) and love is the capstone. Doctrine is the foundation (3:10; Jude 3) and experience is the practical expression which attracts (John 13:35).

See discussion questions on issues raised in chapter 13 of 1 Corinthians on p. 209.

CHAPTER 14

14:1. Like 12:31, this verse is a hinge which connects the preceding to the following.

14:1, 2. Pursue love: The Greek word for pursue (*dioko*) carries such meanings as "hasten," "run," "run after," "aspire to." We can take or leave many things in life, but not love. We should pursue or strive for love as a priceless treasure. The fruit of the Spirit prepares believers for the exercise of the grace-gifts of the Spirit. **desire spiritual gifts** (*pneumatikon;* compare 12:1) Most interpreters take this to mean that believers are to seek certain gifts—prophecy, especially—in order to serve Christ's body. Two matters may speak against such a view.

For a teaching/communication suggestion on chapter 14 of 1 Corinthians, see "Why Go to Church?" on p. 229.

First, the Greek word for desire (*zeloo*) is the same as in 12:31 and may indicate a negative desire, not positive. So 14:1 would then read, "Pursue love, but you are desiring spirituals, when you should rather prophesy." Secondly, *gifts* is not in the Greek text and, as in 12:1, should be omitted. The context seems to indicate that spirituals *(pneumatika)* is an adjective describing specific utterances, perhaps ecstatic tongues. Therefore, in contrast to the "spirituals" (ecstatic tongues?) they desire improperly, they should desire prophesying. Why? Because the main purpose of gifts is to edify one another, but the person who **speaks in a tongue** is understood only by God. Thus **no one understands . . . in the spirit.**

14:3–5. **He who prophesies** here may incorporate all of the speaking gifts (Rom. 12:6; 1 Pet. 4:11) that edify others, as is demonstrated by the results in verses 3 and 4. **edification . . . exhortation . . . comfort:** Paul prefers for the Corinthians to exercise this gift in their midst instead of "speaking in a tongue," by which one merely edifies himself. **I wish you all spoke in tongues:** Perhaps the apostle is contrasting the Spirit-given gift of tongues (note the plural) with speaking in a tongue (the singular), which may be a reference to ecstatic speech. Or perhaps Paul recognizes value in private, personal prayer uttered in a tongue, even as he aims to correct the abuse of tongues in public worship. Another possibility is that we should not read too much into this comment. Elsewhere the apostle wished that all were celibate like him (7:7), but certainly he did not expect such to be the case. Paul saw benefit in the true gift of tongues but a limited one. **prophesies is greater . . . unless indeed he interprets:** When interpreted, the gift of speaking in tongues will benefit the church.

14:6. what shall I profit you: If Paul had first come to the Corinthians speaking in tongues that they did not know, what benefit would it have been to them? Their response would probably have been one of disinterest (v. 11) or derision (v. 23). Rather than this fruitless approach, he came with a **revelation** (compare 2:10), **prophecy** (12:29), **knowledge** (compare 2:12) and **teaching** (12:29; compare 14:26).

14:7–9. Like musical instruments that must be used at the proper time and in the proper way for them to serve their proper function, so tongues being exercised outside these guidelines are like **speaking into the air.** Even if the languages sound beautiful, are spoken fluently, or contain great ideas or even praise of God, they are irrelevant if no one can understand what is being said.

14:10, 11. Paul again forms an analogy to further drive home his point. **many kinds of languages:** No one can master all the languages in the world, but they have one point in common: they all convey meaning **(significance). Meaning** is essential to communication in language, and it is no different with the languages from the Spirit. Without meaning they make the speaker a **foreigner** (literally, barbarian, making meaningless sounds like "barbar") to listeners.

14:12. spiritual gifts: The word for spiritual here is different from Paul's usage to this point (gifts is not in the Greek text). Rather than *pneumatikon* or *pneumatika,* he uses the common word *pneuma,* meaning "spirits." They are desirous for spirits (v. 2). Paul may be speaking with tongue in cheek, describing their fall back to former practices in Greek pagan worship. Or he may be using "spirits" to refer to their speaking in tongues. Paul seeks to redirect their zeal toward legitimate manifestations of the Holy Spirit that will benefit fellow worshipers.

14:13. pray that he may interpret: If one "speaks in a tongue" (possibly with ecstacy), no one around can understand (14:2). Consequently, the speaker should beseech God for the ability to interpret so the entire church may benefit.

14:14. pray in a tongue: But if one prays in a tongue (i.e., without interpreting) and there is no interpretation (which seemed to be the Corinthian practice), then there is no understanding and consequently no benefit to the person or the church.

14:15. Pray with the spirit refers contextually to the spirit of the person, not the Spirit of God (v. 2). Paul desires to pray to God both with his spirit and with **understanding.** Paul is unwilling to become schizoid in his spiritual life, turning off his mind while giving free sway to his spirit.

14:16, 17. Otherwise: From verse 12 on, Paul shows the absurdity of their promoting their favorite "gift" in an unedifying way rather than building the body into unity as taught in chapter 2. Here, then, he forces them through his logic to channel their zeal (12:31; 13:5; 14:1; 14:12). **place of the uninformed:** Possibly a new convert is in view. However, anyone who does not have the gift of interpretation could fill this place. **Amen at your giving of thanks:** It was common in Jewish, and apparently early church, worship for the congregation to indicate its agreement with the prayer by responding with "amen" (Deut.

27:14–26; Rev. 5:14). Such a response would be impossible when no one understands.

14:18, 19. more than you all: Apparently Paul quantitatively spoke numerous languages. Or he spoke in tongues more often than even the zealously tongues-speaking Corinthians. Either way, **in the church** the speaking of five words that were understandable (presumably prophesying) had more benefit than a countless number of words **in a tongue.** All speaking in tongues in Acts occurred in public. Paul's teaching here focuses on such public utterance, although verse 18 may have in view Paul's tongues-speech in private, personal prayer. Possibly, in view of verses 20–22, the apostle prayed publicly in various languages when he visited the different synagogues as he traveled from town to town through the Roman Empire.

14:20–22. Brethren: In this new paragraph (possibly picking up now from 13:11) Paul challenges the Corinthians to reorient their thinking. They are to be **mature,** while in **malice** they are to be **babes.** The Corinthians still had much to learn. At the time of Paul's writing they had poor ethical judgment, though they had a high opinion of themselves. **In the law:** Paul evaluates the purpose of tongues and the mature use of them by the Scriptures rather than by personal experience. The quotation from Isaiah 28:11 indicates that "law" here refers to the Old Testament rather than simply the Pentateuch.

14:23–25. At this point Paul advances from the theological debate to the application to the congregation. Having demonstrated that their tongues–speaking had limited value for the church and was even harmful to it, Paul displays vividly what their disorderly tongues-speaking was doing to unbelievers. Whenever the church met and the **uninformed or unbelievers** entered the assembly and the Corinthians were speaking in tongues (presumably without interpretation), these Christians appeared mad. However, when these non-Christians heard the congregation **prophesy,** the message **convicted** them, so that they fell **down on** their faces and worshiped God.

14:26. Paul now sets forth to the Corinthians a sample of the way a local church meeting should be conducted. If **each of you** brings to the meeting the special ability that God has given and everything is done for **edification,** the church as a whole will be benefited. **Psalm** probably refers to the singing of an Old Testament psalm (compare Col 3:16; Eph. 5:19). **Teaching** would most likely consist of the presentation of some Old Testament truth or teaching of the apostles. Though the apostle has sought to curtail the excess, he still recognizes that there was a proper place for the gift of tongues **(has a tongue)** with **an interpretation.** The one who receives a **revelation** may be the prophet who speaks the word of God (vv. 29–32).

14:27. The apostle puts forth some guidelines designed to keep the gift of tongues under control and yet allow the Spirit of God to use the gift through the church. He limits the number of manifestations of this gift in one church meeting to **three,** and in order **(in turn),** and each one of these manifestations is to be interpreted. Before speaking in tongues, they need to be sure that someone is present to **interpret** or the tongues-speakers themselves should interpret (compare vv. 5, 13).

 For insight on the spiritual gift of speaking in tongues, see the word study on "Tongues" on p. 187.

14:28. if ... no interpreter ... keep silent: If no one interprets what is said, then the tongues-speaker is not to speak. The Greek word for "silent" (*sigao*) means "to say nothing," "stop speaking," "hold one's tongue."

14:29. two or three prophets speak: As beneficial as prophesying is, even here Paul seeks to order the activity. There is only so much time in a meeting of the church and there is much to be done. **Let the others judge** indicates that no one, not even a person exercising a grace-gift, is exempt from the judgment of the church (6:5; 11:29, 31). This judgment might be by the other prophets present.

14:30. Revealed surely indicates that the prophesying is more than what we view as preaching or speaking from the texts of Scripture. This is akin to Old Testament prophecy in which God gives revelation to a servant so he can give that revelation to God's people. **Let the first keep silent** is similar to the admonition in verse 28 concerning tongues-speakers. The speakers are not to be interrupting each other. All things are to be done orderly (v. 41).

14:31, 32. One by one is similar to "in turn" of verse 27 regarding the tongues-speakers. Since the purpose of prophesying is that the congregation may **learn** and **be encouraged,** only this orderly procedure will assure the result. **Subject to the prophets** is added lest someone should claim, "I simply can't help myself when God brings a revelation to me from the Spirit." Paul teaches that the Holy Spirit does not overpower the individual he empowers. The will of the Christian is not broken but must cooperate with the work of God.

14:33. God is not the author of confusion: Confusion is exactly what the Corinthians had been experiencing. This comes not from God but from the sinful flesh. **As in all the churches of the saints** may go with the first part of verse 33 or as the beginning of verse 34. The clause seems to fit better with verse 34 regarding behavior in the church meetings.

14:34. Paul commands that **women** are to be **silent** in the church meetings. This is a stronger and more inclusive statement than is given in 1 Timothy 2:12. In 1 Timothy the reference is to teaching men; here all talking appears prohibited. This seems to disagree, however, with the previous allowance of women prophesying in chapter 11. Some have argued that the speaking refers to speaking in tongues, while others believe disruptive talk is prohibited. Still others believe Paul is attempting to inhibit a feminist group at Corinth. The solution is likely otherwise. The immediate context concerns self-control and judging the prophets. The prohibition relates to women not being involved in judging the prophets. Such judging would be an expression of authority over men, which was forbidden.

14:35. Ask their own husbands at home seems to indicate the **women** are older women who are already married. The idea of younger unmarried women seeking to address the church probably never entered the apostle's mind. **Shameful** indicates the strong feeling of the apostle and the early church in general of having women instruct men in the church or exercise authority over them. However, when women were covered and prophesied, this was acceptable and not viewed as exercising authority over the men (compare 11:3–10).

14:36. Come originally from you is another argument for the Corinthians to accept Paul's teaching. The Corinthians did not invent the truth Paul teaches. It began at Jerusalem and has now traveled throughout most of the Roman world.

14:37. To further establish his arguments and the authority of his teaching, Paul now asserts that as an apostle what he teaches are the **commandments of the Lord.** They are not opinions and are not optional. **Thinks himself to be a prophet or spiritual** further demonstrates that two primary classes of gifted persons are in view in chapter 14, namely, the prophet and the tongues-speaker.

14:38–40. To the person who refuses to heed the apostle's admonition, Paul simply says if that person wants to be **ignorant, let him be ignorant.**

 See discussion questions on issues raised in chapter 14 of 1 Corinthians on *p. 209.*

CHAPTER 15

15:1, 2. Paul's **gospel** to the Corinthians centered on the physical death and resurrection of Jesus Christ, the eternal Son of God who became human yet never sinned (Gal. 1:6–10). Paul had started the Corinthian church; the gospel that the Corinthians had originally **received** came from him (2:2).

 For insight on and a handy review of the central truths of the resurrection presented in chapter 15 of 1 Corinthians, see "Facts About the Resurrection" *on p. 200.*

15:3. Paul did not originate the proclamation of Jesus that he **delivered** to the Corinthians; he simply gave the Corinthians what he himself had **received.**

He viewed himself as a link in a long chain of witnesses to the truth of the death and resurrection of Christ. **Christ died for our sins:** Christ's death dealt decisively with our sins. He suffered in our place to endure the just wrath of God against us. **according to the Scriptures:** Christ lived and died in accordance with the prophecies about Him in the Old Testament (Ps. 16:10; Is. 53:8–10).

15:4. The Resurrection verifies the fact that Christ's death paid the full price for sin. The Greek term translated **rose** here is in the perfect tense, emphasizing the ongoing effects of this historical event. Christ is a risen Savior today.

 For a teaching/communication suggestion on chapter 15 of 1 Corinthians, see "Three Great Possessions of Believers" on p. 230.

15:5–8. At the time of Paul's writing, a person could have verified the truthfulness of the apostle's statements. The majority of the **five hundred** people who saw the risen Christ, as well as **all the apostles** and **James** (the half brother of Jesus), were still living. **Born out of due time** is probably Paul's comment on the unique way he became an apostle. Unlike the other apostles, who had the benefit of an initial training period with Christ, Paul became an apostle abruptly, with no opportunity for earthly contact with Christ or His teaching.

15:9. Paul considered himself **the least of the apostles** because at one time he had persecuted the church (Acts 22:4; Eph. 3:8; 1 Tim. 1:15, 16).

15:10. I labored more abundantly: Even though Paul got a late start and did not have the discipleship training that the other apostles did, he traveled further, established more churches, and wrote more Scripture than all of them (2 Cor. 11:23–27). But Paul attributed his success to **the grace of God.**

15:11. whether . . . I or they: Paul did not care who got credit for the Corinthians' faith. He cared only that the Corinthians believed.

15:12, 13. Some of the Corinthians were teaching **that there is no resurrection.** These opponents of Paul may have been denying the reality of Christ's resurrection. They may also have been teaching that resurrection is only spiritual rather than physical. Or they may have been teaching that the Resurrection had already happened (2 Tim. 2:18). Whatever the case, they contradicted the essential teaching that Christ had been physically raised from the dead and that believers in Him will some day also be resurrected.

15:14. preaching is empty . . . faith is also empty: It is not enough that a person believes something. It is absolutely essential that *what* one believes is true. The object of our faith is important. A dead Savior cannot take away sins, rescue us from God's wrath, or develop a relationship with us.

15:15. false witnesses: In verses 5–8, Paul listed several people, including himself, who had witnessed the resurrected Christ. To deny the Resurrection was to deny the truth of their testimony.

15:16, 17. you are still in your sins: Christ's death without His Resurrection would not succeed in saving us from our sins.

15:18. Without the resurrection of Christ, those who are **asleep in Christ**—the dead—have **perished** or been destroyed. The Greek word translated "futile" in this passage speaks of something that has no results. Without the resurrection of Christ, the Christian faith brings no forgiveness and no future life in God's presence.

 For insight and information on the resurrection of Christ and believers, see the word study on "Resurrection" on p. 187.

15:19. we are of all men the most pitiable: If Christians have no hope for the future, the pagans could justifiably consider Christians fools since believers would have suffered for nothing.

15:20–28. Paul changes mood and tone in these verses. He declares the truthfulness of Christ's and the believer's resurrection.

15:20. Jesus is the **firstfruits** of all others who believe in Him. This is an Old Testament image of the first installment of a crop which anticipates and guarantees the ultimate offering of the whole crop (16:15; Rom. 8:23). Because Christ rose from the dead, those who are **asleep** in Christ (v. 18; 1 Thess. 4:15, 16) have a guarantee of their own resurrection.

15:21, 22. by man came death: The first man, Adam, transgressed God's law and brought sin and death into the world (Gen. 2:17; 3:19; Rom. 5:12–21); the second Man, Jesus Christ, was the perfect sacrifice to take away sin and to bring life and resurrection to those who believe in Him (Rom. 5:15–21). **in Christ all shall be made alive:** The principle here is similar to that in Romans 5:18, 19, where Paul explains that by one man's (Adam's) sin many were made unrighteous, whereas by one Man's (Christ's) obedience many will be made righteous.

15:23. Each one in his own order indicates that God has a certain design for the resurrection. The word *order* is a Greek military term that might also be translated "rank." The Commander is raised first; His troops afterward. In 1 Thessalonians 4:13–18, **His coming** is described as Christ's coming with those who have "fallen asleep" (the dead), who are then united with their physical bodies. Following this is the removal of all living Christians from the earth.

15:24. The end here refers to all remaining prophetic events that will occur after the rapture of the church and during the climax of history, when Christ **puts an end to all rule** (vv. 25–28). **delivers the kingdom to God the Father:** When Christ and the church are joined at His coming, God will establish His *kingdom* on this earth, culminating in a new heaven and a new earth. **puts an end to all rule and all authority:** Until the time of *the end*, the Father subjugates everything to the Son (Ps. 110:1; Dan. 2:44; 7:14, 27). Christ is Lord over the universe (Col. 1:15–17).

15:25, 26. all enemies: God has allowed His enemy Satan to rule as the "prince of the power of the air" (Eph. 2:2) and the "god of this age" (2 Cor. 4:4), but his final judgment before God is certain. **The last enemy . . . death:** The conquering of death is final proof of God's victory and the inauguration of the new day of the Lord (Rev. 20:14).

15:27, 28. it is evident: Paul clarified the verses that he had been quoting from the Old Testament. The texts say that everything is put under the Son, but God the Father **is excepted,** or excluded from this subjugation, because the **Son** must be **subject to** the Father. **God may be all in all** indicates that there will be no challenge to the sovereign rule of God over all the universe. There will be universal peace and prosperity.

15:29. There are scores of interpretations about what is meant in this verse by **baptized for the dead.** The most natural interpretation is that some of the Corinthians, in conformity to their prior pagan practices which allowed such rites, were baptized for some in the Corinthian church who had died without baptism. Certainly whether they were baptized or not relates in no way to whether they were justified or not but may have served some ritualistic function within the church. The apostle does not approve or disapprove of the unusual practice in so many words though it is informative that he says *they* rather than *we* when speaking of the ceremony. No other evidence is found among the church in the first century of such a practice except for a heretical sect (i.e., the Marconites). He desires, rather, to get to the heart of the problem: **If the dead do not rise . . . Why then:** To deny the Resurrection and yet be involved in such activities surely makes that look foolish.

15:30–32. why do we stand in jeopardy: Paul risked his life **daily.** To do so would have been of no **advantage** without the hope of a resurrection. Why else should Paul have endured difficulties like fighting **beasts at Ephesus?** It would have been better for him to take the position of the Epicureans, who sought pleasure and avoided pain. The reference to beasts might be a figurative reference to Paul's human enemies at Ephesus. Acts 19 does not record any confrontation with animals.

15:33, 34. Paul had already warned the Corinthians to avoid fellow believers who lived immoral lives (5:9–13). Quoting a proverb from the poet Menander, **evil company corrupts good habits,** Paul warned the Corinthians to stay away from those who teach false doctrine (2 Cor. 6:14–7:1).

15:35–37. Some people objected to the Resurrection on the grounds that it was too hard to understand. Paul called these people **foolish.** Difficulty understanding the nature of the Resurrection should not cause a person to doubt its reality, any more than not understanding how a seed becomes a plant should cause disbelief in the coming harvest.

15:38–41. The variety found in nature among living beings such as **men, animals, fish,** and **birds,** and among objects such as **celestial bodies and terrestrial bodies** reflects the Creator's power and will. The varying brightness of the **sun, moon,** and **stars** serves as a good illustration of the differences between the earthly human body and the heavenly human body. All these different celestial and terrestrial objects are evidence that God the Creator can certainly create new resurrected human bodies out of our old bodies.

15:42–44. The earthly body has various weaknesses, while the heavenly body is devoid of these weaknesses. The body from the earth is corruptible, has **dishonor,** is weak, and is governed by natural instincts. The body from heaven is incorruptible, glorious, powerful, and is governed by the spirit energized by God.

15:44–49. natural . . . spiritual: The contrast is not between a material body and an immaterial body, but between a body subject to death and a body that is immortal. The Greek term translated "spiritual" here refers to a body directed by the Spirit, as opposed to one dominated by the flesh (2:15; 10:4). **First man . . . second Man** contrasts the sinful nature that every person inherits with the new righteous nature that comes through Christ.

For insight on the new bodies that believers will receive at the resurrection, see the word study on "Life-Giving Spirit" on p. 188.

15:50. Mere **flesh and blood** cannot enter into the glorious existence of an immortal body (vv. 35–49). Something must happen to this *flesh* so that it becomes incorruptible (v. 42).

15:51, 52. we shall all be changed: The teaching here is similar to the teaching given to the Thessalonians (1 Thess. 4:13–18). Whereas the dead in Christ will be raised first, the living believers will be instantly transformed into their immortal bodies when Jesus returns.

15:53–57. The living will receive a body that is not subject to death (v. 50). Satan's apparent victories in the Garden of Eden (Gen. 3:13) and at the Cross (Mark 15:22–24) were reversed by Jesus' death (Col. 2:15) and Resurrection. From the vantage point of Jesus' victorious return, **Death** and **Hades** (the grave) have no power over Christians, because Jesus has already conquered both. We participate in His **victory.**

15:58. The Corinthians were to continue **steadfast** in the **work** of Christ, specifically because of the Resurrection. **your labor is not in vain:** All the work that we do for Christ will be rewarded (2 Cor. 5:10; Rev. 22:12).

 See discussion questions on issues raised in chapter 15 of 1 Corinthians on p. 210.

CHAPTER 16

16:1–4. Now concerning: Paul once again addressed a question asked by the Corinthians (7:1, 25; 8:1; 12:1) about giving (Acts 11:29, 30; 24:17; Rom. 15:25–28; 2 Cor. 8; 9). **The first day of the week** was the regular weekly meeting day of the early church. **Lay something aside** expresses the concept of Christian giving in the New Testament. The Old Testament tithe (altogether coming to about 23 percent) was not adopted by the New Testament church, though certainly Christ practiced it. New Testament believers were encouraged to give liberally, but never a specified amount or percentage (Rom. 12:8). Paul wanted to make sure that the Corinthians' offering would be collected before he arrived so he would not need to pressure the people when he saw them (2 Cor. 9:5). **Whomever you approve** refers to the person who would accompany Paul (v. 4) to **Jerusalem** to deliver the gift on behalf of the Corinthian church.

 For a teaching/communication suggestion on Christian giving, see "Putting Money to Work" on p. 231.

16:5–7. Now I will come to you: Paul had hoped to leave Ephesus soon to visit Corinth, perhaps even spending **the winter** with the Corinthians. Travel by sea during the winter was hazardous (Acts 27:9–44). Paul eventually did make it to Corinth, but not according to the schedule he planned here. This failure to come caused him trouble later with the Corinthians (2 Cor. 1:15–2:1).

 For a teaching/communication suggestion on chapter 16 of 1 Corinthians, see "Expressions of Christian Love" on p. 230.

16:8, 9. The opportunities for Paul's ministry **in Ephesus,** a major city of Asia Minor, were great, as was the persecution he endured there.

16:10–12. Although Paul could not leave immediately for Corinth, he wanted to be represented among the Corinthians by his fellow workers. He planned to send **Timothy,** a young man at this time. Paul encouraged the Corinthians to go easy on Timothy, for although he was trustworthy, he was more timid than Paul.

For insight on Paul's relationship to Timothy, see "Who Was Timothy?" on p. 192.

16:13, 14. Watch is often used in the New Testament to indicate anticipation of some future event (Mark 13:37; Rev. 3:3). Paul's exhortation to **stand fast in the faith** is especially important in view of the susceptibility of the Corinthians to false teaching (2 Cor. 11:3). **Be brave** may also be translated "play the man," emphasizing not only bravery but maturity. Paul's command to do everything **with love** serves as a balance to these strong exhortations.

16:15–18. The household of Stephanas was among the first in **Achaia** to respond to Paul's preaching. **Stephanas, Fortunatus, and Achaicus** probably were the ones who confirmed the bad news brought by Chloe's household in 1:11. They were also probably the bearers of the letter that the Corinthians sent to Paul (7:1).

 For a teaching/communication suggestion on Paul and Christian friendship, see "From Enemies to Family and Friends" on p. 231.

16:19, 20. The churches of Asia may be those mentioned in Revelation 2 and 3. **Aquila and Priscilla** were tentmakers who had met Paul in Corinth. They followed him to Ephesus and made their house available for the meetings of the church (Rom. 16:3–5). They would have been known to many in the Corinthian church. **a holy kiss:** This custom, adopted by the early Christians, symbolized love, forgiveness, and unity.

 For insight on Paul's relationship to Aquila and Priscilla, see "Who Were Aquila and Priscilla?" on p.192.

16:21–24. my own hand: From this point on, Paul stopped dictating (Rom. 16:22; Gal. 6:11) and completed the letter in his own handwriting. **let him be accursed:** It may seem harsh that Paul would wish God's damnation on those who do not love Jesus. But the acceptance or rejection of Christ is serious business. Those who reject the Lord Jesus are enemies of God (Gal. 1:8, 9). In the next breath Paul desires the coming of our Lord with an Aramaic expression, *marana tha,* meaning "Lord, come."

 See discussion questions on issues raised in chapter 16 of 1 Corinthians on p. 211.

5
Extended Commentary on
1 Corinthians

(From *Believer's Bible Commentary*, by William MacDonald)

CHAPTER 1

1:1. Paul was **called to be an apostle of Jesus Christ** on the Damascus road. This call did not come from or through men, but directly from the Lord Jesus. **An apostle** is literally "a sent one." The first apostles were witnesses of Christ in resurrection. They also could perform miracles to confirm that the message they preached was divine. Paul could truly say in the language of Gerhard Tersteegen:

> *Christ the Son of God has sent me*
> *To the midnight lands;*
> *Mine the mighty ordination*
> *Of the pierced hands.*

When Paul wrote, a **brother** named **Sosthenes** was with him, so Paul includes his name in the salutation. It cannot be known for sure whether this is the same Sosthenes as in Acts 18:17, the ruler of the synagogue who was publicly beaten by the Greeks. Possibly this leader had been saved through Paul's preaching and was now helping him in the work of the gospel.

1:2. The letter is addressed first of all **to the church of God which is at Corinth**. It is encouraging that there is no place on earth too immoral for an assembly belonging to God to be established. The Corinthian congregation is further described as **those who are sanctified in Christ Jesus, called . . . saints.** **Sanctified** here means set apart to God from the world, and describes the *position* of all who belong to Christ. As to their *practical condition*, they should set themselves apart day by day in holy living.

 For information on the precise location of Corinth and its significance as a trade center, see "The Peloponnesus, Achaea, and the Isthmus of Corinth" on p.188.

Some people contend that sanctification is a distinct work of grace whereby a person obtains the eradication of the sin nature. Such a teaching is contradicted in this verse. The Corinthian Christians were far from what they should have been in practical holiness, but the fact remains that they were positionally **sanctified** by God.

As saints they were members of a great fellowship: **called to be saints, with all who in every place call on the name of Jesus Christ our Lord, both theirs and ours**. Although the teachings of this epistle were first addressed to the saints in Corinth, they are also intended for all those of the worldwide fellowship who acknowledge the lordship of Christ.

For a teaching/communication suggestion on chapter 1 of 1 Corinthians, see "Divisions in the Church" on p. 213.

1:3. First Corinthians is in a very special way the letter of His lordship. In discussing the many problems of assembly and personal life, the apostle constantly reminds his readers that Jesus Christ is Lord and that all we do should be done in acknowledgment of this great truth.

Paul's characteristic greeting is given in verse 3. **Grace and peace** summarize his entire gospel. **Grace** is the source of every blessing, and **peace** is the result in the life of a man who accepts the grace of God. These great blessings come **from God our Father and the Lord Jesus Christ**. Paul does not hesitate to mention **the Lord Jesus** in the same breath with **God our Father**. This is one of hundreds of similar expressions in the New Testament implying the equality of the Lord Jesus with God the Father.

1:4. Having concluded his salutation, the apostle now turns to thanksgiving for the Corinthians and for the wonderful work of God in their lives (vv. 4–9). It was a noble trait in Paul's life that always sought to find something thankworthy in the lives of his fellow believers. If their practical lives were not very commendable, then he would at least **thank** his **God** for what He had done for them. This is exactly the case here. The Corinthians were not what we would call "spiritual Christians." But Paul can at least give thanks **for the grace of God which was given to** them **by Christ Jesus**.

1:5. The particular way in which God's grace was manifested to the Corinthians was in their being richly endowed with gifts of the Holy Spirit. Paul specifies gifts of **utterance and all knowledge**, presumably meaning that the Corinthians had been given the gifts of tongues, interpretation of tongues, and knowledge to an extraordinary degree. **Utterance** has to do with outward expression and **knowledge** with inward comprehension.

1:6. The fact that they had these gifts was a confirmation of God's work in their lives, and that is what Paul means when he says, **even as the testimony of Christ was confirmed in you.** They heard **the testimony of Christ,** they received it by faith, and God testified that they were truly saved by giving them these miraculous powers.

1:7. As far as the possession of gifts was concerned, the Corinthian church was not inferior to any other. But the mere possession of these gifts was not in itself a mark of true spirituality. Paul was really thanking the Lord for something for which the Corinthians themselves were not directly responsible. Gifts are given by the ascended Lord without regard to a person's own merit. If a person has some gift, he should not be proud of it but use it humbly for the Lord.

The fruit of the Spirit is another matter entirely. This involves the believer's own surrender to the control of the Holy Spirit. The apostle could not commend the Corinthians for evidence of the fruit of the Spirit in their lives, but only for what the Lord had sovereignly bestowed on them—something over which they had no control.

Later in 1 Corinthians the apostle will have to reprove the saints for their abuse of these gifts, but here he is content to express thanks that they had received these gifts in such unusual measure.

The Corinthians were **eagerly waiting for the revelation of our Lord Jesus Christ.** Bible students are not agreed about whether this refers to Christ's coming for His saints (1 Thess. 4:13–18), or to the Lord's coming with His saints (2 Thess. 1:6–10), or both. In the first case it would be a revelation of Christ only to believers, whereas in the second it would be His revelation to the whole world. Both the rapture and the glorious appearing of Christ are **eagerly** awaited by the believer.

1:8. Now Paul expresses the confidence that the Lord **will also confirm** the saints **to the end, that** they might **be blameless in the day of our Lord Jesus Christ.** Once again it is striking that Paul's thanksgiving is concerned with what God will do rather than with what the Corinthians have done. Because they have trusted Christ, and because God confirmed this fact by giving the gifts of the Spirit to them, Paul was confident that God would keep them for Himself until Christ's coming for His people.

 For insight on the meaning of fellowship, see the word study on "Fellowship" on p. 185.

1:9. Paul's optimism concerning the Corinthians is based on the faithfulness of **God** who called them **into the fellowship of His Son.** He knows that since God had gone to such tremendous cost to make them sharers of the life of **our Lord,** He would never let them slip out of His hands.

1:10. The apostle is now ready to take up the problem of **divisions** in the church (1:10–4:21). He begins with a loving exhortation to unity. Instead of commanding with the authority of an apostle, he pleads with the tenderness of a brother. The appeal for unity is based on **the name of our Lord Jesus Christ,** and since the name stands for the Person, it is based on all that the Lord Jesus is and has done. The Corinthians were exalting the name of men; that could only lead to divisions. Paul will exalt the name of the Lord Jesus, knowing that only in this way will unity be produced among the people of God. To **speak the same thing** means to be of **the same mind and** of one accord. It means to be united as to loyalty and allegiance. This unity is produced when Christians have the mind of Christ. In the verses to follow, Paul will tell them in a practical manner how they can think Christ's thoughts after Him.

1:11. News concerning the **contentions** in Corinth had come to Paul from **Chloe's household.** In naming his informers, Paul lays down an important principle of Christian conduct. We should not pass on news about our fellow believers unless we are willing to be quoted in the matter. If this example were followed today, it would prevent most of the idle gossip which now plagues the church.

1:12. Sects or parties were being formed within the local church, each one claiming its distinctive leader. Some acknowledged preference for **Paul,** some for **Apollos,** some for **Cephas** (Peter). Some even claimed to belong to **Christ,** probably meaning that they *alone* belonged to Him, to the exclusion of others!

 For insight on the Apollos faction at Corinth, see "Who Was Apollos?" on p. 189.

1:13. Paul's indignant rebuke of sectarianism is found in verses 13–17. To form such parties in the church was to deny the unity of the body of **Christ.** To follow human leaders was to slight the One who had been crucified for them. To take the name of a man was to forget that in baptism, they had acknowledged their allegiance to the Lord Jesus.

1:14. The rise of parties in Corinth made Paul thankful **that** he **had baptized** only a few in the assembly there. He mentions **Crispus and Gaius** as among those whom he had baptized.

1:15, 16. He would never want anyone to **say that** he **had baptized in** his **own name.** In other words, he was not trying to win converts to himself or to make a name for himself. His sole aim was to point men and women to the Lord Jesus Christ.

On further reflection Paul remembered that he had **also baptized the household of Stephanas,** but he could **not** think of **any other.**

1:17. He explains that **Christ did not send** him primarily **to baptize, but**

to preach the gospel. This does not mean for a moment that Paul did not believe in baptism. He has already mentioned the names of some whom he *did* baptize. Rather, it means that his main business was not to baptize; he probably entrusted this work to others, perhaps to some of the Christians in the local church. This verse, however, does lend its testimony against any idea that baptism is essential to salvation. If that were true, then Paul would be saying here that he was thankful that he saved none of them except Crispus and Gaius! Such an idea is untenable.

In the latter part of verse 17, Paul is making an easy transition to the verses that follow. He did not **preach the gospel** by using **wisdom of words, lest the Cross of Christ should be made of no effect**. He knew that if men were impressed by his oratory or rhetoric, then to that extent he had defeated himself in his efforts to set forth the true meaning of **the Cross of Christ**.

It will help us to understand the section that follows if we remember that the Corinthians, being Greeks, were great lovers of human wisdom. They regarded their philosophers as national heroes. Some of this spirit had apparently crept into the assembly at Corinth. There were those who desired to make the gospel more acceptable to the intelligentsia. They did not feel that it had status among scholars, and so they wanted to intellectualize the message. This worship of intellectualism was apparently one of the issues that was causing the people to form parties around human leaders. Efforts to make the gospel more acceptable are completely misguided. There is a vast difference between God's wisdom and man's, and there is no use trying to reconcile them.

Paul now shows the folly of exalting men, and emphasizes that to do this is inconsistent with the true nature of the gospel (1:18–3:4). His first point is that the message of the cross is the opposite of all that men consider to be true wisdom (1:18–25).

1:18. The message of the cross is foolishness to those who are perishing. As Barnes so aptly stated: "The death on the cross was associated with the idea of all that is shameful and dishonorable; and to speak of salvation only by the sufferings and death of a crucified man was fitted to excite in their bosoms only unmingled scorn." The Greeks were lovers of wisdom (the literal meaning of the word *philosophers*). But there was nothing in the gospel message to appeal to their pride of knowledge.

To those **who are being saved**, the gospel **is the power of God**. They hear the message, they accept it by faith, and the miracle of regeneration takes place in their lives. Notice the solemn fact in this verse that there are only two classes of people—those who perish and those who are saved. There is no in-between class. People may love their human wisdom, but only the gospel leads to salvation.

1:19. The fact that the gospel would be offensive to human wisdom was prophesied by Isaiah: "I will destroy the wisdom of the wise, and bring to nothing the understanding of the prudent" (29:14).

S. Lewis Johnson in *The Wycliffe Bible Commentary* notes that in context these "words are God's denouncement of the policy of the 'wise' in Judah in seeking an alliance with Egypt when threatened by Sennacherib." How true it is that God delights to accomplish His purposes in ways that seem foolish to men. How often He uses methods that the wise of this world would ridicule, yet they achieve the desired results with wonderful accuracy and efficiency. For example, man's wisdom assures him that he can earn or merit his own salvation. The gospel sets aside all man's efforts to save himself and presents Christ as the only way to God.

1:20. Paul next hurls out a defiant challenge: **Where is the wise? Where is the scribe? Where is the disputer of this age?** Did God consult them when He devised His plan of salvation? Could they ever have worked out such a plan of redemption if left to their own wisdom? Can they rise to disprove anything that God ever said? The answer is an emphatic "No!" **God** has **made foolish the wisdom of this world.**

1:21. Man cannot by his own **wisdom** come to the knowledge of God. For centuries God gave the human race this opportunity, and the result was failure. Then **it pleased God** by the preaching of the cross, a message that seems foolish to men, **to save those who believe.** The foolishness of the thing preached refers to the cross. Of course, we know that it is not foolishness, but it seems foolish to the unenlightened mind of man. Godet says that verse 21 contains a whole philosophy of history, the substance of entire volumes. We should not hurry over it quickly, but ponder deeply its tremendous truths.

1:22. It was characteristic of the **Jews** to **request a sign.** Their attitude was that they would believe if some miracle were shown to them. The **Greeks** on the other hand searched for **wisdom.** They were interested in human reasonings, in arguments, in logic.

1:23. But Paul did not cater to their desires. He says, **We preach Christ crucified.** As someone has said, "He was not a sign-loving Jew, nor a wisdom-loving Greek, but a Savior-loving Christian."

To the Jews, Christ crucified was **a stumbling block.** They looked for a mighty military leader to deliver them from the oppression of Rome. Instead of that, the gospel offered them a Savior nailed to a cross of shame. **To the Greeks,** Christ crucified was **foolishness.** They could not understand how One who died in such seeming weakness and failure could ever solve their problems.

1:24. But strangely enough, the very things that the Jews and the Gentiles sought are found in a wonderful way in the Lord Jesus. To those who hear His call and trust in Him, **both Jews and Greeks, Christ** becomes **the power of God and the wisdom of God.**

1:25. Actually there is neither foolishness nor weakness with God. But the apostle is saying in verse 25 that what seems to be **foolishness** on God's part, in the eyes of men, is actually **wiser than men** at their very best. Also, what seems to be **weakness** on God's part, in the eyes of men, turns out to be **stronger than** anything that **men** can produce.

1:26. Having spoken of the gospel itself, the apostle now turns to the people whom God calls by the gospel (vv. 26–29). He reminds the Corinthians that **not many wise according to the flesh, not many mighty, not many noble are called.** It has often been pointed out that the text does not say "not any" but **not many.** Because of this slight difference, one English lady of noble blood used to testify that she was saved by the letter "m."

The Corinthians themselves had not come from the upper intellectual crust of society. They had not been reached by high-sounding philosophies but by the simple gospel. Why, then, were they putting such a premium on human wisdom and exalting preachers who sought to make the message palatable to the worldly-wise?

If men were to build a church, they would want to enroll the most prominent members of the community. But verse 26 teaches us that the people whom men esteem so highly, God passes by. The ones He calls are not generally the ones the world considers great.

1:27. God has chosen the foolish things of the world to put to shame the wise, and God has chosen the weak things of the world to put to shame the things which are mighty. As Erich Sauer says: "The more primitive the material, the greater—if the same standard of art can be reached—the honor of the Master; the smaller the army, the mightier—if the same great victory can be won—the praise of the conqueror."

God used trumpets to bring down the walls of Jericho. He reduced Gideon's army from 32,000 to 300 to rout the armies of Midian. He used an oxgoad in the hand of Shamgar to defeat the Philistines. With the jawbone of a donkey He enabled Samson to defeat a whole army. And our Lord fed over 5,000 with nothing more than a few loaves and fishes.

1:28. To make up what someone has called "God's five-ranked army of fools," Paul adds **the base things of the world and the things which are despised** and **the things which are not.** Using such unlikely materials, God brings **to nothing the things that are.** In other words, He loves to take up people who are of no esteem in the eyes of the world and use them to glorify Himself. These verses should serve as a rebuke to Christians who curry the favor of prominent and well-known personalities and show little or no regard for the more humble saints of God.

1:29. God's purpose in choosing those of no account in the eyes of the world is that all the glory should accrue to Himself and not to man. Since salvation is entirely of Him, He alone is worthy to be praised.

1:30. Verse 30 emphasizes even further that all we are and have comes from Him—not from philosophy, and that there is therefore no room for human glory. First of all, Christ **became for us wisdom.** He is the wisdom of God (v. 24), the One whom God's wisdom chose as the way of salvation. When we have Him we have a positional wisdom that guarantees our full salvation. Secondly, He is our **righteousness.** Through faith in Him we are reckoned righteous by a holy God. Thirdly, He is our **sanctification.** In ourselves we have nothing in the way of personal holiness, but in Him we are positionally sanctified, and by His power we are transformed from one degree of sanctification to another. Finally, He is our **redemption,** and this speaks of redemption in its final aspect when the Lord will come and take us home to be with Himself, and when we shall be redeemed—spirit, soul, and body.

Traill delineated the truth sharply: "Wisdom out[side] of Christ is damning folly—righteousness out[side] of Christ is guilt and condemnation—sanctification out[side] of Christ is filth and sin—redemption out[side] of Christ is bondage and slavery."

A. T. Pierson relates verse 30 to the life and ministry of our Lord: "His deeds and His words and His practices, these show Him as the wisdom of God. Then come His death, burial, and resurrection: these have to do with our righteousness. Then His forty days' walk among men, His ascension up on high, the gift of the Spirit, and His session at the right hand of God, have to do with our sanctification. Then His coming again, which has to do with our redemption."

1:31. God has so arranged it that all these blessings should come to us **in the LORD.** Paul's argument therefore is, "Why glory in men? They cannot do any one of these things for you."

👓 See discussion questions on issues raised in chapter 1 of 1 Corinthians on p. 203.

CHAPTER 2

2:1. The apostle now reminds the saints of his ministry among them and how he sought to glorify God and not himself. He came to them proclaiming **the**

testimony of God, not **with excellence of speech or of wisdom.** He was not interested in showing himself off as an orator or philosopher. This shows that the apostle Paul recognized the difference between ministry that is soulish and that which is spiritual. By soulish ministry, we mean that which amuses, entertains, or generally appeals to man's emotions. Spiritual ministry, on the other hand, presents the truth of God's Word in such a way as to glorify Christ and to reach the heart and conscience of the hearers.

 For a teaching/communication suggestion on chapter 2 of 1 Corinthians, see "Wisdom and Power Go Together" on p. 213.

2:2. The content of Paul's message was **Jesus Christ and Him crucified. Jesus Christ** refers to His person, while **Him crucified** refers to His work. The person and work of the Lord Jesus form the substance of the Christian witness.

2:3. Paul further emphasizes that his personal demeanor was neither impressive nor attractive. He was with the Corinthians **in weakness, in fear, and in much trembling.** The treasure of the gospel was contained in an earthen vessel that the excellence of the power might be of God and not of Paul. He himself was an example of how God uses weak things to confound the mighty.

2:4. Neither Paul's **speech** nor his **preaching** were in **persuasive words of human wisdom, but in demonstration of the Spirit and of power.** Some suggest that his **speech** refers to the material he presented and his **preaching** to the manner of its presentation. Others define his **speech** as his witness to individuals and his **preaching** as his messages to groups. According to the standards of this world, the apostle might never have won an oratorical contest. In spite of this, **the Spirit** of God used the message to produce conviction of sin and conversion to God.

2:5. Paul knew that there was the utmost danger that his hearers might be interested in himself or in his own personality rather than in the living Lord. Conscious of his own inability to bless or to save, he determined that he would lead people to trust in **God** alone rather than **in the wisdom of men.** All who proclaim the gospel message or teach the word of God should make this their constant aim.

2:6. First of all, the **wisdom** shown in the gospel is divine in its origin (vv. 6, 7). **We speak wisdom among those who are mature** or full-grown. **Yet** it is **not the wisdom of this age,** nor would it be wisdom in the eyes of **the rulers of this age.** Their wisdom is a perishable thing which, like themselves, is born for one brief day.

2:7. We speak the wisdom of God in a mystery. A mystery is a New

Testament truth not previously revealed, but now made known to believers by the apostles and prophets of the early church age. This mystery is the **hidden wisdom which God ordained before the ages for our glory**. The mystery of the gospel includes such wonderful truths as the fact that *now* Jews and Gentiles are made one in Christ; that the Lord Jesus will come and take His waiting people home to be with Himself; and that not all believers will die but all will be changed.

2:8. **The rulers of this age** may refer to demonic spirit beings in the heavenlies or to their human agents on earth. They didn't understand the hidden wisdom of God (Christ on a cross) or realize that their murder of the Son of God would result in their own destruction. **Had they known** the ways of God, **they would not have crucified the Lord of glory**.

2:9. The process of revelation, inspiration, and illumination are described in verses 9–16. They tell us how these wonderful truths were made known to the apostles by the Holy Spirit, how they in turn passed on these truths to us by inspiration of the Holy Spirit, and how we understand them by the illumination of the Holy Spirit.

The quotation in verse 9 from Isaiah 64:4 is a prophecy that God had treasured up wonderful truths which could not be discovered by the natural senses but which in due time He would reveal to **those who love Him**. Three faculties (**eye** and **ear** and **heart**, or mind) by which we learn earthly things, are listed, but these are not sufficient for the reception of divine truths, because the Spirit of God is necessary for this.

This verse is commonly interpreted to refer to the glories of heaven, and once we get that meaning in our minds, it is difficult to dislodge it and accept any other meaning. But Paul is really speaking here about the truths that have been revealed for the first time in the New Testament. Men could never have arrived at these truths through scientific investigations or philosophical inquiries. The human mind, left to itself, could never discover the wonderful mysteries which were made known at the beginning of the gospel era. Human reason is totally inadequate to find the truth of God.

2:10. That verse 9 does not refer to heaven is proven by the statement that **God has revealed them to us through His Spirit**. In other words, these truths foretold in the *Old Testament* were made known to the apostles of the *New Testament* era. The **us** refers to the writers of the New Testament. It was by the **Spirit** of God that the apostles and prophets were enlightened, because **the Spirit searches all things, yes, the deep things of God**. In other words, the Spirit of God, one of the members of the Godhead, is infinite in wisdom and understands all the truths of God and is able to impart them to others.

2:11. Even in human affairs no one knows what a **man** is thinking but he himself. No one else can possibly find out unless the man himself chooses to make it known. Even then, in order to understand a man, a person must have **the spirit of** a **man**. An animal could not fully understand our thinking. So it is with God. The only one who can understand the things of God is **the Spirit of God.**

2:12. The **we** of verse 12 refers to the writers of the New Testament, although it is equally true of all the Bible writers. Since the apostles and prophets had received the Holy Spirit, He was able to share with them the deep truths of God. That is what the apostle means when he says in this verse: **Now we have received, not the spirit of the world, but the Spirit who is from God, that we might know the things that have been freely given to us by God.** Apart from **the Spirit who is from God**, the apostles could never have received the divine truths of which Paul is speaking and which are preserved for us in the New Testament.

2:13. Having described the process of revelation by which the writers of sacred Scripture received truth from God, Paul now goes on to describe the process of inspiration, by which that truth was communicated to us. Verse 13 is one of the strongest passages in the Word of God on the subject of verbal inspiration. The apostle Paul clearly states that in conveying these truths to us, the apostles did **not** use **words** of their own choosing or words dictated by **man's wisdom.** Rather, they used the very words **which the Holy Spirit** taught them to use. And so we believe that the actual words of Scripture, as found in the original autographs, were the very words of God (and that the Bible in its present form is entirely trustworthy).

A howl of objection arises at this point since to some people what we have said implies *mechanical dictation,* as if God did not allow the writers to use their own style. Yet we know that Paul's writing style is quite different from Luke's, for example. How, then, can we reconcile verbal inspiration with the obvious individual style of the writers? In some way that we do not understand, God gave the very words of Scripture, and yet He clothed those words with the individual style of the writers, letting their human personality be part of His perfect word.

The expression **comparing spiritual things with spiritual** can be explained in several ways. It may mean (1) teaching spiritual truths with Spirit-given words; (2) communicating spiritual truths to spiritual men; or (3) comparing spiritual truths in one section of the Bible with those in another. We believe that the first explanation fits the context best. Paul is saying that the process of inspiration involves the conveying of divine truth with words that are especially chosen for that purpose by the Holy Spirit. Thus we could paraphrase: "presenting spiritual truths in spiritual words."

It is sometimes objected that this passage cannot refer to inspiration because Paul says we **speak**, not "we write." But it is not uncommon to find the verb "to speak" used of inspired writings (e.g., John 12:38, 41; Acts 28:25; 2 Pet. 1:21).

2:14. Not only is the gospel divine in its revelation and divine in its inspiration, but now we learn that it can only be received by the power of **the Spirit of God**. Unaided, **the natural man does not receive the things of the Spirit of God. They are foolishness to him.** He cannot possibly understand them because they can only be **spiritually** understood.

The colorful Vance Havner advises:

> The wise Christian wastes no time trying to explain God's program to unregenerate men; it would be casting pearls before swine. He might as well try to describe a sunset to a blind man or discuss nuclear physics with a monument in the city park. The natural man cannot receive such things. One might as well try to catch sunbeams with a fishhook as to lay hold of God's revelation unassisted by the Holy Spirit. Unless one is born of the Spirit and taught by Him, all this is utterly foreign to him. Being a Ph.D. does not help, for in this realm it could mean "Phenomenal Dud!"

2:15. On the other hand, the man who is illuminated by the Spirit of God can discern these wonderful truths even though **he himself** cannot be **rightly judged** by the unconverted. Perhaps he is a carpenter, or plumber, or fisherman; yet he is an able student of the Holy Scriptures. "The Spirit-controlled Christian investigates, inquires into, and scrutinizes the Bible and comes to an appreciation and understanding of its contents" (Kenneth S. Wuest). To the world he is an enigma. He may never have been to college or seminary, yet he can understand the deep mysteries of the Word of God and perhaps even teach them to others.

 For a teaching/communication suggestion on the theme of judgment (1 Cor. 2:15), see "What About Judging All Things?" on p. 214.

2:16. The apostle now asks with Isaiah the rhetorical question: **Who has known the mind of the LORD that he may instruct Him?** To ask the question is to answer it. God cannot be known through the wisdom or power of men. He is known only as He chooses to make Himself known. However, those who have **the mind of Christ** are able to understand the deep truths of God.

To review then, first there is *revelation* (vv. 9–12). This means that God revealed previously unknown truths to men by the Holy Spirit. These truths were made known supernaturally by the Spirit of God.

Secondly, there is *inspiration* (v. 13). In transmitting these truths to others, the apostles (and all other writers of the Bible) used the very words which the Holy Spirit taught them to use.

Finally, there is *illumination* (vv. 14–16). Not only must these truths be miraculously *revealed* and miraculously *inspired,* but they can only be *understood* by the supernatural power of the Holy Spirit.

 See discussion questions on issues raised in chapter 2 of 1 Corinthians on p. 203.

CHAPTER 3

3:1. When Paul first visited Corinth, he had fed the believers with the elementary milk of the Word because they were weak and young in the faith. The teaching that had been given to them was suitable to their condition. They could not receive deeply spiritual instruction because they were new believers. They were mere **babes in Christ.**

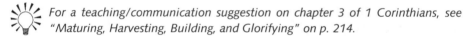 For a teaching/communication suggestion on chapter 3 of 1 Corinthians, see "Maturing, Harvesting, Building, and Glorifying" on p. 214.

3:2. Paul had taught them only the elementary truths concerning Christ, which he speaks of as **milk.** They were not able to take **solid food** because of their immaturity. In the same vein, the Lord Jesus said to His disciples, "I still have many things to say to you, but you cannot bear them now" (John 16:12). With regard to the Corinthians, the tragic thing was that they still had not improved sufficiently to receive deeper truth from the apostle.

3:3. The believers were **still** in a **carnal** or fleshly state of soul. This was evidenced by the fact that there was **envy** and **strife** among them. Such behavior is characteristic of the people of this world, but not of those who are led by the Spirit of God.

3:4. In forming parties around human leaders, such as **Paul** and **Apollos,** they were acting on a purely human level. That is what Paul means when he asks, "Are you not . . . behaving like mere men?"

Up to this point, the apostle Paul has been showing the folly of exalting men by a consideration of the true nature of the gospel message. He now turns to the subject of the Christian ministry and shows from this standpoint also that it is foolishness to exalt religious leaders by building parties around them.

3:5. **Apollos** and **Paul** were *servants* (*minister* is Latin for "servant")

through whom the Corinthians had come to believe in the Lord Jesus. They were simply agents and not the heads of rival schools. How unwise then of the Corinthians to raise servants to the rank of master. Ironside quaintly comments at this point, "Imagine a household divided over servants!"

3:6. Using a figure from agriculture, Paul shows that the servant is after all very limited in what he can do. **Paul** himself could plant and **Apollos** could water, but only **God** could give **the increase.** So today, some of us can preach the word and all of us can pray for unsaved relatives and friends, but the actual work of salvation can be done only by the Lord.

3:7. Looking at it from this point, we can readily see that the planter and the one who waters are really not very important, relatively speaking. They have not the power in themselves to bring forth life. Why then should there be any envy or rivalry among Christian workers? Each should do the work that has been allotted to him, and rejoice when the Lord shows His hand in blessing.

3:8. He who plants and he who waters are one in the sense that they both have the same object and aim. There should be no jealousy between them. As far as service is concerned, they are on the same level. In a coming day, **each one will receive his own reward according to his own labor.** That day is the judgment seat of Christ.

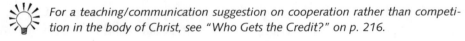 *For a teaching/communication suggestion on cooperation rather than competition in the body of Christ, see "Who Gets the Credit?" on p. 216.*

3:9. God is the One to whom all are responsible. All His servants are **fellow workers,** laboring together in **God's** tilled harvest **field,** or, to change the picture, working together on the same **building.** Erdman renders the thought as follows: "We are fellow-workers who belong to God and are working with one another."

3:10. Continuing with the idea of building, the apostle first of all acknowledges that anything he has been able to accomplish has been due to **the grace of God.** By this he means the undeserved ability from God to do the work of an apostle. Then he goes on to describe his part in the beginning of this assembly at Corinth: **As a wise master builder, I have laid the foundation.** He came to Corinth preaching Christ and Him crucified. Souls were saved and a local church was planted. Then he adds: **And another builds on it.** By this, he doubtless refers to other teachers who subsequently visited Corinth and built on the foundation which had already been established there. However, the apostle cautions: **But let each one take heed how he builds on it.** He means that it is a solemn thing to exercise a teaching ministry in the local church. Some had come to Corinth with divisive doctrines and teachings contrary to the Word of God. Paul was doubtless conscious of these teachers as he wrote the words.

3:11. Only one foundation is required for a building. Once it is laid, it never needs to be repeated. The apostle Paul had laid the foundation of the church at Corinth. That **foundation** was **Jesus Christ**, His person and work.

 For a teaching/communication suggestion on unity in the church, see "How to Cure Divisions in the Church" on p. 215.

3:12. Subsequent teaching in a local church may be of varying degrees of value. For instance, some teaching is of lasting worth, and it might be compared to **gold, silver,** or **precious stones.** Here **precious stones** probably does not refer to diamonds, rubies, or other gems but rather to the granite, marble, or alabaster used in the construction of costly temples. On the other hand, teaching in the local church might be of passing value or of no value at all. Such teaching is compared to **wood, hay,** and **straw.**

This passage of Scripture is commonly used in a general way to refer to the lives of all Christian believers. It is true that we are all building, day by day, and the results of our work will be manifested in a coming day. However, a careful student of the Bible will want to note that the passage does not refer primarily to all believers but rather to preachers and teachers.

3:13. In a coming day, **each one's work will become clear.** The word **Day** refers to the judgment seat of Christ when all service for the Lord will be reviewed. The process of review is compared to the action of **fire.** Service that has brought glory to God and blessing to man, like gold, silver, and precious stones, will not be affected by the fire. On the other hand, that which has caused trouble among the people of God or failed to edify them will be consumed. **The fire will test each one's work, of what sort it is.**

3:14. Work in connection with the church may be of three types. In verse 14 we have the first type—service that has been of a profitable nature. In such a case, the servant's life work **endures** the test of the judgment seat of Christ and the worker **will receive a reward.**

3:15. The second type of work is that which is useless. In this case, the servant **will suffer loss,** although **he himself will be saved, yet so as through fire.** E. W. Rogers points out: "Loss does not imply the forfeiture of something once possessed." It should be clear from this verse that the judgment seat of Christ is not concerned with the subject of a believer's sins and their penalty. The penalty of a believer's sins was borne by the Lord Jesus Christ on the Cross of Calvary, and that matter has been settled once for all. Thus the believer's salvation is not at all in question at the judgment seat of Christ; rather, it is a matter of his service.

 For a teaching/communication suggestion on God's judgment of our works, see "The Ultimate Performance Review" on p. 216.

Through failure to distinguish between salvation and rewards, the Roman Catholic Church has used this verse to try to support its teaching of purgatory. However, a careful examination of the verse reveals no hint about purgatory. There is no thought that the fire purifies the character of a person. Rather, the fire tests a man's work or service, of what sort it is. The man is saved despite the fact that his works are consumed by the fire.

An interesting thought in connection with this verse is that the Word of God is sometimes compared to fire (see Is. 5:24 and Jer. 23:29). The same Word of God that will test our service at the judgment seat of Christ is available to us now. If we are building in accordance with the teachings of the Bible, then our work will stand the test in that coming day.

3:16. Paul reminds the believers that they **are the temple** (Gk., the inner shrine or sanctuary) **of God and that the Spirit of God dwells in** them. It is true that every individual believer is also a temple of God indwelt by the Holy Spirit, but that is not the thought here. The apostle is looking at the church as a collective company, and he wishes them to realize the holy dignity of such a calling.

3:17. A third class of work in the local church is that which may be spoken of as destructive. Apparently there were false teachers who had come into the church at Corinth and whose instruction tended more to sin than to holiness. They did not think it a serious matter to thus cause havoc in a temple of God, so Paul thunders out this solemn declaration: **If anyone defiles the temple of God, God will destroy him.** Viewed in its local setting, this means that if any man enters a local church and wrecks its testimony, **God will destroy him.** The passage is speaking of false teachers who are not true believers in the Lord Jesus. The seriousness of such an offense is indicated by the closing words of verse 17: **For the temple of God is holy, which temple you are.**

3:18. In Christian service, as in all of the Christian life, there is always the danger of self-deception. Perhaps some of those who came to Corinth as teachers posed as people of extreme wisdom. Any who have an exalted view of their own worldly wisdom must learn that they must become fools in the eyes of the world in order to **become wise** in God's estimation. Godet helpfully paraphrases at this point: "If any individual whatever, Corinthian or other, while preaching the gospel *in your assemblies* assumes the part of a wise man and reputation of a profound thinker, let him assure himself that he will not attain true wisdom until he has passed through a crisis in which that wisdom of his with which he is puffed up will perish and after which only he will receive the wisdom which is from above."

3:19. The wisdom of this world is foolishness with God. Man by searching could never find out God. Neither would human wisdom ever have devised a plan of salvation by which God would become man in order to die for guilty, vile, rebel sinners. Job 5:13 is quoted in verse 19 to show that God triumphs over the supposed wisdom of men to work out His own purposes. Man with all his learning cannot thwart the plans of the Lord; instead, God often shows them that in spite of their worldly wisdom, they are utterly poor and powerless.

3:20. Psalm 94:11 is quoted here to emphasize that **the LORD knows** all the reasonings **of the wise** men of this world, and He further knows **that they are futile**, empty, and fruitless. But why is Paul going to such pains to discredit worldly wisdom? Simply for this reason—the Corinthians were placing a great premium on such wisdom and were following those leaders who seemed to exhibit it in a remarkable degree.

 For insight on the futility of human wisdom, see the word study on "Futile" on p. 186.

3:21. In view of all that had been said, **no one** should **boast in men**. And as far as true servants of the Lord are concerned, we should not boast that we belong to them but rather realize that they all belong to us. **All things are yours.**

3:22. Someone has called verse 22 "an inventory of the possessions of the child of God." Christian workers belong to us, whether **Paul** the evangelist, or **Apollos** the teacher, or **Cephas** the pastor. Since they all belong to us, it is folly for us to claim that we belong to any *one* of them. Then **the world** is ours. As joint heirs with Christ, we will one day come into possession of it, but in the meantime it is ours by divine promise. Those who tend its affairs do not realize that they are doing so for us. **Life** is ours. By this we do not mean merely existence on earth but life in its truest, fullest sense. And **death** is ours. For us it is no longer a dread foe that consigns the soul to the dark unknown; rather, it is now the messenger of God that brings the soul to heaven. **Things present** and **things to come—all are** likewise ours. It has been truly said that all things serve the man who serves Christ. A. T. Robertson once said: "The stars in their courses fight for the man who is partner with God in the world's redemption."

3:23. All Christians belong to Christ. Some in Corinth were claiming to belong to Him to the exclusion of all others. They formed the "Christ-party." But Paul refutes any such contention. We are all **Christ's, and Christ is God's.** By thus showing the saints their true and proper dignity, Paul reveals in bold relief the folly of forming parties and divisions in the church.

 See discussion questions on issues raised in chapter 3 of 1 Corinthians on p. 204.

CHAPTER 4

4:1. In order that they might properly appraise Paul and the other apostles, he says that the saints should look upon them **as servants** or assistants **of Christ and stewards of the mysteries of God.** A steward is a servant who cares for the property of another. **The mysteries of God** were the previously hidden secrets that God revealed to the apostles and prophets of the New Testament period.

 For a teaching/communication suggestion on chapter 4 of 1 Corinthians, see "The Dimensions of Life" on p. 217.

4:2. A major requirement **in stewards** is to **be found faithful.** Man values cleverness, wisdom, wealth, and success; but God is looking for those who will be faithful to Jesus in all things.

4:3. The faithfulness required in stewards is a difficult thing for people to evaluate. That is why Paul says here that with him **it is a very small thing that** he **should be judged by** the Corinthians **or by a human court.** Paul realizes how utterly unable man is to form a competent judgment of true faithfulness to God. He adds: **In fact, I do not even judge myself.** He realized that he was born into the human family with a judgment that was constantly biased in his own favor.

4:4. When the apostle says **I know of nothing against myself,** he means that in the matter of Christian service, he is not conscious of any charge of unfaithfulness that might be brought against him. He does not mean for a moment that he does not know of any sin in his life or any way in which he falls short of perfection! The passage should be read in the light of the context, and the subject here is Christian service and faithfulness in it. But even if he did not know anything against himself, **yet** he was **not justified by this.** He simply was not competent to judge in the matter. After all, the Lord is the judge.

4:5. In view of this, we should be extremely careful in our appraisal of Christian service. We tend to exalt the spectacular and sensational, and depreciate that which is menial or inconspicuous. The safe policy is to **judge nothing before the time,** but to wait **until the Lord comes.** He will be able to judge, not only what is seen by the eye, but also the motives of the hearts—not only what was done, but *why* it was done. He will **reveal the counsels of the hearts**, and anything that was done for self-display or self-glory will fail to receive a reward.

That **each one's praise will come from God** is not to be taken as a flat promise that every believer's service will show up in a favorable way in that day. The meaning is that everyone who *deserves* praise will receive praise **from God** and not from men.

In the next eight verses, the apostle states quite clearly that pride is the cause of the divisions that have come into the church at Corinth.

4:6. He first explains that in speaking about the Christian ministry and the tendency to follow human leaders (3:5–4:5), he used himself and **Apollos** as the examples. The Corinthians were not forming parties around Paul and Apollos alone, but also around other men who were then in their church. However, out of a sense of Christian courtesy and delicacy, Paul **transferred** the entire matter to himself **and Apollos** so that by their example the saints would learn not to have exaggerated opinions of their leaders or to gratify their pride by the formation of parties. He wanted the saints to evaluate everything and everyone by the Scriptures.

4:7. If one Christian teacher is more gifted than another, it is because God made him so. Everything he has, he received from the Lord. In fact it is true of all of us that everything we have has been given to us by God. That being the case, why should we be proud or puffed up? Our talents and gifts are not the result of our own cleverness.

4:8. The Corinthians had become self-sufficient; they were **already full**. They prided themselves on the abundance of spiritual gifts in their midst; they were **already rich**. They were living in luxury, comfort, and ease. There was no sense of need. They acted as if they were already reigning, but they were doing so without the apostles. Paul states that he **could wish** that the time to reign had already come so that he **might reign with** them! But in the meantime, "lifetime is training time for reigning time," as someone has said. Christians will reign with the Lord Jesus Christ when He comes back and sets up His kingdom on earth. In the meantime, their privilege is to share the reproach of a rejected Savior. H. P. Barker warns: "It is positive disloyalty to seek our crown before the King gets his. Yet this is what some of the Christians at Corinth were doing. The apostles themselves were bearing the reproach of Christ. But the Corinthian Christians were 'rich' and 'honorable.' They were seeking a good time where their Lord and Master had such a hard time."

At coronations, peers and peeresses never put on their coronets until the sovereign has been crowned. The Corinthians were reversing this; they were already reigning while the Lord was still in rejection!

4:9. In contrast to the self-satisfaction of the Corinthians, Paul describes the lot of **the apostles**. He pictures them as thrown into the arena with wild beasts while **men** and **angels** look on. As Godet has said: "It was not time for the Corinthians to be self-complacent and boasting, while the church was on the throne and the apostles were under the sword."

4:10. While the apostles were treated as **fools for Christ's sake,** the saints enjoyed prestige in the community as **wise** Christians. The apostles were **weak,** but the Corinthians suffered no infirmity. In contrast to the dishonor of the apostles was the eminence of the saints.

4:11. It did not seem to the apostles that the hour of triumph or of reigning had come. They were suffering from **hunger and thirst** and nakedness and persecution. They were hunted, pursued, and **homeless.**

4:12. They supported themselves by **working** with their **own hands.** For reviling, they returned blessing. When they were **persecuted,** they did not fight back, but patiently endured.

4:13. When **defamed,** they entreated men to accept the Lord Jesus. In short, they were **made as the filth of the world,** the scum **of all things.** This description of suffering for the sake of Christ should speak to all our hearts. If the apostle Paul were living today, could he say to us, as he said to the Corinthians, "You have reigned as kings without us"?

4:14. In verses 14–21, Paul gives a final admonition to the believers on the subject of divisions. Conscious of the fact that he has been using irony, he explains that he has not done so **to shame** the Christians, but rather to **warn** them as his **beloved children.** He was not inspired by bitterness to speak as he had done, but rather by a sincere interest in their spiritual welfare.

4:15. The apostle reminds them that though they **might have ten thousand instructors in Christ,** yet they have only one father in the faith. Paul himself had led them to the Lord; he was their spiritual father. Many others might come along to teach them, but no others could have the same tender regard for them as the one who pointed them to the Lamb. Paul does not at all intend to depreciate the ministry of teaching, but is simply stating what we all know to be true—that many can be engaged in Christian service without the personal interest in the saints that is characteristic of one who has pointed them to Christ.

4:16. Paul **therefore** urges them to be imitators of himself, that is, in his unselfish devotion to Christ and in his tireless love and service for his fellow believers, such as he has described in verses 9–13.

4:17. In order to help them reach this goal, Paul **sent Timothy** to them, his **beloved and faithful son in the Lord**. Timothy was instructed to **remind** them of Paul's **ways in Christ,** ways which he taught in all the churches. Paul is saying that he practiced what he preached, and this should be true of everyone who engages in Christian service.

4:18. When Paul explained that he was sending Timothy to them, perhaps some of his detractors in Corinth would rise quickly to suggest that Paul was afraid to come himself. These men were **puffed up** in suggesting that Paul was **not coming** personally.

4:19. But he promises that he **will come** in the near future, **if the Lord wills**. When he does, he will expose the pride of those who can talk so freely, but have no spiritual **power.**

4:20. After all, it is **power** that counts, **for the kingdom of God is not** concerned principally with words but with action. It does not consist of profession, but of reality.

4:21. The manner in which Paul comes to them will depend on themselves. If they show a rebellious spirit, he will come to them **with a rod.** If, on the other hand, they are humble and submissive, he will come **in love and a spirit of gentleness.**

 See discussion questions on issues raised in chapter 4 of 1 Corinthians on p. 204.

CHAPTER 5

Chapter 5 deals with the necessity for disciplinary action in a church when one of the members has committed serious sin of a public nature. Discipline is necessary for the church to retain its holy character in the eyes of the world and also so the Holy Spirit may work ungrieved in its midst.

 For a teaching/communication suggestion on chapter 5 of 1 Corinthians, see "Separation, Celebration, and Isolation" on p. 218.

5:1. Apparently it had become widely **reported** that one of the men in the fellowship at Corinth had committed **sexual immorality**. Here it was a very extreme form of sin, one that was not even practiced among the ungodly **Gentiles**. Specifically, the sin was that this man had had illicit intercourse with **his father's wife**. The man's own mother had no doubt died and the father had married again. So his father's wife, in this case, would then refer to his stepmother. She was probably an unbeliever, because nothing is said about taking action against her. The church did not have jurisdiction in her case.

5:2. How had the Corinthian Christians reacted to all this? Instead of plunging into deep mourning, they were proud and haughty. Perhaps they were proud of their tolerance in not disciplining the offender. Or perhaps they were so proud of the abundance of spiritual gifts in the church that they did not give serious thought to what had taken place. Or perhaps they were more interested in numbers than in holiness. They were not sufficiently shocked by sin.

You are puffed up, and have not rather mourned, that he who has done this deed might be taken away from among you. This implies that if the believers had taken the proper attitude of humiliation before the Lord, He Himself would have acted in the matter, taking some form of disciplinary action on the offender. Erdman says: "They should have understood that the true glory of the Christian church consists not in the eloquence and gifts of its great teachers, but in the moral purity and the exemplary lives of its members."

5:3. In contrast to their indifference, the apostle states that even though he was **absent**, yet he had **already judged** the matter as if he were present.

5:4. He pictures the church being assembled to take action against the offender. Although he is not present bodily, yet he is there in **spirit** as they meet **in the name of our Lord Jesus Christ.** The Lord Jesus had given authority to the church and to the apostles to exercise discipline in all such cases. Thus Paul says he would act with the **power** (or authority) **of our Lord Jesus.**

5:5. The action he would take would be to **deliver such a one to Satan for the destruction of the flesh, that his spirit may be saved in the day of the Lord Jesus.** Commentators disagree on the meaning of this expression. Some feel that it describes the act of excommunication from the local church. Outside the church is the sphere of Satan's dominion (1 John 5:19). Therefore, "to deliver to Satan" would be simply to excommunicate the man from the church. Others feel that the power to deliver to Satan was a special power granted to apostles but no longer in existence today.

Again, there is disagreement about the meaning of the expression **the destruction of the flesh.** Many feel that it describes physical suffering that would be used by God to break the power of sinful lusts and habits in the man's life. Others feel that **the destruction of the flesh** is a description of slow death, which would give him time to repent and be spared.

In any case, we should remember that the discipline of believers is always calculated to bring about their restoration to fellowship with the Lord. Excommunication in never an end in itself, but always a means toward an end. The ultimate purpose is **that his spirit may be saved in the day of the Lord Jesus.** In other words, there is no thought of the man's eternal damnation. He is disciplined by the Lord in this life because of the sin he has committed, but he is **saved in the day of the Lord Jesus.**

 For a teaching/communication suggestion on discipline in the body of Christ, see "Guidelines for Redemptive Church Discipline" on p. 218.

5:6. Paul now reproves the Corinthians for their **glorying** or boasting. Maybe they excused themselves by saying that it happened only once. They should have known **that a little leaven leavens the whole lump.** Leaven here is a picture of moral sin. The apostle is saying that if they tolerate a little moral sin in the church, it will soon grow and expand until the whole fellowship is seriously affected. Righteous, godly discipline is necessary in order to maintain the character of the church.

 For insight on the problem of blatant immorality in the Corinthian church, see "The Problem with Cover-Ups" on p. 193.

5:7. Thus they are commanded to **purge out the old leaven.** In other words, they should take stern action against evil so that they might be a **new—** in the sense of a pure—**lump.** Then Paul adds: **Since you truly are unleavened.** God sees them in Christ as holy, righteous, and pure. Now the apostle is saying that their state should correspond with their standing. As to *position* they were unleavened. Now as to their *practice* they should also be unleavened. Their natures should correspond with their name, and their conduct with their creed.

For indeed Christ, our Passover, was sacrificed for us. In thinking about the unleavened bread, Paul's mind goes back to the Passover Feast where, on the eve of the first day of the feast, the Jew was required to remove all leaven from his house. He went to the kneading trough and scraped it clean. He scrubbed the place where the leaven was kept until not a trace remained. He searched the house with a lamp to make sure none had been overlooked. Then he lifted up his hands to God and said, "Oh God, I have cast out all the leaven from my house, and if there is any leaven that I do not know of, with all my heart I cast it out too." That pictures the kind of separation from evil to which the Christian is called today.

The slaying of the Passover lamb was a type or picture of the death of our Lord Jesus Christ on the Cross. This verse is one of many in the New Testament that establishes the principle of *typical* teaching. By this we mean that persons and events of the Old Testament were *types* or shadows of things that were to come. Many of them pointed forward directly to the coming of the Lord Jesus to put away our sins by the sacrifice of Himself.

5:8. The feast here does not refer to the Passover or to the Lord's Supper but rather is used in a general way to describe the whole life of the believer. Our entire existence is to be a festival of joy, and it is to be celebrated **not with the old leaven** of sin **nor with the leaven of malice and wickedness.** As we rejoice in Christ, we must have no evil thoughts in our hearts toward others. From this we see that the apostle Paul was not speaking about literal leaven, such as the yeast that is used in making bread. Rather, he was using leaven in a spiritual sense to describe the manner in which sin defiles what it touches. We are to live our lives **with the unleavened bread of sincerity and truth.**

5:9. Now Paul explains to them that he had previously written in a letter that they were **not to keep company with sexually immoral people.** The fact that such an epistle is lost does not affect the inspiration of the Bible at all. Not every letter Paul wrote was inspired, but only those which God has seen fit to include in the Bible.

5:10. The apostle now goes on to explain that in warning them to have no company with **sexually immoral people,** he did not mean to imply that they should separate themselves from any contact at all with ungodly men. As long as we are in the world, it is necessary for us to do business with unsaved people and we have no way of knowing the depths of sin to which they have descended. In order to live a life of complete isolation from sinners, **you would need to go out of the world.**

So Paul says that he did not at all mean complete separation from **the sexually immoral people of this world,** or the covetous, or extortioners, or idolaters. **Covetous** people are those who are convicted of dishonesty in business or financial affairs. For instance, anyone who is found guilty of tax fraud is subject to excommunication for covetousness. **Extortioners** are those who enrich themselves by using violent means, such as threats of harm or death. **Idolaters** are those who are given over to the worship of anyone or anything other than the true God, and who practice the terrible sins of immorality that are connected with idolatry.

5:11. What Paul really wants to warn them against is having fellowship with a professing **brother** who engages in any of these terrible sins. We might paraphrase his words as follows: "What I meant to say and what I now repeat is that you should not even eat a common meal with any professing Christian who is sexually immoral, or a covetous man, or an idolater, or a reviler, or a drunkard, or an extortioner."

It is often necessary for us to have contact with the unsaved, and we can often use these contacts in order to witness to them. Such contact is not as dangerous to the believer as having fellowship with those who profess to be

Christians and yet live in sin. We should never do anything that such a person might interpret as condoning his sin.

To the list of sinners mentioned in verse 10, Paul adds revilers and drunkards in verse 11. **A reviler** is a man who uses strong, intemperate language against another. But we would add a word of caution here. Should a man be excommunicated from the church if on one occasion only he should lose his temper and use unguarded words? We would think not, but would suggest that this expression refers to habitual practice. In other words, **a reviler** would be one who is known as being characteristically abusive toward others. At any rate, this should be a warning to us to exercise control of our language. As Dr. Ironside has mentioned, many people say that they are just *careless* with their tongue, but he points out that they might just as well say that they are careless with a machine gun.

A drunkard is one given to excess in the use of alcoholic beverages.

Does the apostle Paul mean that we are **not even to eat** with a Christian who engages in these practices? That is exactly what the verse teaches! We are not to eat with him at the Lord's Supper, nor are we to enjoy a social meal with him. There may be exceptional cases. A Christian wife, for instance, would still be obligated to eat with her husband who had been disfellowshiped. But the general rule is that professing believers who are guilty of the sins listed should be subjected to social ostracism in order to impress on them the enormity of their transgression and to bring them to repentance. If it is objected that the Lord ate with publicans and sinners, we would point out that these men did not profess to be His followers, and in eating with them He did not recognize them as His disciples. What this passage teaches is that we should not fellowship with *Christians* who are living wicked lives.

5:12. Paul's two questions in verse 12 mean that Christians are not responsible for the judgment of the unsaved. Wicked men in the world about us will be brought into judgment by the Lord Himself in a coming day. But we do have a responsibility as far as judging **those who are inside** the confines of the church. It is the duty of the local church to exercise godly discipline.

Again, if it is objected that the Lord taught, "Judge not that you be not judged," we would reply that there He is speaking about motives. We are not to judge men's motives because we are not competent for that type of judgment. But the Word of God is equally clear that we are to judge known sin in the assembly of God in order to maintain its reputation for holiness and to restore the offending brother to fellowship with the Lord.

5:13. Paul explains that **God** will take care of the judgment of **those who are outside**, that is, of the unsaved. In the meantime, the Corinthians should exercise the judgment that God has committed to them by putting away **the evil person** from among themselves. This calls for a public announcement in the church that this brother is no longer in fellowship. The announcement should be made in genuine sorrow and humiliation and should be followed by continual prayer for the spiritual restoration of the wanderer.

 See discussion questions on issues raised in chapter 5 of 1 Corinthians on p. 204.

CHAPTER 6

The first eleven verses of chapter 6 have to do with lawsuits among believers. News had come to Paul that some Christians were going to court against their fellow believers—before the judges of this world. So he lays down these instructions of lasting value for the church. Note the repetition of the expression "Do you not know . . . ?" (vv. 2, 3, 9, 15, 16, 19).

6:1. The opening question expresses shocked surprise that any of them would think of taking a brother **to law before the unrighteous**, that is, before unsaved judges or magistrates. He finds it rather inconsistent that those who know true righteousness should go before people who are not characterized by righteousness. Imagine Christians looking for justice from those who have none to give!

 For a teaching/communication suggestion on chapter 6 of 1 Corinthians, see "Basic Truths of the Christian Life" on p. 204.

6:2. A second glaring inconsistency is that those who one day **will judge the world** should be incapable of judging trivial matters that come up among themselves. The Scriptures teach that believers will reign with Christ over the earth when He returns in power and glory, and that matters of judgment will be committed to them. If Christians are going to **judge the world**, should they not be able to handle petty differences that plague them now?

6:3. Paul reminds the Corinthians that they will **judge angels**. It is almost astounding to consider the manner in which the apostle injects such a momentous statement into the discussion. Without fanfare or build-up, he states the amazing fact that Christians will one day **judge angels**. We know from Jude 6 and 2 Peter 2:4, 9 that angels will be judged. We also know that Christ will be the judge (John 5:22). It is because of our union with Him that we can be spoken of as judging angels in a coming day. If we are considered qualified to judge angels, we should be able to handle the everyday problems that arise in **this life.**

6:4. If then you have judgments concerning things pertaining to this life, do you appoint those who are least esteemed by the church to judge? Unsaved judges are not given places of honor or esteem by the local church. They are, of course, respected for the work they are doing in the world, but as far as church matters are concerned they do not have any jurisdiction. Thus Paul is asking the Corinthians: "When matters arise between you requiring the impartial judgment of some third party, do you go outside the confines of the church and set men to judge you who are not recognized by the church for spiritual discernment?"

6:5. Paul asks this question to move them to **shame**. Is it true that in an assembly that boasted of its wisdom and of the rich bestowment of gifts on its members, **not** one **wise man** could be found to settle these quarrels **between his brethren?**

6:6. Apparently not one such wise man was available, since a Christian **brother** was going **to law against** his own **brother** in Christ, taking family matters before the unbelieving world. Truly a deplorable situation!

6:7. The expression **Now therefore, it is already an utter failure for you** shows they were entirely wrong in this situation. They shouldn't even think of going to law against one another. But perhaps one of the Christians would object at this point: "Paul, you don't understand. Brother so-and-so cheated me in business dealings." Paul's answer is: **Why do you not rather accept wrong? Why do you not rather let yourselves be cheated?** This would be the truly Christian attitude to take. It is much better to receive a wrong than to commit a wrong.

For insight on the problem of lawsuits at Corinth, see "Lawsuits Among Believers" on p. 194.

6:8. But this was not the attitude among the Corinthians. Instead of being willing to accept wrong and be cheated, they were actually committing **wrong** against others, even their own brothers in Christ.

6:9. Had they forgotten that people whose lives are characteristically **unrighteous will not inherit the kingdom of God**? If they have forgotten, then he will remind them of a list of sinners who will have no part in God's **kingdom**. He does not mean to imply that Christians can practice such sins and be lost, but rather he is saying that people who practice such sins are not Christians.

In this list, **fornicators** are distinct from **adulterers**. Here fornication means illicit sexual intercourse on the part of an unmarried person, whereas adultery would mean such conduct on the part of a married person. **Idolaters** are mentioned again, as in the two previous lists in chapter 5. **Homosexuals** means those who allow their bodies to be used in a perverted way, while **sodomites** are those who practice sodomy on other people.

6:10. To the list are added thieves, covetous, drunkards, revilers, and extortioners. **Thieves** are those who take what does not belong to them. Notice that the sin of covetousness is always listed among the most wicked vices. Though men might excuse it and think lightly of it, God condemns it vigorously. A **covetous** man is one with an inordinate desire for possessions that often drives him to use unjust means of acquiring the same. **Drunkards** are primarily those who are addicted to the use of alcohol. **Revilers** are those who use abusive speech against others. **Extortioners** are those who take advantage of others' poverty or necessities to secure exorbitant gain.

6:11. Paul does not imply that these sins were practiced by the Corinthian believers, but he is warning them that such things characterized them before they were saved—**such were some of you.** But they had been washed and sanctified and justified. They had been **washed** from their sin and impurity through the precious blood of Christ, and they were being continually washed from defilement through the word of God. They were **sanctified** by the operation of the Spirit of God, being set apart to God from the world. They had been **justified in the name of the Lord Jesus Christ and by the Spirit of God**; that is, they had been reckoned righteous before God on the basis of the work of the Lord Jesus on the cross for them. What is Paul's argument here? It is simply this, as so aptly expressed by Godet: "Such a fathomless depth of grace is not to be recrossed."

6:12. In the concluding verses of this chapter, the apostle lays down some principles for judging between right and wrong. The first principle is that a thing may be lawful and yet not helpful. When Paul says, **All things are lawful for me,** he does not mean all things in an absolute sense. For instance, it would not be lawful for him to commit any of the sins mentioned above. He is here speaking only about those things that are morally indifferent. For example, the question about whether a Christian should eat pork was a very real issue among believers in Paul's time. Actually, it was a matter of moral indifference. It did not really matter to God whether a man ate pork. Paul is simply saying that certain things might be legitimate and yet not profitable. There might be certain things which would be permissible for me to do and yet if someone else saw me doing them, he might be hindered by my action. In such a case, it would not be at all suitable for me.

The second principle is that some things might **be lawful** and yet they might be enslaving. Paul states: **I will not be brought under the power of any.**

This would have a very direct message today with regard to the subjects of liquor, tobacco, and drugs. These things, as well as many others, are enslaving, and the Christian should not allow himself to be put in such bondage.

For a teaching/communication suggestion on authentic Christian freedom, see "What Controls You?" on p. 220.

6:13. A third principle is that some things are perfectly lawful for the believer and yet their value is temporary. Paul says: **Foods for the stomach, and the stomach for foods, but God will destroy both it and them.** This means that the human **stomach** has been so constructed that it can receive **foods** and digest them. Likewise, God has wonderfully designed **foods** so they can be received by the human **stomach**. And yet we should not live for foods, because they are only of temporary value. They should not be given an undue place in the life of the believer. Don't live as if the greatest thing in life is to gratify your appetites.

Although the body is wonderfully designed by God for the reception and assimilation of food, there is one thing that is certain: **the body is not for sexual immorality** but **for the Lord, and the Lord for the body.** In planning the human body, God never intended that it should be used for vile or impure purposes. Rather, He planned that it should be used for the glory of the Lord and in His blessed service.

There is something amazing in this verse which should not escape notice. Not only is **the body for the Lord,** but even more wonderful is the thought that **the Lord is for the body.** This means that the Lord is interested in our bodies, their welfare, and their proper use. God wants our bodies to be presented to Him a living sacrifice, holy, and acceptable (Rom. 12:1). As Erdman says: "Without the Lord, the body can never attain its true dignity and its immortal destiny."

6:14. The fact that the Lord is for the body is further explained in this verse. God has not only **raised up the Lord** Jesus from among the dead, but He **will also raise us up by His power.** His interest in our body does not end at the time of death. He is going to **raise** the body of every believer to fashion it like the glorious body of the Lord Jesus. We will not be disembodied spirits in eternity. Rather, our spirit and soul will be reunited with our glorified body, thus to enjoy the glories of heaven forever.

6:15. To further emphasize the need for personal purity in our lives and for guarding our bodies from impurity, the apostle reminds us that our **bodies are members of Christ.** Every believer is a member of the body of Christ. Would it be proper, then, to **take the members of Christ and make them**

members of a harlot? To ask the question is to answer it, as Paul does with an indignant **Certainly not!**

6:16. In the act of sexual union, two bodies become **one**. It was so stated at the dawn of creation: **For the two, He says, shall become one flesh** (Gen. 2:24). This being so, if a believer should be **joined to a harlot**, it would be the same as making a member of Christ a member of a harlot. The two would become **one body.**

6:17. Just as in the physical act there is a union of two into one, so when a person believes on the Lord Jesus Christ and is **joined** to Him, the believer and Christ become so united that they can henceforth be spoken of as **one spirit**. This is the most perfect merging of two persons that is possible. It is the closest type of union. Paul's argument, therefore, is that those who are thus **joined to the Lord** should never tolerate any type of union that would be in conflict with this spiritual wedlock.

A. T. Pierson writes: "The sheep may wander from the shepherd, and the branch be cut off from the vine; the member be severed from the body, the child alienated from the father, and even the wife from the husband; but when two spirits blend in one, what shall part them? No outward connection or union, even of wedlock is so emphatically expressive of perfect merging of two lives in one."

6:18. And so the apostle warns the Corinthians to **flee sexual immorality**. They are not to dabble with it, trifle with it, study it, even talk about it. They are to **flee** from it! A beautiful Bible illustration of this is found in the account of Joseph when he was tempted to sin by Potiphar's wife (Gen. 39). While there may be safety in numbers, sometimes there is more safety in flight!

Then Paul adds: **Every sin that a man does is outside the body; but he who commits sexual immorality sins against his own body.** Most sins have no direct effect on one's **body**, but **sexual immorality** is unique in the sense that it does *directly* affect one's body: a person reaps the consequences of this sin in his own body. The difficulty is that the verse says that *every* sin that a man commits is outside the body. But we believe that the apostle is speaking here in a comparative sense. While it is true that gluttony and drunkenness, for example, affect a person's body, most sins do not. And not even gluttony or drunkenness affect the body as directly, as extensively, or as destructively as immorality. Sex outside marriage inevitably and irresistibly works havoc on the offender.

6:19. Again Paul reminds the Corinthians that theirs was a holy and dignified calling. Had they forgotten that their bodies were a **temple of the Holy Spirit**? That is the solemn truth of Scripture, that every believer is indwelt by the Spirit of God. How could we ever think of taking a body in which the *Holy* Spirit dwells and using it for *vile* purposes? Not only is our body the shrine of the Holy Spirit, but in addition, **we are not** our **own.** It is not for us to take our bodies and use them the way we desire. In the final analysis, they do not belong to us; they belong to the Lord.

 For insight on the meaning of the body as God's temple, see the word study on "Temple" on p. 185.

6:20. We are the Lord's both by creation and redemption. Here the latter is particularly in view. His ownership of us dates back to Calvary. We **were bought at a price.** At the Cross, we see the price tag that the Lord Jesus put on us. He thought us to be of such value that He was willing to pay for us with the price of His own precious blood. How greatly Jesus must have loved us to bear our sins in His body on the cross!

That being the case, I can no longer think of my body as my own. If I am to take it and use it in the way I desire, then I am acting as a thief, taking what does not belong to me. Rather, I must use my **body** to **glorify God,** the One to whom it belongs.

Bates exclaimed: "Head! Think of Him whose brow was thorn-girt. Hands! Toil for Him whose hands were nailed to the Cross. Feet! Speed to do His behests whose feet were pierced. Body of mine! Be His temple whose body was wrung with pains unspeakable."

We should also glorify God **in** our **spirit,** since both material and immaterial parts of man **are God's.**

 See discussion questions on issues raised in chapter 6 of 1 Corinthians on p. 205.

CHAPTER 7

7:1. Up to this point, Paul has been dealing with various abuses in the church at Corinth which he had heard of by direct report. Now he is about to answer questions which the saints at Corinth sent to him. The first has to do with marriage and the single state. He therefore first lays down the broad principle that **it is good for a man not to touch a woman.** To touch a woman, in this case, means to have a physical relationship. The apostle does *not* imply that the unmarried state is holier than marriage, but simply that it is better to be unmarried if one desires to give oneself to the service of the Lord without distraction. This will be explained in later verses.

 For a teaching/communication suggestion on chapter 7 of 1 Corinthians, see "The Meanings of Marriage" on p. 220.

7:2. Paul recognizes, however, that the single state carries with it great temptations to impurity. Thus he qualifies the first statement by saying: **Because of sexual immorality, let each man have his own wife, and let each woman have her own husband.** For **each man** to **have his own wife** means monogamous marriage. Verse 2 establishes the principle that God's order for His own people continues to be what it always was—that a person should have only one spouse.

7:3. In the married state, each one should **render to** his partner the obligations of married life, since there is a mutual dependence. When it says: **Let the husband render to his wife the affection due her,** it means, "Let him carry out his obligations to her as a husband." She should, of course, **do likewise** to him. Note the delicacy Paul uses on this topic. There is no coarseness or vulgarity. How different from the world!

7:4. In marital union there is a dependence of **the wife** upon the **husband** and vice versa. In order to carry out God's order in this holy union, both husband and wife must recognize their interdependence.

 For insight on the meaning of marriage, see "Practical Lessons on Marriage" on p. 194.

7:5. Christenson writes: "In plain language this means that if one partner desires the sexual relationship, the other should respond to that desire. The husband and wife who adopt this down-to-earth approach to sex will find it a wonderfully satisfying aspect of their marriage—for the simple reason that the relationship is rooted in reality, and not in some artificial or impossible ideal."

Perhaps when some of these Corinthians were first saved, they began to think that the intimacies of married life were not consistent with Christian holiness. Paul will disabuse their minds of any such idea. Here he firmly tells them that Christian couples are **not** to **deprive one another,** that is, to deny one's partner's rights as far as the other partner's body is concerned. There are only two exceptions. First of all, such an abstinence should only be by mutual **consent** so the husband and wife **may give** themselves to **fasting and prayer.** The second condition is that such abstinence should only be temporary. Husband and wife should **come together again,** lest Satan tempt them because of their **lack of self-control.**

 For insight on sexuality in marriage, see "A New View of Sexuality" on p. 195.

7:6. Verse 6 has given rise to a great deal of speculation and controversy. Paul says: **But I say this as a concession, not as a commandment.** Some interpreters have taken this to mean that the apostle did not consider the foregoing words to be inspired by God. Such an interpretation is untenable, since he claims in 1 Corinthians 14:37 that the things which he was writing to the Corinthians were the commandments of the Lord. We feel rather that the apostle was saying that under certain circumstances, it was all right for a married couple to abstain from the marriage act, but that this abstinence is a permission, **not a commandment**. Christian people do not have to refrain from this act in order to give themselves undividedly to prayer. Others feel that verse 6 refers to the whole idea of marriage, that is, that Christians are permitted to marry but are not commanded to do so.

7:7. Paul now begins advice to the unmarried. It is clear, first of all, that he considered the unmarried state preferable, but he recognized that it could be followed only as God enabled. When he says: **For I wish that all men were even as I myself,** it is obvious from the context that he means "unmarried." There is much diversity of opinion about whether Paul had always been a bachelor, or whether he was a widower at the time he wrote this. However, for present purposes, it is not necessary to settle the debate, even if we could. Where Paul says: **But each one has his own gift from God, one in this manner, and another in that,** he means that God gives grace to some to remain unmarried whereas He definitely calls others to the married state. It is an individual matter, and no general legislation can be adopted that can be applicable to all.

7:8. Therefore he advises **the unmarried and the widows** to **remain even as** he is himself.

For insight on Paul's personal experience with marriage, see "Paul's Marital Status" on p. 195.

7:9. However, if they lack the power of **self-control** in the unmarried state, then they are permitted to **marry. For it is better to marry than to burn with passion.** This passionate burning involves the grave danger of falling into sin.

7:10. The next two verses are addressed to **married** couples, where both partners are believers. **Now to the married I command, yet not I, but the Lord** simply means that what Paul was teaching here had already been taught by **the Lord** Jesus when He was on earth. Christ had already given an explicit command on this subject. For instance, He had forbidden divorce except on the ground of unfaithfulness (Matt. 5:32; 19:9). The overall instruction that Paul gives is that **a wife is not to depart from her husband.**

7:11. However, he recognizes that there are extreme cases where it might be necessary for a wife to leave her husband. In such a case, she is obligated to

remain unmarried, or be reconciled to her husband. Separation does not break the marriage tie; rather, it gives opportunity for the Lord to heal the differences that have come between and to restore both parties to fellowship with Him and with each other. The **husband** is commanded **not to divorce his wife.** No exception is made in his case.

7:12. Verses 12–24 deal with the problem of a marriage where only one party is a believer. Paul prefaces his remarks with the statement: **But to the rest I, not the Lord, say.** Again, we strongly emphasize that this does not mean that what Paul is saying represents his own viewpoints and not the Lord's. He is simply explaining that what he is about to say had **not** been previously taught by **the Lord** Jesus when He was here on earth. There is no instruction in the Gospels similar to this. The Lord Jesus simply did not take up the case of a marriage where only one member was a believer. But now Christ has instructed His apostle in this matter, and what Paul says here is the inspired word of God.

But to the rest means to those whose partners are not believers. This passage does *not* condone a Christian's marrying an unsaved person. It probably has in view the situation where one of the partners was saved after marriage.

If any brother has a wife who does not believe, and she is willing to live with him, let him not divorce her. In order to appreciate this passage of Scripture properly, it is helpful to remind ourselves of God's commandment to His people in the Old Testament. When Jews married heathen wives and had children by them, they were commanded to put both the wives and the children away. This is clearly seen in Ezra 10:2, 3 and Nehemiah 13:23–25.

Now the question has arisen in Corinth about what a wife who had been converted should do about her husband and children, or what a man who has an unbelieving wife should do with her. Should he put her away? The answer is obviously negative. The Old Testament commandment no longer applies to the people of God under grace. If a Christian has a non-Christian wife, **and she is willing to live with him,** he should not leave her. This does not mean that it is all right for a man to marry a non-believer, but simply that being married to her when he was converted, he should not leave her.

7:13. Likewise, **a woman who has a** non-Christian **husband** who **is willing to live with her** should stay with her husband. Perhaps by her meek and godly testimony before him, she will win him to the Lord.

7:14. Actually the presence of a believer in a non-Christian home has a sanctifying influence. As mentioned before, to *sanctify* means to set apart. Here it does not mean that the unbelieving husband is saved by his wife;

neither does it mean that he is made holy. Rather, it means that he is set apart in a position of external privilege. He is fortunate to have a Christian wife who prays for him. Her life and testimony are an influence for God in the home. Speaking from a human point of view, the likelihood of that man being saved is greater when he has a godly, Christian wife than if he had an unbelieving wife. As Vine puts it: "He receives a spiritual influence holding the possibility of actual conversion." The same would hold true, of course, in the case of an **unbelieving wife** and a Christian **husband**. The unbelieving wife would be **sanctified** in such a case.

Then the apostle adds, **otherwise your children would be unclean; but now they are holy.** We have already mentioned that in the Old Testament the children were to be put away as well as the heathen wife. Now Paul explains that in the dispensation of grace, children born of a marriage where one partner is a believer and the other is not **are holy.** The word **holy** comes from the same root word translated **sanctified** in this verse. It does not mean that the children are made holy in themselves, that is, that they necessarily live clean and pure lives. Rather, it means that they are set apart in a place of privilege. They have at least one parent who loves the Lord, and who tells them the gospel story. There is a strong possibility of their being saved. They are privileged to live in a home where one of the parents is indwelt by the Spirit of God. In this sense, they are sanctified.

This verse also includes the assurance that it is not wrong to have children when one parent is a Christian and the other is not. God recognizes the marriage, and the children are not illegitimate.

7:15. But what should be the attitude of a Christian if the unsaved partner desires to leave? The answer is that he or she should be allowed to **depart.** The expression **a brother or a sister is not under bondage in such cases** is very difficult to explain with finality. Some believe that it means that if the unbeliever deserts the believer, and there is every reason to believe that the desertion is final, then the believer is free to obtain a divorce. Those who hold this view teach that verse 15 is a parenthesis, and that verse 16 is connected with verse 14 as follows:

1. Verse 14 states that the ideal situation is for a believer to remain with an unbelieving partner because of the sanctifying influence of a Christian in the home.
2. Verse 16 suggests that through staying in the home, the believer may win the unbeliever to Christ.
3. Verse 15 is a parenthesis, allowing the believer to be divorced (and possibly to remarry) if he or she is deserted by the unbeliever.

The hope of eventual salvation is connected with continued union rather than with the unbeliever's leaving the home.

But other Bible students insist that verse 15 deals only with the subject of separation and not with divorce and remarriage. To them, it simply means that if the unbeliever departs, he should be allowed to do so peacefully. The wife is not under any obligation to keep the marriage together beyond what she has already done. **God has called us to peace**, and we are not required to use emotional displays or legal processes to prevent the unbeliever from departing.

Which is the right interpretation? We find it impossible to decide definitely. It does seem to us that the Lord taught in Matthew 19:9 that divorce is permitted where one party has been guilty of unfaithfulness (adultery). We believe that in such a case, the innocent party is free to remarry. As far as 1 Corinthians 7:15 is concerned, we cannot be positive that it permits divorce and remarriage where an unbeliever has deserted his Christian partner. However, anyone who is guilty of this form of desertion will almost inevitably enter into a new relationship very soon, and thus the original union will be broken anyway. J. M. Davies writes: "The unbeliever who departs would very soon be married to another, which would automatically break the marriage bond. To insist that the deserted party remain unmarried would put a yoke upon him/her which in the majority of cases, they would not be able to bear."

7:16. One's understanding of verse 16 varies somewhat depending on the interpretation of verse 15.

If a person believes that verse 15 does not sanction divorce, he points to this verse as proof. He argues that the believer should permit separation but should not divorce the unbeliever because that would prevent the possibility of the restoration of the marriage union and the likelihood of the unbeliever's being saved. If, on the other hand, a person believes that divorce is permitted when a believer has been deserted, then this verse is linked with verse 14, and verse 15 is considered as a parenthesis.

7:17. There is sometimes a feeling among new converts that they must make a complete break with every phase of their former life, including institutions such as marriage which are not in themselves sinful. In the newfound joy of salvation, there is the danger of using forcible revolution to overthrow all that a person has previously known. Christianity does not use forcible revolution in order to accomplish its purposes. Rather, its changes are made by peaceful means. In verses 17–24, the apostle lays down the general rule that becoming a Christian need not involve violent revolution against existing ties. Doubtless he has marriage ties primarily in view, but he also applies the principle to racial and social ties.

Each believer is to walk in accordance with the calling of the Lord. If He has called one to married life, then he should follow this in the fear of the Lord. If God has given grace to live a celibate life, then a man should follow that calling. In addition, if at the time of a person's conversion, he is married to an unsaved wife, then he need not overturn this relationship, but should continue to the best of his ability to seek the salvation of his wife. What Paul is stating to the Corinthians is not for them alone; this is what he taught **in all the churches**.

 For insight on the nature of Christian vocation, see "Living Out God's Call Where We Are" on p. 196.

Vine writes: "When Paul says, 'and so ordain I in all the churches,' he is not issuing decrees from a given center, but is simply informing the Church at Corinth that the instructions he was giving them were what he gave in every church."

7:18. Paul deals with the subject of racial ties in verses 18 and 19. If a man was a Jew at the time of his conversion, and bore in his body the mark of circumcision, he need not take a violent revulsion at this and seek to obliterate all physical marks of his former way of life. Likewise, if a man were a heathen at the time of his new birth, he does not have to seek to hide his heathen background by taking on the marks of a Jew.

We might also interpret this verse to mean that if a Jew were converted, he should not be afraid to live on with his Jewish wife, or if a Gentile were converted he should not try to flee from that background. These external differences are not what really count.

7:19. As far as the essence of Christianity is concerned, **circumcision is nothing and uncircumcision is nothing**. What really counts is **keeping the commandments of God**. In other words, God is concerned with what is inward, not with what is outward. The relationships of life need not be violently forsaken by the entrance of Christianity. "Rather," Kelly says, "by the Christian faith, the believer is raised to a position where he is superior to all circumstances."

7:20. The general rule is that **each one** should **remain** with God in that state **in which he was called**. This, of course, only refers to callings that are not in themselves sinful. If a person were engaged in some wicked business at the time of conversion, he would be expected to leave it! But the apostle here is dealing with things not wrong in themselves. This is proved in the following verses where the subject of slaves is discussed.

7:21. What should **a slave** do when he is saved? Should he rebel against his owner and demand his freedom? Does Christianity insist that we go around seeking our "rights"? Paul gives the answer here: **Were you called while a slave? Do not be concerned about it.** In other words, "Were you a slave at the time of your conversion? Do not be needlessly concerned about that. You can be a slave and still enjoy the highest blessings of Christianity."

But if you can be made free, rather use it. There are two interpretations of this passage. Some feel that Paul is saying, "If you can become free, by all means avail yourself of this opportunity." Others feel that the apostle is saying that even if a slave could become free, Christianity does not require him to avail himself of that freedom. Rather, he should use his bondage as a testimony to the Lord Jesus. Most people will prefer the first interpretation (and it is probably correct), but they should not overlook the fact that the second would be more nearly in accord with the example left to us by the Lord Jesus Christ Himself.

7:22. He who is called in the Lord while a slave is the Lord's freedman. This does not mean a man who was freeborn but rather one who was made free, that is, a slave who obtained his freedom. In other words, if a man were a slave at the time of his conversion, he should not let that worry him, because he **is the Lord's freedman.** He has been set free from his sins and from the bondage of Satan. On the other hand, if a man were **free** at the time of his conversion, he should realize that from now on he is a **slave,** bound hand and foot to the Savior.

7:23. Every Christian has been **bought at a price.** He henceforth belongs to the One who bought him, the Lord Jesus. We are to be Christ's bondslaves and **not become slaves of men.**

7:24. Therefore, no matter what one's social state, he can consistently **remain with God** in that state. These two words *with God* are the key that unlocks the whole truth. If a man is **with God,** then even slavery can be made true freedom. "It is that which ennobles and sanctifies any position in life."

7:25. In verses 25–38, the apostle is addressing himself to the unmarried, whether male or female. The word **virgins** can be used to apply to either. Verse 25 is another verse that some interpreters have used to teach that the contents of this chapter are not necessarily inspired. They even go to such extremes as to say that Paul, being a bachelor, was a male chauvinist and that his personal prejudices are reflected in what he says here! To adopt such an attitude, of course, is to deal a vicious attack on the inspiration of Scriptures. When Paul says he has **no commandment from the Lord** about **virgins,** he simply means that during the Lord's earthly ministry He did not leave any explicit instruction on this subject. Therefore Paul gives his own **judgment, as one whom the Lord in His mercy has made trustworthy**, and this judgment is inspired of God.

7:26. In general, it **is good** to be unmarried, **because of the present distress.** "The present distress" refers to the sufferings of this earthly life in general. Perhaps there was a special time of distress at the time Paul wrote this letter. However, distress has continued to exist and will last until the Lord comes.

7:27. Paul's advice is that those who are already married should **not seek** to be separated. On the other hand, if a man **is loosed from a wife,** he should **not seek a wife.** The expression **loosed from a wife** does not only mean widowed or divorced. It simply means free from the marriage bond, and could include those who never married.

7:28. Nothing Paul says should be construed to indicate that it is a sin to marry. After all, marriage was instituted by God in the Garden of Eden before sin entered the world. It was God Himself who decreed: "It is not good that man should be alone" (Gen. 2:18). "Marriage is honorable among all, and the bed undefiled" (Heb. 13:4). Paul elsewhere speaks of those who forbid to marry as a sign of latter-day apostasy (1 Tim. 4:1–3).

Thus Paul states, **But even if you do marry, you have not sinned; and if a virgin marries, she has not sinned.** New converts to Christianity should not think that there is anything wrong in the marriage relationship. Yet Paul adds that those women who do marry **will have trouble in the flesh.** This may include the travail connected with childbirth, etc. When Paul says **But I would spare you,** he may mean (1) I would spare you the physical suffering which accompanies the marriage state, particularly the troubles of family life, or (2) I would spare the reader the enumeration of all these troubles.

7:29. Paul would like to emphasize that because **the time is short** we should subordinate even these legitimate relationships of life in order to serve the Lord. Christ's coming is near, and although husbands and wives should perform their mutual duties with faithfulness, they should seek to put Christ first in all their lives. Ironside expresses it in this way: "Everyone is to act in view of the fact that the time is indeed fleeting, the Lord's return is nearing, and no consideration of personal comfort is to be allowed to hinder devotion to the will of God."

W. E. Vine says: "The meaning is not, of course, that a married man is to refrain from behaving as a husband should, but that his relationship to his wife should be entirely subservient to his higher relationship with the Lord . . . who is to have the first place in the heart; he is not to permit a natural relation to obstruct his obedience to Christ."

7:30. The sorrows and joys and possessions of life should not be given a place of undue consideration in our lives. All these must be subordinated in our endeavor to buy up the opportunity to serve the Lord while it is still day.

7:31. In living our lives on earth, it is inevitable that we have a certain amount of contact with mundane things. There is a legitimate use of these things in the life of the believer. However, Paul warns that while we may **use** them, we should not *misuse* them. For instance, the Christian should not live for food, clothes, and pleasure. He may use food and clothes as essentials, but they should not become the god of his life. Marriage, property, commerce, or political, scientific, musical, and artistic activity have their place in the world, but all may become a distraction to spiritual life.

The expression **the form of this world is passing away** is borrowed from the theater and refers to the changing of scenes. It speaks of the transience of all that we see about us today. Its short-lived character is well expressed in Shakespeare's famous lines: "All the world's a stage, and all the men and women merely players. They have their exits and their entrances, and one man in his time plays many parts."

7:32. Paul wants the Christians **to be without care**. He means the cares that would hinder them from serving the Lord. And so he goes on to explain that **he who is unmarried cares for the things of the Lord—how he may please the Lord**. This does not mean that all unmarried believers actually do give themselves without distraction to the Lord, but it means that the unmarried state provides the opportunity for doing so in a way that the married state does not.

7:33. Again this does not mean that a **married** man cannot be very attentive to the things of the Lord, but it is a general observation that married life requires that a man **please his wife**. He has additional obligations to think of. As Vine has pointed out: "In general, if a man is married, he has limited his range of service. If he is unmarried, he can go on to the ends of the earth and preach the gospel."

7:34. **The unmarried woman cares about the things of the Lord, that she may be holy both in body and in spirit. But she who is married cares about the things of the world—how she may please her husband.** A word of explanation is needed here also. The unmarried woman, or the **virgin**, is able to give a greater portion of her time to **the things of the Lord**. The expression **that she may be holy both in body and in spirit** does not mean that the unmarried state is more holy, but simply that she can be more *set apart* in both body and spirit to the work of the Lord. She is not essentially purer, but her time is freer.

Again, **she who is married cares about the things of the world**. That does not mean that she is more worldly than the unmarried woman, but that her day must be devoted in part to mundane duties such as care of the home. These things are legitimate and right, and Paul is not criticizing them or depreciating them; he is merely stating that an unmarried woman has wider avenues for service and more time than a married woman.

7:35. Paul is not setting forth this teaching in order to put people under a rigid system of bondage. He is instructing them for their own **profit** so that when they think of their lives and of the service of the Lord, they may judge His guidance in the light of all this instruction. His attitude is that celibacy is good, and it enables a person to **serve the Lord without distraction**. As far as Paul is concerned, man is free to choose either marriage or celibacy. The apostle does not want to **put a leash** on anyone or to put people in bondage.

For insight on marital roles in Paul's time, see "Women and Work in the Ancient World" on p. 190.

7:36. Verses 36–38 are perhaps the most misunderstood verses in this chapter, and perhaps in the entire epistle. The common explanation is this: In Paul's day a man exercised rigid control over his home. It was up to him whether his daughters married or not. They could not do so without his permission. Thus these verses are taken to mean that if a man refuses to allow his daughters to marry, that is a good thing, but if he allows them to marry, then he is not sinning.

Such an interpretation seems almost meaningless as far as instruction for the people of God in this day is concerned. The interpretation does not fit in with the context of the rest of the chapter, and seems hopelessly confusing.

The RSV translates *virgin* as "betrothed." The thought would then be that if a man marries his betrothed or fiancée, he does not sin; but if he refrains from marrying her, it is better. Such a view is loaded with difficulties.

In his commentary on 1 Corinthians, William Kelly presents an alternate view that seems to have great merit. Kelly believes that the word **virgin** (*parthenos*) may also be translated "virginity." Thus the passage is not speaking about a man's virgin daughters, but about *his own virginity*. According to this interpretation, the passage is saying that if a man maintains the unmarried state he does well, but if he decides to get married, **he does not sin**.

John Nelson Darby adopts this same interpretation in his New Translation: "But if anyone think that he behaves unseemly to his virginity, and if he is beyond the flower of his age, and so it must be, let him do what he will, he does not sin: let them marry. But he who stands firm in his heart, having no need, but has authority over his own will, and has judged this in his heart to keep his own virginity, he does well. So that he that marries himself does well: and he that does not marry does better."

Looking at verse 36 in greater detail then, we take it as meaning that if a man has come to full manhood, and if he does not feel that he has the gift of continence, **he does not sin** in marrying. He feels that the need requires him to do so, and so he should **do what he wishes** in this case, that is, get married.

7:37. Nevertheless, if a man has determined to serve the Lord without distraction, and if he has sufficient self-control so that there is **no necessity** for his marrying, if he has determined to maintain the unmarried state, and this with a view to glorifying God in service, then he **does well.**

7:38. The conclusion is that **he who gives** himself **in marriage** does well, **but he who** maintains the unmarried state for greater service for the Lord **does better.**

7:39. The last two verses of the chapter contain advice to widows. **A wife is bound by law** to her husband **as long as** he **lives.** The **law** referred to here is the marriage law, instituted by God. **If** a woman's **husband dies, she is at liberty to be married to** another man. This same truth is enunciated in Romans 7:1–3, namely, that death breaks the marriage relationship. However, the apostle adds the qualification that she is free to marry **whom she wishes, only in the Lord.** This means, first of all, that the person she marries must be a Christian, but it means more than this. **In the Lord** means "in the will of the Lord." In other words, she might marry a Christian and still be out of the will of the Lord. She must seek the guidance of the Lord in this important matter and marry the believer whom the Lord has for her.

7:40. Paul's frank judgment is that a widow **is happier if she remains** unmarried. This does not contradict 1 Timothy 5:14 where Paul expresses his judgment that younger widows should marry. Here he is stating his general idea—in 1 Timothy a specific exception.

Then he adds, **I think I also have the Spirit of God.** Some interpreters misunderstand these words to mean that Paul was not sure of himself in stating these things! Again we protest vigorously against any such interpretation. There can be no question about the inspiration of what Paul wrote in this portion. He is using irony here. His apostleship and his teaching had been under attack by some people at Corinth. They professed to have the mind of the Lord in what they were saying. Paul is saying in effect, "Whatever else others may say of me, I think that I also have the Spirit of God. They profess to have Him but surely they do not think that they have a monopoly on the Holy Spirit."

We know that Paul did indeed **have the Spirit** in all that he wrote to us, and that the path of happiness for us is to follow his instructions.

 See discussion questions on issues raised in chapter 7 of 1 Corinthians on p. 206.

CHAPTER 8

The question of eating meat offered to idols is taken up in 8:1–11:1, a real problem to those believers who were recently converted to Christ from paganism. Perhaps they would be invited to a social event at a temple where a great feast would be spread with meat previously offered to idols. Or perhaps they would go to the market to buy meat and find that the butcher was selling meat that had been offered to idols. This would not affect the quality of the meat, of course, but should a Christian buy it? In another scenario, a believer might be invited to a home and be served food that had been offered up to some idol deity. If he knew that this had been the case, should he partake of the food? Paul addresses himself to these questions.

 For a teaching/communication suggestion on chapter 8 of 1 Corinthians, see "Life, Conscience, and Knowledge" on p. 221.

8:1. The apostle begins by stating that **concerning things offered to idols,** both the Corinthians and he himself had **knowledge.** It was not a subject about which they were completely ignorant. They **all** knew, for instance, that the act of offering a piece of meat to an idol had not changed it in any sense. Its flavor and nutritional value remained the same. However, Paul points out that **knowledge puffs up, but love edifies.** By this he means that knowledge in itself is not a sufficient guide in these matters. If knowledge were the only principle applied, then it might lead to pride. Actually in all such matters the Christian must use not only knowledge but also love. He must not only consider what is lawful for himself, but what would be best for others.

8:2, 3. Vine paraphrases verse 2 as follows: "If a man imagines he has fully acquired knowledge, he has not even begun to know how it ought to be gained." Without love there can be no true knowledge. On the other hand, **if anyone loves God, this one is known by Him** in the sense that God approves him. In one sense, of course, God knows everybody, and in another sense He knows especially those who are believers. But here the word *know* is used to denote favor or approval. If anyone makes his decisions in such matters as meats offered to idols out of love to God and man and not out of mere knowledge, that person wins the smile of God's approval.

8:4. As far as things **offered to idols** are concerned, believers understand that **an idol is** not a real god with power, knowledge, and love. Paul was not denying the existence of idols themselves; he knew that there were such things as images carved out of wood or stone. Later on he acknowledges that behind these idols there are demon-powers. But what he emphasizes here is that the gods which these idols purport to represent do not exist. **There is no other God but one**—the God and Father of our Lord Jesus Christ.

8:5. Paul admits that there were many **so-called gods** in heathen mythology, such as Jupiter, Juno, and Mercury. Some of these gods were supposed to live **in heaven**, and others, such as Ceres and Neptune, here **on earth**. In this sense **there are many gods and many lords**, that is, mythological beings which people worshiped and were in bondage to.

8:6. Believers know that **there is one** true **God, the Father, of whom are all things, and we for Him.** This means that God, our Father, is the Source or Creator of **all things** and that **we** were created **for Him.** In other words, He is the purpose or goal of our existence. We also know that there is **one Lord,** namely **Jesus Christ,** through whom all things exist, and through whom all people live. The expression **through whom are all things** describes the Lord Jesus as the mediator or agent of God, whereas the expression **through whom we live** indicates that it is through Him that we have been created and redeemed.

When Paul says that **there is one God, the Father,** and **one Lord Jesus Christ,** he does not mean that the Lord Jesus Christ is not God. Rather, he simply indicates the respective roles that these two persons of the Godhead fulfilled in creation and in redemption.

8:7. However, not all Christians, especially new converts, understand the liberty that they have in Christ Jesus. Having come from backgrounds of idolatry and being used to idols, they think they are committing idolatry when they eat meat that has been **offered to an idol.** They think that the idol is a reality and therefore **their conscience, being weak, is defiled.**

The expression **weak** here does not mean physically weak or even spiritually weak. It is a term describing those who are unduly scrupulous in matters of moral indifference. For instance, as far as God is concerned, it is not wrong for a believer to eat pork. It would have been wrong for a Jew to do so in the Old Testament, but a Christian is at perfect liberty to partake of such food. However, a Jew converted to Christianity might still have scruples about this. He might feel that it is wrong to eat a roast pork dinner. He is what the Bible calls a "weak brother." It means that he is not living in the full enjoyment of his Christian liberty. Actually, as long as he thinks that it is wrong to eat pork, he would sin if he went ahead and did it. That is what is meant by the expression **their conscience, being weak, is defiled**. If my conscience condemns a certain act and I go ahead and commit it, then I have sinned. "Whatever is not from faith is sin" (Rom. 14:23).

8:8. **Food** in itself is not a matter of great consequence **to God**. Refraining from certain foods does not give us favor with God, nor does partaking of such foods make us better Christians.

8:9. But although there is nothing to gain by eating these foods, there might be much to lose if in so doing I cause a **weak** Christian to stumble. This is where the principle of love must come in. A Christian has liberty to eat meat that has been previously offered in sacrifice to idols, but it would be utterly wrong for him to eat if in so doing he offends a **weak** brother or sister.

8:10. The danger is that the weak brother might be encouraged to do what his conscience condemns, if he **sees** another doing something which to him is questionable. In this verse, the apostle condemns **eating in an idol's temple** because of the effect it would have on others. Of course, when Paul speaks here of **eating in an idol's temple,** he is referring to some social event or some general celebration, such as a wedding. It would never be right to eat in such a temple if the meal involved participation in idol worship in any way. Paul later condemns that (10:15–26). The expression **for if anyone sees you who have knowledge** means if anybody sees you, who have a full measure of Christian liberty, who know that meat offered to idols is not unclean or impure, etc. The important principle here is that we must not only consider what effect such an action would have on ourselves, but even more important, what effect it would have on others.

8:11. A person may so parade his **knowledge** of what is legitimate for a Christian that he causes a brother in Christ to stumble. The word **perish** does not mean that he would lose his eternal salvation. It means not the loss of *being* but the loss of *well-being*. This weak brother's testimony would be hurt and his life would be adversely affected as far as usefulness for God is concerned. The seriousness of offending a weak brother in Christ in such a way is indicated by the words **for whom Christ died**. Paul's argument is that if the Lord Jesus Christ loved this man so much that He was willing to die for him, we should not dare to hinder his spiritual progress by doing anything that would cause him to stumble. A few slices of meat are not worth it!

8:12. It is not just a matter of sinning against a brother in Christ, or of wounding his **weak conscience**. It constitutes sin **against Christ** Himself. Whatever we do to the least of His brethren, we do to Him. What hurts one of the members of the body hurts the head as well. Vine points out that in dealing with each subject, the apostle leads his readers to view it in the light of the atoning death of Christ. Barnes says, "It is an appeal drawn from the deep and tender love, the sufferings, and the dying groans of the Son of God." **Sin against Christ** is what Godet calls "the highest of crimes." Realizing this, we should be very careful to examine all our actions in the light of their effect on others, and to refrain from doing anything that would cause a brother to be offended.

For insight on the responsible use of Christian freedom, see "Dealing with Gray Areas" on p. 196.

8:13. Because it is sin against Christ to make one's **brother stumble**, Paul states that he **will never again eat meat** if in so doing he makes his **brother stumble**. The work of God in the life of another person is far more important than a tender roast! Although the subject of meats offered to idols is not a problem for most Christians today, the *principles* which the Spirit of God gives us in this section are of abiding value. There are many things today in the Christian life, which, while not forbidden in the Word of God, would cause needless offense to weaker Christians. While we might have the right to participate in them, a greater right is to forego that right for the spiritual welfare of those whom we love in Christ, our fellow-believers.

See discussion questions on issues raised in chapter 8 of 1 Corinthians on p. 206.

CHAPTER 9

At first glance, chapter 9 might seem to indicate a new subject. However, the question of meats offered to idols continues for two more chapters. Paul is merely turning aside here to give *his own example* of self-denial for the good of others. He was willing to forego his right to financial support as an apostle in accordance with the principle set forth in 8:13. Thus this chapter is closely linked with chapter 8.

For a teaching/communication suggestion on chapter 9 of 1 Corinthians, see "Giving Up Our Rights" on p. 221.

9:1. Some people in Corinth questioned Paul's authority. They said he was not one of the Twelve, and therefore was not a genuine apostle. Paul protests that he was free from human authority, a genuine **apostle** of the Lord Jesus. He bases his claim on two facts. First of all, he had **seen Jesus Christ our Lord** in resurrection. This took place on the road to Damascus. He also points to the Corinthians themselves as proof of his apostleship by asking, **Are you not my work in the Lord?** If they had any doubt about his apostleship, they should examine themselves. Were they saved? Of course they would say they were. Well, who pointed them to Christ? The apostle Paul did! Therefore, they themselves were proof of the fact that he was a genuine apostle of the Lord.

9:2. Others may not recognize him as **an apostle**, but surely the Corinthians themselves should. They were **the seal of** his **apostleship in the Lord.**

9:3. Verse 3 probably refers to what has gone before (and not to what follows, as the NKJV punctuates it). Paul is saying that what he has just said is his **defense to those who examine** him, or who question his authority as an apostle.

9:4. In verses 4–14, the apostle discusses his **right** to financial support as an apostle. As one who had been sent by the Lord Jesus, Paul was entitled to financial remuneration from the believers. However, he had not always insisted on this right. He had often worked with his hands, making tents, in order that he might be able to preach the gospel freely to men and women. No doubt his critics took advantage of this, suggesting that the reason he did not take support was that he knew he was not a real apostle. He introduces the subject by asking a question: **Do we have no right to eat and drink?**—that is—without having to work for it? Are we not entitled to be supported by the church?

9:5. Do we have no right to take along a believing wife, as do also the other apostles, and **the brothers of the Lord, and Cephas?** Perhaps some of Paul's critics suggested that Paul did not marry because he knew that he and his wife would not be entitled to the support of the churches. Peter and the other apostles were married, as were also **the brothers of the Lord.** Here the apostle is stating that he would have just as much right to be married and enjoy the support of the Christians for both his wife and himself. The expression **to take along a believing wife** refers not only to the right to marry, but also to the right of support for both husband and wife. The phrase **the brothers of the Lord** probably means His actual half brothers, or possibly His cousins. This text alone does not solve the problem, although other Scriptures indicate that Mary did have other children after Jesus, her firstborn (Luke 2:7; see Matt. 1:25; 12:46; 13:55; Mark 6:3; John 2:12; Gal. 1:19).

9:6. It appears that **Barnabas,** like Paul, had worked to provide for his material needs while preaching the gospel. Paul asked if they both did not have the **right to refrain from working** and to be cared for by the people of God.

9:7. The apostle based his first claim to financial support on the example of the other apostles. He now turns to an argument from human affairs. A soldier is not sent to war **at his own expense.** Whoever **plants a vineyard** is never expected to do so without receiving some recompense from **its fruit.** Finally, a shepherd is not expected to keep **a flock** without being given a right to partake **of the milk**. Christian service is like warfare, agriculture, and pastoral life. It involves fighting against the enemy, caring for God's fruit trees, and serving as an under-shepherd for His sheep. If the right of support is recognized in these earthly occupations, how much more should it be in the service of the Lord!

 For insight on support of the ministry, see "Paying Vocational Christian Workers" on p. 197.

9:8. Paul next turns to the Old Testament for further proof of his point. Does he have to base his argument merely on these mundane things of life, such as warfare, agriculture, and shepherding? **Does not the** Scripture **say the same** thing?

9:9. It is clearly stated in Deuteronomy 25:4 that **an ox** should **not** be muzzled **while it treads out the grain.** That is, when an animal is used in a harvesting operation, it should be allowed to partake of some of the harvest. **Is it oxen God is concerned about?** God does care for oxen, but He didn't cause these things to be written in the Old Testament merely for the sake of dumb animals. There was a spiritual principle involved to be applied to our life and service.

9:10. Or does He say it altogether for our sakes? The answer is "yes," our welfare was in His mind when these words were **written**. When a man plows, he **should plow** with the expectation of some remuneration. So likewise, when a man threshes, he should be able to look forward to some of the harvest in recompense. Christian service resembles plowing and threshing, and God has decreed that those who engage in these aspects of His service should not do so at their own expense.

9:11. Paul speaks of himself as having **sown spiritual things** for the Christians at Corinth. In other words, he came to Corinth preaching the gospel to them and teaching them precious spiritual truths. That being so, is it asking too much in return that they minister to him of their finances or other **material things**? The argument is that the wages of the preacher are inferior in value to what he has given. Material benefits are small compared with spiritual blessings.

9:12. Paul was aware that the church at Corinth was supporting **others** who were preaching or teaching there. They recognized this obligation to other people but not to the apostle Paul, and so he asks: **If others are partakers of this right over you, are we not even more?** If they recognized the right of others to financial support, why should they not recognize that he, their father in the faith, had this right? Doubtless some of those who were being supported were the Judaizing teachers. Paul adds that, although he had **this right**, he did not use it with the Corinthians but endured **all things** lest he **hinder the gospel of Christ**. Rather than insist on his right to receive support from them, he bore privations and hardships so the gospel would not be hindered.

9:13. Paul next introduces the argument from the support of those who served in the Jewish temple. Those who had official duties in connection with the temple service were supported from the income the temple received. In this sense they lived off **the things of the temple**. Also, the priests themselves who served **at the altar** were given a certain portion **of the offerings** that were brought to the altar. In other words, both the Levites, who had the ordinary duties around the temple, and the priests, to whom were entrusted the more sacred duties, were supported for their service.

9:14. Finally, Paul introduces the definite command of **the Lord** Himself. He **commanded that those who preach the gospel should live from the gospel**. This would be conclusive proof alone of Paul's right to support from the Corinthians. But this raises the question of why he did not insist on being supported by them. The answer is given in verses 15–18.

9:15. He explains that he **used none of these things**, that is, he did not insist on his rights. Neither was he writing **these things** at the present time in order that they might send money to him. He would rather **die than that anyone should** be able to rob him of his **boasting**.

9:16. Paul is saying that he cannot **boast** in the fact that he preaches the gospel. A divine compulsion **is laid upon** him. It is not a vocation that he chose for himself. He received the "tap on the shoulder," and he would have been a miserable man if he had not obeyed the divine commission. This does not mean the apostle was not willing to preach the gospel, but rather that the decision to preach did not come from himself, but from the Lord.

9:17. If the apostle Paul preached the gospel **willingly**, he would have the **reward** that goes with such service—the right of maintenance. Throughout the Old and New Testaments, it is clearly taught that those who serve the Lord are entitled to support from the Lord's people. In this passage, Paul does not mean that he was an unwilling servant of the Lord, but is simply stating that there was a divine compulsion in his apostleship. He goes on to emphasize this in the latter part of the verse. If he preached **against** his **will**, that is, if he preached because there was a fire burning within him and he could not refrain from preaching, then he had **been entrusted with a stewardship** of the gospel. He was a man acting under orders, and therefore he could not boast in that.

Verse 17 is admittedly difficult, and yet the meaning seems to be that Paul would not claim his right of maintenance from the Corinthians because the ministry was not an occupation that he chose on his own. He was placed in it by the hand of God. The false teachers in Corinth might claim their right to be supported by the saints, but the apostle Paul would seek his reward elsewhere.

Knox's translation of this verse is as follows: "I can claim a reward for what I do of my own choice; but when I act under constraint, I am only executing a commission."

Ryrie comments: "Paul could not escape his responsibility to preach the gospel, because a stewardship (responsibility) had been committed to him and he was under orders to preach even though he was never paid (compare Luke 17:10)."

9:18. If then he could not boast in the fact that he preached the gospel, of what would he boast? Of something that was a matter of his own choice— that he presented **the gospel of Christ without charge**. This is something he could determine to do. He would preach the gospel to the Corinthians, at the same time earning his own living, not using to the full his right for maintenance **in the gospel**.

 For insight on the meaning of genuine freedom, see the word study on "Liberty" on p. 186.

To summarize the apostle's argument here, he is making a distinction between what was obligatory and what was optional. There is no thought of any reluctance in his preaching the gospel. He did that cheerfully. But in a very real sense, it was a solemn obligation that rested upon him. Therefore in the discharge of that obligation there was no reason for his boasting. In preaching the gospel, he could have insisted on his right to financial support, but he did not do this; rather, he decided to give the gospel **without charge** to the Corinthians. Since this was a matter of his own will, he would glory in this. As we have suggested, Paul's critics claimed that his working as a tentmaker indicated that he did not consider himself to be a true apostle. Here he turns his self-support in such a way as to prove that his apostleship was nonetheless real; in fact, it was of a very high and noble character.

In verses 19–22, Paul cites his example of the waiving of legitimate rights for the gospel's sake. In studying this section, it is important to remember that Paul does not mean that he ever sacrificed important principles of the Scripture. He did not believe that the end justified the means. In these verses he is speaking about matters of moral indifference. He accommodated himself to the customs and habits of the people with whom he worked in order that he might gain a ready ear for the gospel. But never did he do anything that might compromise the truth of the gospel.

9:19. In one sense Paul was **free from all men**. No one could exercise jurisdiction or compulsion over him. Yet he brought himself under bondage **to all** people in order **that** he **might win the more**. If he could make a concession without sacrificing divine truth, he would do it in order to win souls to Christ.

9:20. To the Jews he **became as a Jew, that** he **might win Jews**. This cannot mean that he put himself back under the Law of Moses in order to see Jews saved. What it does mean might be illustrated in the action that Paul took in connection with the circumcision of Timothy and Titus. In the case of Titus, there were those who insisted that unless he was circumcised, he couldn't be saved. Realizing that this was a frontal attack on the gospel of the grace of God, Paul stoutly refused to have Titus circumcised (Gal. 2:3). However, in the case of Timothy it seems that no such issue was involved. Therefore, the apostle was willing that Timothy should be circumcised if this would result in a wider hearing of the gospel (Acts 16:3).

To those who are under the law, as under the law, that I might win those who are under the law. The phrase "Those who are under the law" refers to the Jewish people. But Paul had already spoken of his dealings with the Jews in the first part of the verse. Why does he then repeat the subject here? The explanation that has often been offered is that when he speaks of Jews in the first part of the verse, he is referring to their national customs, whereas here he is referring to their religious life.

At this point a brief word of explanation is necessary. As a Jew, Paul had been born under the law. He sought to obtain favor with God by keeping the law, but he found that he was unable to do so. The law only showed him what a wretched sinner he was, and it utterly condemned him. Eventually he learned that the law was not a way of salvation, but only God's method of revealing to man his sinfulness and his need of a Savior. Paul then trusted in the Lord Jesus Christ, and in so doing he became free from the condemning voice of the law. The penalty of the law that he had broken was paid by the Lord Jesus at Calvary.

After his conversion, the apostle learned that the law was not the way of salvation, nor was it the rule of life for one who had been saved. The believer is not under law but under grace. This does not mean that he can do as he pleases. Rather, it means that a true sense of the grace of God will prevent him from even wanting to do these things. Indwelt by the Spirit of God, the Christian is raised to a new level of behavior. He now desires to live a holy life, not out of fear of punishment for having broken the law, but out of love for Christ, who died for him and rose again. Under law the motive was fear, but under grace the motive is love. Love is a far higher motive than fear. People will do out of love what they would never do from terror.

Arnot says: "God's method of binding souls to obedience is similar to His method of keeping the planets in their orbits—that is, by flinging them out free. You see no chain keeping back these shining worlds to prevent them from bursting away from their center. They are held in the grip of an invisible principle. . . . And it is by the invisible bond of love—love to the Lord who bought them—that ransomed men are constrained to live soberly and right-eously and godly."

With that brief background in mind, let us now get back to the latter half of verse 20. **To those who are under the law, as under the law, that I might win those who are under the law.** When he was with Jewish people, Paul behaved as a Jew in matters of moral indifference. For instance, he ate the foods that the Jewish people ate and refrained from eating such things as pork which were forbidden to them. Perhaps Paul also refrained from working on the Sabbath, realizing that if he did this the gospel might gain a more ready hear-ing from the people.

As a born-again believer in the Lord Jesus, the apostle Paul was not under the law as a rule of life. He merely adapted himself to the customs, habits, and prejudices of the people in order that he might win them to the Lord.

9:21. Ryrie writes: "Paul is not demonstrating two-facedness or multi-facedness, but rather he is testifying of a constant, restrictive self-discipline in order to be able to serve all sorts of men. Just as a narrowly channeled stream is more powerful than an unbounded marshy swamp, so restricted liberty results in more powerful testimony for Christ."

To **those who are without law,** Paul acted as one **without law** (although he himself was **not without law toward God, but under law toward Christ).** The phrase "Those who are without law" does not refer to rebels or outlaws who do not recognize any law, but is a general description of Gentiles. The law was given to the Jewish nation and not to the Gentiles. Thus when Paul was with the Gentiles he complied with their habits and feelings as far as he could possibly do so and still be loyal to the Savior. The apostle explained that even while he thus acted as **without law,** he was nevertheless **not without law toward God.** He did not consider that he was free to do as he pleased, **but** he was **under law toward Christ.**

In other words, he was bound to love, honor, serve, and please the Lord Jesus, not now by the Law of Moses, but by the law of love. He was "enlawed" to Christ. We have an expression "When in Rome, do as the Romans do." Paul is saying here that when he was with the Gentiles, he adapted himself to their manner of living as far as he could consistently do so and still be loyal to Christ. But we must keep in mind that this passage deals only with cultural things and not with doctrinal or moral matters.

9:22. Verse 22 speaks of those who are **weak** or overscrupulous. They were excessively sensitive about matters that were not of fundamental importance. **To the weak,** Paul **became as weak,** that he **might win** them. He would be a vegetarian if necessary rather than offend them by eating meat. In short, Paul became **all things to all men, that** he **might by all means save some.** These verses should never be used to justify a sacrifice of scriptural principle. They describe a readiness to accommodate to the customs and habits of the people in order to win a hearing for the Good News of salvation. When Paul says **that I might by all means save some,** he does not think for a moment that he could save another person, because he realized that the Lord Jesus was the only person who could save. At the same time it is wonderful to notice that those who serve Christ in the gospel are so closely identified with Him that He even allows them to use the word *save* to describe a work in which they are involved. How this exalts and ennobles and dignifies the gospel ministry!

Verses 23–27 describe the peril of losing one's reward through lack of self-discipline. To Paul the refusal of financial help from the Corinthians was a form of rigid discipline.

9:23. Now this I do for the gospel's sake, that I may be partaker of it with you. In the preceding verses Paul had been describing how he submerged his own rights and desires in the work of the Lord. Why did he do this? He did it **for the gospel's sake,** in order that he might share in the triumphs of the gospel in a coming day.

9:24. As the apostle wrote the words in verse 24, he was reminded of the Isthmian games that were held not far from Corinth. The Corinthian believers would be well acquainted with those athletic contests. Paul reminds them that while many **run in a race,** not all receive **the prize.** The Christian life is like a race. It requires self-discipline. It calls for strenuous effort. It demands definiteness of purpose. The verse does not, however, suggest that in the Christian race only one person can win the prize. It simply teaches that we should all run as winners. We should all practice the same kind of self-denial that the apostle Paul himself practiced. Here, of course, the prize is not salvation, but a reward for faithful service. Salvation is nowhere stated to be the result of our faithfulness in running the race. Salvation is the free gift of God through faith in the Lord Jesus Christ.

For insight on athletic metaphors used by Paul, see "Paul and the Greek Games" on p. 190.

9:25. Now Paul changes the figure from running to wrestling. He reminds his readers that **everyone who competes** in the games—that is, wrestles—exercises self-control **in all things**. A wrestler once asked his coach, "Can't I smoke and drink and have a good time and still wrestle?" The coach replied, "Yes, you can, but you can't win!" As Paul thinks of the contestants at the games, he sees the winner stepping up to receive his prize. What is it? It is **a perishable crown**, a garland of flowers or a wreath of leaves that will soon wither away. But in comparison he mentions **an imperishable crown** which will be awarded to all those who have been faithful in their service to Christ.

> We thank Thee for the crown
> Of glory and of life;
> 'Tis no poor withering wreath of earth,
> Man's prize in mortal strife;
> 'Tis incorruptible as is the Throne,
> The kingdom of our God and
> His Incarnate Son.
>
> —*Horatius Bonar*

9:26. In view of this imperishable crown, Paul states that he therefore runs **not with uncertainty**, and fights **not as one who beats the air**. His service was neither purposeless nor ineffectual. He had a definite aim, and his intention was that every action should count. There must be no wasted time or energy. The apostle was not interested in wild misses.

9:27. Instead, he disciplined his **body, and** brought **it into subjection**, lest when he had **preached to others**, he himself might be rejected or **disqualified**. In the Christian life, there is a necessity for self-control, for temperance, for discipline. We must practice self-mastery.

The apostle Paul realized the dread possibility that after he had **preached to others**, he himself might be **disqualified**. Considerable debate has centered on the meaning of this verse. Some hold that it teaches that a person can be saved and then subsequently lost. This, of course, is in conflict with the general body of teaching in the New Testament that no true sheep of Christ will ever perish.

Others say that the word translated "disqualified" is a strong word and refers to eternal damnation. However, they interpret the verse to mean that Paul is not teaching that a person who was ever saved could be disqualified, but simply that one who failed to exercise self-discipline had never been saved in the first place. Thinking of the false teachers and how they indulged every passion and appetite, Paul sets forth the general principle that if a person does not keep his body in subjection, this is proof that he never was born again; and although he might preach to others, he himself will be disqualified.

A third explanation is that Paul is not speaking here of salvation at all but of service. He is not suggesting that he might ever be lost, but that he might not stand the test as far as his service was concerned and might be rejected for the prize. This interpretation exactly fits the meaning of the word *disqualified* and the athletic context. Paul recognizes the awful possibility that, having **preached to others,** he himself might be *put on the shelf* by the Lord as no longer usable by Him.

In any event, the passage is an extremely serious one and should cause deep heart-searching on the part of everyone who seeks to serve the Lord Christ. Each one should determine that by the grace of God he will never have to learn the meaning of the word by experience.

 See discussion questions on issues raised in chapter 9 of 1 Corinthians on p. 207.

CHAPTER 10

As Paul has been thinking of the necessity for self-control, the example of the Israelites comes before his mind. In chapter 10, he remembers how they became self-indulgent and careless in the discipline of their bodies, and thus became disqualified and disapproved.

First of all, he speaks of the privileges of Israel (vv. 1–4); then the punishment of Israel (v. 5); and finally the causes of Israel's downfall (vv. 6–10). Then he explains how these things apply to us (vv. 11–13).

 For a teaching/communication suggestion on chapter 10 of 1 Corinthians, see "How to Face Difficult Decisions" on p. 222.

10:1. The apostle reminds the Corinthians **that all** the Jewish **fathers were under the cloud** and **all passed through the sea.** The emphasis is on the word **all.** He is thinking back to the time of their deliverance from Egypt and how they were guided miraculously by a pillar of **cloud** by day and a pillar of fire by night. He is thinking back to the time when they passed through the Red Sea and escaped into the wilderness. As far as privilege was concerned, they enjoyed divine guidance and divine deliverance.

10:2. Not only that, but **all were baptized into Moses in the cloud and in**

the sea. To be **baptized into Moses** means to be identified with him and to acknowledge his leadership. As Moses led the children of Israel out of Egypt toward the Promised Land, the entire nation of Israel pledged allegiance to Moses at first and recognized him as the divinely appointed deliverer. It has been suggested that the expression "under the cloud" refers to that which identified them with God, and the expression "through the sea" describes that which separated them from Egypt.

10:3. They **all ate the same spiritual food.** This refers to the manna that was provided miraculously for the people of Israel as they journeyed through the wilderness. The expression **spiritual food** does not mean that it was non-material. It does not mean that it was invisible or unreal. Rather, **spiritual** simply means that the material food was a type or picture of spiritual nourishment, and that the spiritual reality is what the writer had primarily in mind. It may also include the idea that the food was supernaturally given.

10:4. All through their journeyings, God provided water for them to drink. It was real water, but again it is called **spiritual drink** in the sense that it was typical of spiritual refreshment, and miraculously provided. They would have died from thirst many times if the Lord had not given them this water in a miraculous way. The expression **they drank of that spiritual Rock that followed them** does not mean that a literal, material rock journeyed behind them as they traveled. The Rock signifies the river that flowed from it and followed the Israelites. **That Rock was Christ** in the sense that He was the One who provided it and the One it represents, providing living water to His people.

10:5. After enumerating all these marvelous privileges which they enjoyed, the apostle must now remind the Corinthians that **with most of** the Israelites **God was not well pleased, for their bodies were scattered in the wilderness.** Although all Israel left Egypt and all professed to be one in heart and soul with their leader Moses in the wilderness, yet the sad truth is that their hearts were still back in Egypt. They enjoyed a physical deliverance from the bondage of Pharaoh, but they still lusted after the sinful pleasures of that country. Of all the warriors over twenty years of age who left Egypt, only two, Caleb and Joshua, won the prize—they reached the Promised Land. The carcasses of the rest of them fell **in the wilderness** as evidence of God's displeasure.

Note the contrast between the word *all* in the first four verses and the word *most* in verse 5. They were all privileged, but **most of them** perished. Godet marvels: "What a spectacle is that which is called up by the apostle before the eyes of the self-satisfied Corinthians: all those bodies, sated with miraculous food and drink, strewing the soil of the desert!"

10:6. In the events that happened in the time of the Exodus, we see teaching that applies to us. The children of Israel were actually **examples** for us, showing us what will happen to us if we also **lust after evil things** as they did. As we read the Old Testament, we should not read it merely as history, but as containing lessons of practical importance for our lives today.

In the verses to follow, the apostle will list some of the specific sins into which they fell. It is worth noticing that many of these sins are concerned with the gratification of bodily appetites.

10:7. Verse 7 refers to the worship of the golden calf and the feast that followed it, as recorded in Exodus 32. When Moses came down from Mount Sinai, he found that the people had made a golden calf and were worshiping it. We read in Exodus 32:6 how **the people sat down to eat and drink, and rose up to play**, that is, to dance.

10:8. The sin mentioned in verse 8 refers to the time when the sons of Israel intermarried with the daughters of Moab (Num. 25). Seduced by Balaam the prophet, they disobeyed the word of the Lord and fell into immorality. We read in verse 8 that **in one day twenty-three thousand fell**. In the Old Testament, it says that twenty-four thousand died in the plague (Num. 25:9). Critics of the Bible have often used this to try to show a contradiction in the sacred Scriptures. If they would read the text more carefully, they would see that there is no contradiction. Here it simply states that *twenty-three thousand* fell *in one day*. In the Old Testament, the figure of *twenty-four thousand* describes the entire number that died *in the plague*.

10:9. Paul next alludes to the time when the Israelites complained about the food and expressed doubt about the goodness of the Lord. At that time God sent **serpents** among them and many people died (Num. 21:5, 6). Here again, it is noticeable how food gratification was their downfall.

10:10. The sin of Korah, Dathan, and Abiram is referred to here (Num. 16:14–47). Again there was complaining against the Lord because of the food situation (Num. 16:14). The Israelites did not practice self-control with regard to their bodies. They did not discipline their bodies or put them under subjection. Rather, they made provision for the lusts of the flesh, and this proved to be their downfall.

10:11. The next three verses give the practical application of the events. First of all, Paul explains that the meaning of these events is not limited to their historical value. They have a significance for us today. **They were written** as a warning to us who are living after the close of the Jewish age and during the gospel age, "to us to whom the revenues of the past ages have descended," as Rendall Harris put it so well.

10:12. This verse is a warning to the self-confident: **Let him who thinks he stands take heed lest he fall**. Perhaps this refers especially to the strong believer who thinks he can dabble with self-gratification and not be affected by it. Such a person is in danger of falling under the disciplinary hand of God.

10:13. But then Paul adds a marvelous word of encouragement for those who are tempted. He teaches that the testings, trials, and temptations that face us are **common** to all. However, **God is faithful, who will not allow** us to be tested **beyond what** we **are able**. He does not promise to deliver us from temptation or testing, but He does promise to limit its intensity. He further promises to provide **the way of escape,** that we **may be able to bear it**. Reading this verse, one is struck by the comfort it has brought to tested saints of God through the centuries. Young believers have clung to it as to a lifeline and older believers have rested on it as upon a pillow. Perhaps some of Paul's readers were being fiercely tempted at the time to go into idolatry. Paul would comfort them with the thought that God would not allow any unbearable temptation to come their way. At the same time they should be warned that they should not expose themselves to temptation.

 For teaching/communication suggestions on facing temptations, see "Dealing with Trials and Temptations" on p. 222 and "How to Deal with Temptation" on p. 223.

10:14. The section from 10:14 through 11:1 returns to deal more specifically with the subject of meat offered to idols. First of all, Paul takes up the question about whether believers should participate in feasts in idol temples (vv. 14–22).

Therefore, my beloved, flee from idolatry. Perhaps it was a real test for the believers at Corinth to be invited to participate in an idol feast at one of the temples. Some might feel that they were above temptation. Perhaps they would say that surely it would not hurt to go just once. The apostle's inspired advice is to **flee from idolatry**. He does not say to study about it, to become better acquainted with it, or to trifle with it in any way. They should run in the opposite direction.

 For insight on worship of false gods, see the word study on "Idolatry" on p. 186.

10:15, 16. Paul knows that he is addressing himself to intelligent people who can understand what he is saying. In verse 16 he makes reference to the Lord's Supper. He says first of all: **The cup of blessing which we bless, is it not the communion of the blood of Christ? The cup of blessing** refers to the cup of wine that is used at the Lord's Supper. It is a cup that speaks of the tremendous blessing that has come to us through the death of Christ; therefore it is called **the cup of blessing**. The clause **which we bless** means "for which we give thanks." When we take that cup and press it to our lips, we are saying in effect that we are participants in all the benefits that flow from the blood of Christ. Therefore we might paraphrase this verse as follows: "The cup which speaks of the tremendous blessings which have come to us through the blood of the Lord Jesus, and the same cup for which we give thanks, what is it but a testimony to the fact that all believers are partakers of the benefits of the blood of Christ?"

The same thing is true of **the bread which we break**, the Communion loaf. As we eat the bread, we say, in effect, that we have been saved through the offering of His body on the Cross and that we are therefore members of His body. In short, the cup and the loaf speak of fellowship with Christ, of participating in His glorious ministry.

The question has been raised about why the blood should be mentioned first in this verse whereas in the institution of the Lord's Supper, the bread is mentioned first. A possible answer is that Paul is speaking here of the order of events when we come into the Christian fellowship. Usually a new convert understands the value of the blood of Christ before he recognizes the truth of the one body. Thus this verse might give the order in which we understand salvation.

10:17. All believers, **though many, are one body in Christ**, represented by **that one** loaf of **bread. All partake of that one bread** in the sense that all have fellowship in the benefits that flow from the giving of the body of Christ.

10:18. What Paul is saying in these verses is that eating at the Lord's Table signifies fellowship with Him. The same was true of those Israelites who ate **of the sacrifices**. It meant that they had fellowship with **the altar**. The reference, no doubt, is to the peace offering. The people brought their sacrifices to the temple. A portion of the offering was burned on the altar with fire; another portion was reserved for the priests; but the third part was set aside for the person making the offering and his friends. They ate of the offering on the same day. Paul is emphasizing that all who ate of the offering identified themselves with God and with the nation of Israel and, in short, with all of which **the altar** spoke.

But how does this fit in with the portion of the Scripture that we are studying? The answer is quite simple. Just as partaking of the Lord's Supper speaks of fellowship with the Lord, and just as the Israelites, partaking of the peace offering, spoke of fellowship with the altar of Jehovah, so eating at an idol feast in the temple speaks of fellowship with the idols.

10:19. What am I saying then? That an idol is anything, or that what is offered to idols is anything? Does Paul mean to imply by all this that meat offered to idols changes its character or quality? Or does he mean to say that an idol is real, that it hears, sees, and has power? Obviously the answer to both of these questions is "No."

10:20. What Paul does want to emphasize is that **the things which the Gentiles sacrifice** are offered **to demons.** In some strange and mysterious way, idol worship is linked with demons. Using the idols, the demons control the hearts and minds of those who worship them. There is one devil, Satan, but there are many demons who serve as his messengers and agents. Paul adds: **I do not want you to have fellowship with demons.**

10:21. You cannot drink the cup of the Lord and the cup of demons; you cannot partake of the Lord's Table and of the table of demons. In this verse **the cup of the Lord** is a figurative expression to describe the benefits which come to us through Christ. It is a figure of speech known as metonymy, where the container is used to denote the thing contained. The expression **the Lord's Table** is likewise a figurative expression. It is not the same as the Lord's Supper, although it might include the latter. A table is an article of furniture where food is set out and where fellowship is enjoyed. Here the **table** of the Lord means the sum total of the blessings which we enjoy in Christ.

When Paul says that **you cannot drink the cup of the Lord and the cup of demons,** that **you cannot partake of the Lord's Table and of the table of demons,** he does not mean that it is a physical impossibility. It would be a physical possibility, for instance, for a believer to go to an idol temple and to participate in a feast there. But what Paul means here is that it would be morally inconsistent. It would be an act of treachery and disloyalty to the Lord Jesus to profess adherence or allegiance to Him, on the one hand, and then to go and have fellowship with those who sacrifice to idols. It would be morally improper and utterly wrong.

10:22. Not only that, it would not be possible to do this without provoking **the Lord to jealousy.** As William Kelly said, "Love cannot but be jealous of wandering affections; it would not be love if it did not resent unfaithfulness." The Christian should fear to thus displease the Lord, or to provoke His righteous indignation. Do we think that we are **stronger than He?** That is, do we dare to grieve Him and risk an exhibition of His disciplinary judgment upon us?

10:23. The apostle turns from the subject of participation in idol feasts and takes up some general principles that should govern Christians in their daily life. When he says **all things are lawful,** he does not mean all things in an absolute sense. For instance, he is not implying that it would be lawful for him to commit murder or to get drunk! Here again we must understand the expression as referring only to matters of moral indifference. There is a great area in the Christian life where things are perfectly legitimate in themselves and yet where for other reasons it would not be wise for a Christian to participate. Thus Paul says: **All things are lawful for me, but all things are not helpful.**

For instance, a thing might be quite lawful for a believer and yet might be equally unwise in view of the national customs of the people where he lives. Also, things that are lawful in themselves might not be edifying. That is, a thing might not result in building up a brother in his most holy faith. Should I then be high-handed in demanding my own rights or should I consider what would help my brother in Christ?

10:24. In all the decisions we make, we should not be thinking selfishly of what will benefit ourselves, but we should be thinking of what would be for our neighbor's **well-being.** The principles we are studying in this section could be applied to matters of dress, food and drink, standards of living, and the entertainments in which we participate.

10:25. If a believer went to **the meat market** to buy some meat, he was not required to ask the merchant whether that meat had been previously offered to idols. The meat itself would not be affected in one way or another, and there would be no question of loyalty to Christ involved.

10:26. In explanation of this advice, Paul quotes from Psalm 24:1: **The earth is the LORD'S, and all its fullness.** The thought here is that the food we eat has been graciously provided by the Lord for us and is specifically intended for our use. Heinrici tells us that these words from Psalm 24 are commonly used among the Jews as a thanksgiving at the table.

10:27. Now Paul takes up another situation that might cause the believers to ask questions. Suppose an unbeliever **invites** a believer to his home for **dinner.** Would a Christian be free to accept such an invitation? Yes. If you are invited to a meal in an unbeliever's home and you are disposed to go, you are at liberty to **eat whatever is set before you, asking no question for conscience' sake.**

10:28. If, during the course of the meal, another Christian should be present who has a weak conscience and informs you that the meat you are eating has been **offered to idols,** should you eat it? No. You should not indulge, because in so doing you might be causing him to stumble and hurt his conscience. Neither should you eat if an unbeliever would be hindered from accepting the Lord through this action. At the end of verse 28, Psalm 24:1 is once again quoted: **The earth is the LORD'S, and all its fullness.**

10:29. In the case just cited you would not refrain from eating because of *your own* conscience. You would have perfect liberty, as a believer, to eat the meat. But the weak brother sitting by has a **conscience** about it, and so you refrain from eating out of respect to his conscience.

The question, **For why is my liberty judged by another man's conscience?** could perhaps be paraphrased as follows: "Why should I selfishly display my freedom to eat the meat and in so doing be condemned by the other man's conscience? Why should I expose my freedom to the condemnation of his conscience? Why should I let my good be evil spoken of? (see Rom. 14:16)."

Is a piece of meat so important that I would cause offense to a fellow believer in the Lord Jesus Christ? (However, many commentators believe that here Paul is quoting the objection of the Corinthians, or asking a rhetorical question, before answering it in the following verses.)

10:30. What the apostle seems to be saying is that to him it seems very contradictory to give **thanks** to God on the one hand, when by so doing he is wounding a brother. It is better to deny oneself a legitimate right than to give thanks to God for something that will cause others to speak **evil** of you. William Kelly comments that it is "better to deny one's self and not allow one's liberty to be condemned by another or incur evil speaking for that for which one gives thanks." Why make such a use of freedom as to give offense? Why let my giving of thanks be exposed to misconstruction or be called sacrilege or scandal?

10:31. There are two great rules to guide us in our daily walk with Christ. The first is **the glory of God**, and the second is the welfare of others. Paul gives the first of these here: **Therefore, whether you eat or drink, or whatever you do, do all to the glory of God.** Christian young people are often faced with decisions about whether a certain course of action would be right or wrong for them. Here is a good rule to apply: Is there any **glory** for **God** in it? Can you bow your head before you participate in it and ask the Lord that He will be magnified by what you are about to do?

10:32. The second rule is the welfare of others. We should **give no offense** or occasion for stumbling, **either to the Jews or to the Greeks or to the church of God.** Here Paul divides all mankind into three classes. **The Jews**, of course, are the nation of Israel. **The Greeks** are the unconverted Gentiles, whereas **the church of God** includes all true believers in the Lord Jesus Christ, whether of Jewish or Gentile stock. In one sense we are bound to offend others and excite their wrath if we witness faithfully to them. However, that is not what is spoken of here. Rather, the apostle is thinking of *needless* **offense.** He is cautioning us against using our legitimate rights in such a way as to cause others to stumble.

10:33. Paul can honestly say that he seeks to **please all men in all things, not seeking** his **own profit, but the profit of many.** Probably few people have ever lived so unselfishly for others as the great apostle Paul.

 See discussion questions on issues raised in chapter 10 of 1 Corinthians on p. 207.

CHAPTER 11

11:1. Verse 1 of chapter 11 probably goes better with chapter 10. Paul had just been speaking of how he tried to gauge all his actions in the light of their effect on others. Now he tells the Corinthians to **imitate** him, **just as** he **also** copied **Christ.** He renounced personal advantages and rights in order to help others. The Corinthians should do likewise and not selfishly parade their freedoms in such a way that they would hinder the gospel of Christ or offend the weak brother.

 For a teaching/communication suggestion on chapter 11 of 1 Corinthians, see "Questions to Ask About Worship" on p. 225.

11:2–34. Verses 2–16 of chapter 11 are devoted to the subject of women's head coverings. The remaining verses deal with abuses in connection with the Lord's Supper (vv. 17–34). The first section of the chapter has been much disputed. Some interpreters think the instruction given here was applicable only to Paul's day. Some even go so far as to contend that these verses reflect Paul's prejudice against women, since he was a bachelor! Still others simply *accept* the teaching of this portion, seeking to *obey* its precepts even if they do not understand them all.

11:2. The apostle first of all commends the Corinthians for the way in which they remembered him **in all things,** and held fast **the traditions** just as he had **delivered them. Traditions** refer not to habits and practices that have arisen in the church down through the years, but in this case to the inspired instructions of the apostle Paul.

11:3. Paul now introduces the subject of women's head coverings. Behind his instruction is the fact that every ordered society is built on two pillars—authority and subjection to that authority. It is impossible to have a well-functioning community where these two principles are not observed. Paul mentions three great relationships involving authority and subjection. First, **the head of every man is Christ;** Christ is Lord and man is subject to Him. Secondly, **the head of woman is man;** the place of headship was given to the man, and the woman is under his authority. Third, **the head of Christ is God;** even in the Godhead, one person has the place of rule and another takes the place of willing subordination. These examples of headship and submission were designed by God Himself and are fundamental in His arrangement of the universe.

 For insight on the meaning of man as the "head," see "What Is Headship?" on p. 198.

At the outset it should be emphasized that subjection does *not* mean inferiority. Christ is subject to God the Father but He is not inferior to Him. Neither is woman inferior to man, although she is subordinate to him.

11:4. Every man who prays or prophesies with **his head covered dishonors his head**, that is, Christ. It is saying, in effect, that the man does not acknowledge Christ as **his head**. Thus it is an act of gross disrespect.

11:5. Every woman who prays or prophesies with her head uncovered dishonors her head, that is, the man. She is saying, in effect, that she does not recognize man's God-given headship and will not submit to it.

If this were the only verse in the Bible on the subject, then it would imply that it is all right for a woman to pray or prophesy in the assembly as long as she has a veil or other covering on her head. But Paul teaches elsewhere that women should be silent in the assembly (1 Cor. 14:34), that they are not permitted to teach or to have authority over the man but to be silent (1 Tim. 2:12).

 For insight on why Paul exhorted female believers to keep their heads covered at church, see "Head Coverings" on p. 191.

The passage is admittedly a difficult one. What does seem clear is that in the matter of covering, the woman's duty is the exact opposite of the man's. In other words, it is proper for a woman to be *covered* whenever it is proper for a man to be *uncovered* in situations involving prayer and prophesying.

11:6. If a woman is not covered, she might as well **be shorn. But if it is shameful for a woman to be shorn or shaved,** then she should be **covered.** The unveiled head of a woman is as shameful as if her hair were cut off. The apostle is *not* commanding a barber's operation but telling what moral consistency would require!

11:7. In verses 7–10, Paul teaches the subordination of the woman to the man by going back to creation. This should forever lay to rest any idea that his teaching about women's covering was what was *culturally* suitable in his day but not applicable to us today. The headship of man and the subjection of woman have been God's order from the very beginning.

First of all, man **is the image and glory of God** whereas **woman is the glory of man**. This means that man was placed on earth as God's representative, to exercise dominion over it. Man's uncovered head is a silent witness to this fact. The woman was never given this place of headship; instead she **is the glory of man** in the sense that she "renders conspicuous the authority of man," as W. E. Vine expresses it.

Man indeed ought not to cover his head in prayer; it would be tantamount to veiling the **glory of God,** and this would be an insult to the divine majesty.

11:8. Paul next reminds us that **man** was **not** created **from woman but woman** was created **from man.** The man was first, then the woman was taken from his side. This priority of the man strengthens the apostle's case for man's headship.

11:9. The purpose of creation is next alluded to in order to press home the point. **Nor was man created** primarily **for the woman, but** rather **woman for the man.** The Lord distinctly stated in Genesis 2:18, "It is not good that man should be alone; I will make him a helper comparable to him."

11:10. Because of her position of subordination to man, **the woman ought to have a symbol of authority on her head.** This symbol of authority is the head covering and here it indicates *not* her own authority but subjection to the authority of her husband.

Why does Paul add **because of the angels?** We would suggest that **the angels** are spectators of the things that are happening on earth today, as they were of the things that happened at creation. In the first creation, they saw how woman usurped the place of headship over the man. She made the decision that Adam should have made. As a result of this, sin entered the human race with its unspeakable aftermath of misery and woe. God does not want what happened in the first creation to be repeated in the new creation. When the angels look down, He wants them to see the woman acting in subjection to the man, and indicating this outwardly by a covering on her head.

We might pause here to state that the head covering is simply an outward sign, and it is of value only when it is the outward sign of an inward grace. In other words, a woman might have a covering on her head and yet not truly be submissive to her husband. In such a case, to wear a head covering would be of no value at all. The most important thing is to be sure that the heart is truly subordinate; then a covering on a woman's head becomes truly meaningful.

11:11. Paul is not implying that man is at all independent of the woman, so he adds: **Nevertheless, neither is man independent of woman, nor woman independent of man, in the Lord.** In other words, man and woman are mutually dependent. They need each other, and the idea of subordination is not in conflict with the idea of mutual interdependence.

11:12. Woman came from man by creation, that is, she was created from

Adam's side. But Paul points out that **man also comes through woman.** Here
he is referring to the process of birth. The woman gives birth to the man child.
Thus God has created this perfect balance to indicate that the one cannot
exist without the other.

All things are from God means that He has divinely appointed **all** these
things, so there is no just cause for complaint. Not only were these relationships created by **God,** but the purpose of them is to glorify Him. All of this
should make the man humble and the woman content.

11:13. The apostle now challenges the Corinthians to **judge among** themselves if it is **proper for a woman to pray to God with her head uncovered.** He
appeals to their instinctive sense. The suggestion is that it is not reverent or
decorous for a woman to enter into the presence of God unveiled.

11:14 Just how **nature itself teaches** us that it is a shame for **a man** to have
long hair is not made clear. Some have suggested that a man's hair will not
naturally grow into tresses as long as a woman's. For a man to have long hair
makes him appear effeminate. In most cultures, the male wears his hair
shorter than the female.

11:15. Verse 15 has been greatly misunderstood by many. Some have
suggested that since a woman's **hair is given to her for a covering,** it is not
necessary for her to have any other covering. But such a teaching does grave
violence to this portion of Scripture. Unless one sees that *two* coverings are
mentioned in this chapter, the passage becomes hopelessly confusing. This
may be demonstrated by referring back to verse 6. There we read: "For if a
woman is not covered, let her also be shorn." According to the interpretation
just mentioned, this would mean that if a woman "does not have her hair on,"
then she might just as well be shorn. But this is ridiculous. If she does not
"have her hair on," she could not possibly be shorn!

The actual argument in verse 15 is that there is a real analogy between the
spiritual and the natural. God gave woman a natural covering of **glory** in a way
He did not give to man. There is a spiritual significance to this. It teaches that
when a woman prays to God, she should wear a covering on her head. What
is true in the natural sphere should be true in the spiritual realm.

11:16. The apostle closes this section with the statement: **But if anyone
seems to be contentious, we have no such custom, nor do the churches of God.**
Does Paul mean, as has been suggested, that the things he has just been saying
are not important enough to contend about? Does he mean that there was no
such custom of women veiling their heads in the churches? Does he mean that
these teachings are optional and not to be pressed upon women as the
commandments of the Lord? It seems strange that any such interpretations

would ever be offered; yet they are commonly heard today. This would mean that Paul considered these instructions as of no real consequence, and he had just been wasting over half a chapter of holy Scripture in setting them forth!

There are at least two possible explanations of this verse that fit in with the rest of the Scripture. First of all, the apostle may be saying that he anticipates that certain people will **be contentious** about these matters, but he adds that **we have no such custom,** that is, the custom of contending about this. We do not argue about such matters, but accept them as the teaching of the Lord. Another interpretation, favored by William Kelly, is that Paul was saying that **the churches of God** did not have any such custom as that of women praying or prophesying without being covered.

11:17. The apostle rebukes the Corinthians for the fact that there were divisions among them as they gathered together (vv. 17–19). Note the repetition of the expression "when you come together" or related words (11:17, 18, 20, 33, 34; 14:23, 26). In 11:2 Paul had praised them for keeping the traditions which he had delivered to them, but there was one matter in which he could **not praise** them. When they gathered together for public meetings, they came **together not for the better but for the worse.** This is a solemn reminder to all of us that it is possible to go away from meetings of the church and to have been harmed rather than benefited.

11:18. The **first** reason for rebuke was the existence of **divisions** or schisms. This does not mean that parties had broken away from the church and formed separate fellowships, but that there were cliques and factions within the congregation. A schism is a party inside, whereas a sect is a different party outside. Paul could **believe** these reports of divisions because he knew that the Corinthians were in a carnal state, and he had previous occasion in this epistle to rebuke them because of their divisions.

F. B. Hole writes:

Paul was prepared to give at least partial credence to the reports of the divisions at Corinth, since he knew that, owing to their carnal state, there were bound to be these opinionated factions in their midst. Here Paul reasons forward from their state to their actions. Knowing them to be carnal and walking as men, he knew that they would certainly fall victims to the inveterate tendency of the human mind to form its strong opinions, and the factions founded in those opinions, ending in the schisms and divisions. He knew, too, that God could overrule their folly and take occasion to make manifest those that were approved of Him, walking according to the Spirit and not as man; and consequently eschewing the whole of this divisive business.

11:19. Paul foresaw that the schisms already begun in Corinth would increase until they became more serious. Although in general this would be detrimental to the church, yet one good thing would come out of it—those who were truly spiritual and who were **approved** of God would **be recognized among** the Corinthians. When Paul says in this verse **there must also be factions among you,** this does not mean that it is a *moral* necessity. God is not condoning splits in the church. Rather, Paul means that because of the carnal conditions of the Corinthians, it was inevitable that **factions** would result. Divisions are proof that some people have failed to discern the mind of the Lord.

11:20. Paul now directs his second rebuke against abuses in connection with the Lord's Supper. When the Christians gathered together, ostensibly to celebrate **the Lord's Supper,** their conduct was so deplorable that Paul says they could not possibly remember the Lord in the way in which He appointed. They might go through the outward motions, but their behavior would preclude any true remembrance of the Lord.

11:21. In the early days of the church, Christians celebrated the "agapē," or love feast along with the Lord's Supper. The love feast was something like a common meal, shared in a spirit of love and fellowship. At the end of the love feast, the Christians often had the remembrance of the Lord with the bread and wine. But before very long, abuses crept in. For instance, in this verse it is implied that the love feast lost its real meaning. Not only did the Christians not wait for one another, but the rich believers shamed their poorer brethren by having lavish meals and not sharing them. Some went away **hungry,** whereas others were actually **drunk!** Since the Lord's Supper often followed the love feast, they would still be drunk when they sat down to partake of the Lord's Supper.

11:22. The apostle rebukes such disgraceful conduct. If they insist on carrying on in such a way, then they should at least have the reverence not to do it in a **church** meeting. To practice intemperance at such a time and to **shame** one's poorer brethren is inconsistent with the Christian faith. Paul withholds **praise** from the saints for acting in this way; and in withholding **praise,** he thereby condemns them strongly.

11:23. To show the contrast between their conduct and the real meaning of the Lord's Supper, he goes back to its original institution. He shows that it was not a common meal or a feast, but a solemn ordinance of the Lord. Paul **received** his knowledge concerning this directly **from the Lord** and he mentions this to show that any violation would be actual disobedience. What he is teaching, then, he received by revelation.

First of all, he mentions how **the Lord Jesus on the** very **night in which He**

was betrayed took bread. The literal rendering is "while He was being betrayed." While the foul plot to deliver Him up was going on outside, **the Lord Jesus** gathered in the upper room with His disciples and **took** the **bread.**

The fact that this occurred at **night** does not necessarily mean that the Lord's Supper must thereafter be observed only at night. At that time, sundown was the beginning of the Jewish day. Our day begins at sunrise. Also it has been remarked that there is a difference between apostolic *example* and apostolic *precepts.* We are not obligated to do all that the apostles *did,* but we are certainly obligated to obey all that they *taught.*

11:24. The Lord Jesus took the bread, first of all, and gave **thanks** for it. Since the bread was typical of His body, He was, in effect, thanking God that He had been given a human body in which He might come and die for the sins of the world.

When the Savior said, **This is My body,** did He mean that the bread actually *became* His body in some real sense? The Roman Catholic dogma of *transubstantiation* insists that the bread and the wine are literally changed into the body and the blood of Christ. The Lutheran doctrine of *consubstantiation* teaches that the true body and blood of Christ are in, with, and under the bread and wine on the table.

In answer to these views, it should be sufficient to remember that when the Lord Jesus instituted this memorial, His body had not yet been given, nor had His blood been shed. When the Lord Jesus said, **This is My body,** He meant, "This is symbolic of My body" or "This is a picture of My body which is broken for you." To eat the bread is to remember Him in His atoning death for us. There is inexpressible tenderness in our Lord's expression "in remembrance of Me."

11:25. **In the same manner** the Lord Jesus **also took the cup** after the Passover **supper, saying, This cup is the new covenant in My blood. This do, as often as you drink it, in remembrance of Me.** The Lord's Supper was instituted immediately after the Passover Feast. That is why it says that the Lord Jesus **took the cup after supper.** In connection with **the cup,** He said that it was **the new covenant** in His **blood.** This refers to the covenant that God promised to the nation of Israel in Jeremiah 31:31–34. It is an unconditional promise by which He agreed to be merciful to their unrighteousness and to remember their sins and iniquities no more. The terms of the new covenant are also given in Hebrews 8:10–12.

The covenant is in force at the present time, but unbelief keeps the nation of Israel from enjoying it. All who do trust the Lord Jesus receive the benefits that were promised. The **new covenant** was ratified by the **blood** of Christ, and that is why He speaks of **the cup** as being **the new covenant in** His **blood.** The foundation of the new covenant was laid through the cross.

11:26. Verse 26 touches on the question about how frequently the Lord's Supper should be observed. **For as often as you eat . . . and drink. . . .** No legalistic rule is laid down; neither is any fixed date given. It seems clear from Acts 20:7 that the practice of the disciples was to meet on the first day of the week to remember the Lord. That this ordinance was not intended simply for the early days of the church is proved by the expression **until He comes.** Godet beautifully points out that the Lord's Supper is "the link between His two comings, the monument of the one, the pledge of the other."

In all this instruction concerning the Lord's Supper, it is notable that there is not a word about a minister or priest officiating. It is a simple memorial service left for all the people of God. Christians gather together simply as believer-priests to thus proclaim the Lord's death **until He comes.**

 For a teaching/communication suggestion on the Lord's Supper, see "The Meaning of the Lord's Supper" on p. 225.

11:27. Having discussed the origin and purpose of the Lord's Supper, the apostle now turns to the consequences of participating in it in the wrong way. Whoever **eats this bread or drinks this cup of the Lord in an unworthy manner will be guilty of the body and blood of the Lord.** We are all unworthy to partake of this solemn Supper. In that sense, we are unworthy of any of the Lord's mercy or kindness to us. But that is not the subject here. The apostle is not speaking of our own personal unworthiness. Cleansed by the blood of Christ, we can approach God in all the worthiness of His own beloved Son. But Paul is speaking here of the disgraceful conduct that characterized the Corinthians as they gathered together for the Lord's Supper. They were **guilty** of careless, irreverent behavior. To act thus is to **be guilty of the body and blood of the Lord.**

11:28. As we come to the Lord's Supper, we should do so in a judged condition. Sin should be confessed and forsaken; restitution should be made; apologies should be offered to those we have offended. In general we should make sure that we are in a proper state of soul.

11:29. To eat and to drink in an inconsistent manner is to eat and drink **judgment to** oneself, **not discerning the Lord's body.** We should realize that the Lord's body was given in order that our sins might be put away. If we go on living in sin, while at the same time partaking of the Lord's Supper, we are living a lie. F. G. Patterson writes, "If we eat the Lord's Supper with unjudged sin upon us, we do not discern the Lord's body which was broken to put it away."

11:30. Failure to exercise self-judgment resulted in God's disciplinary judgment upon some people in the church at Corinth. **Many** were **weak and sick,** and not a few slept. In other words, physical illness had come upon some, and some were taken home to heaven. Because they did not judge sin in their lives, the Lord was required to take disciplinary action against them.

11:31. On the other hand, if we exercise this self-judgment, it will not be necessary for Him to so chasten us.

11:32. God is dealing with us as with His own children. He loves us too dearly to allow us to go on in sin. Thus we soon feel the shepherd's crook on our necks pulling us back to Himself. As someone has said, "It is possible for the saints to be fit for heaven (in Christ) but not fitted to remain on the earth in testimony."

11:33. **When** the believers **come together** for the love feast, or agape, they should **wait for one another**, and not selfishly proceed without regard for the other saints. "Waiting for one another" is in contrast to verse 21, "each one takes his own supper ahead of others."

11:34. But if anyone is hungry, let him eat at home. In other words, the love feast, linked as it was with the Lord's Supper, was not to be mistaken for a common meal. To disregard its sacred character would be to **come together for judgment.**

And the rest I will set in order when I come. Undoubtedly there were other minor matters which had been mentioned to the apostle in the letter from the Corinthians. Here he assures them that he will deal with these matters personally when he visits them.

 See discussion questions on issues raised in chapter 11 of 1 Corinthians on p. 207.

CHAPTER 12

Chapters 12–14 deal with the gifts of the Spirit. There had been abuses in the assembly in Corinth, especially in connection with the gift of tongues, and Paul writes in order to correct those abuses.

Some believers in Corinth had received the gift of tongues. This means they were given the power to speak foreign languages without having studied those languages. But instead of using this gift to magnify God and edify other believers, they were using it to show off. They stood up in the meetings and spoke in languages which no one else understood, hoping that others would be impressed by their linguistic proficiency. They exalted the sign-gifts above the others, and claimed superior spirituality for those who spoke in tongues.

This led to pride on the one hand, and to feelings of envy, inferiority, and worthlessness on the other. So it was necessary for the apostle to correct these erroneous attitudes and to establish controls in the exercise of the gifts, especially tongues and prophecy.

 For a teaching/communication suggestion on chapter 12 of 1 Corinthians, see "Some Truths About Spiritual Gifts" on p. 227.

12:1. He does **not want** the saints at Corinth **to be ignorant** in the matter of **spiritual** manifestations or **gifts**. The literal reading here is **Now concerning "spirituals," brethren, I do not want you to be ignorant.** Most versions supply the word *gifts* to complete the sense. However, the next verse suggests that Paul might have been thinking not only of manifestations of the Holy Spirit but of evil spirits as well.

12:2. Before conversion the Corinthians had been idolaters, enslaved by evil spirits. They lived in fear of the spirits and were led about by these diabolical influences. They witnessed supernatural manifestations of the spirit world and heard spirit-inspired utterances. Under the influence of evil spirits, they sometimes surrendered self-control, and said and did things beyond their own conscious powers.

12:3. Now that they are saved, the believers must know how to judge all spirit-manifestations, that is, how to discern between the voice of evil spirits and the authentic voice of the Holy Spirit. The crucial test is the testimony that is given concerning the Lord Jesus. If a man says, **Jesus is accursed,** you can be sure that he is demon-inspired, because evil spirits characteristically blaspheme and curse the name of Jesus. **The Spirit of God** would never lead anyone to speak of the Savior in this way; His ministry is to exalt the Lord Jesus. He leads people to **say that Jesus is Lord,** not just with their lips, but with the warm, full confession of their hearts and lives.

Notice that the three persons of the Trinity are mentioned in verse 3 and also in verses 4–6.

12:4. Paul next shows that while there is a variety **of gifts** of the Holy Spirit in the church, there is a basic, threefold unity, involving the three persons of the Godhead.

First of all, **there are diversities of gifts, but the same Spirit.** The Corinthians were acting as if there was only one gift—tongues. Paul says, "No, your unity is not found in the possession of one *common* gift, but rather in possession of the Holy Spirit who is the source of *all* the gifts."

12:5. Next the apostle points out that **there are differences of ministries**

or services in the church. Everyone does not have the same work. But what we have in common is that whatever we do is done for **the same Lord** and with a view to serving others (not self).

12:6. Then again, though **there are diversities of activities** as far as spiritual gifts are concerned, **it is the same God who** empowers each believer. If one gift seems more successful or spectacular or powerful than another, it is not because of any superiority in the person who possesses it. It is God who supplies the power.

12:7. The **Spirit** manifests Himself in the life of **each** believer by imparting some gift. There is no believer who does not have a function to perform. And the gifts are given **for the profit of** the entire body. They are not given for self-display or even for self-gratification but in order to help others. This is a pivotal point in the entire discussion.

That leads quite naturally to a list of some of the gifts of the Spirit.

12:8. **The word of wisdom** is the supernatural power to speak with divine insight, whether in solving difficult problems, defending the faith, resolving conflicts, giving practical advice, or pleading one's case before hostile authorities. Stephen so demonstrated the word of wisdom that his adversaries "were not able to resist the wisdom and the Spirit by which he spoke" (Acts 6:10).

The word of knowledge is the power to communicate information that has been divinely revealed. This is illustrated in Paul's use of such expressions as "Behold, I tell you a mystery" (1 Cor. 15:51) and "For this we say to you by the word of the Lord" (1 Thess. 4:15). In that primary sense of conveying new truth, the word of knowledge has ceased, because the Christian faith has been once for all delivered to the saints (Jude 3). The body of Christian doctrine is complete. In a secondary sense, however, **the word of knowledge** may still be with us. There is still a mysterious communication of divine knowledge to those who live in close fellowship with the Lord (see Psalm 25:14). The sharing of that knowledge with others is **the word of knowledge**.

12:9. The gift of **faith** is the divine ability to remove mountains of difficulty in pursuing the will of God (13:2) and to do great exploits for God in response to some command or promise of God as found in His word or as communicated privately. George Müller is a classic example of a man with the gift of faith. Without making his needs known to anyone but God, he cared for ten thousand orphans over a period of sixty years.

The **gifts of healings** have to do with the miraculous power to heal diseases.

12:10. Working of miracles could include casting out demons, changing matter from one form to another, raising the dead, and exercising power over the elements. Philip worked miracles in Samaria, and thereby gained a hearing for the gospel (Acts 8:6, 7).

The gift of **prophecy,** in its primary sense, signified that a person received direct revelations from God and transmitted them to others. Sometimes the prophets predicted future events (Acts 11:27, 28; 21:11); more often they simply expressed the mind of God. Like the apostles, they were concerned with the foundation of the church (Eph. 2:20). They themselves were not the foundation, but they laid the foundation in what they taught concerning the Lord Jesus. Once the foundation was laid, the need for the prophets ceased. Their ministry is preserved for us in the pages of the New Testament. Since the Bible is complete, we reject any so-called prophet who claims to have additional truth from God.

In a weaker sense, we use the word *prophet* to describe any preacher who declares the word of God authoritatively, incisively, and effectively. Prophecy can also include the ascription of praise to God (Luke 1:67, 68) and the encouragement and strengthening of His people (Acts 15:32).

Discerning of spirits describes the power to detect whether a prophet or other person is speaking by the Holy Spirit or by Satan. A person with this gift has special ability to discern if a man is an imposter and an opportunist, for instance. Thus Peter was able to expose Simon as one who was poisoned by bitterness and in the bond of iniquity (Acts 8:20–23).

The gift of **tongues,** as has been mentioned, is the ability to speak a foreign language without having learned it. Tongues were given for a sign, especially to Israel.

The interpretation of tongues is the miraculous power to understand a language that the person has never known before and to convey the message in the local language.

It is perhaps significant that this list of gifts begins with those connected primarily with the intellect and closes with those dealing primarily with the emotions. The Corinthians had reversed this in their thinking. They exalted the gift of tongues above the other gifts. They thought that the more a person had of the Holy Spirit, the more he was carried off by a power beyond himself. They confused power with spirituality.

12:11. All the gifts mentioned in verses 8–10 are produced and controlled by **the same Spirit.** Here again we see that He does not give the same gift to everyone. He distributes **to each one individually as He wills.** This is another important point—the Spirit sovereignly apportions the gifts. If we grasp this, it will eliminate pride on the one hand, because we don't have anything that we didn't receive. And it will eliminate discontent on the other hand, because

God decided what gift we should have, and His choice is perfect. It is wrong for everyone to desire the same gift. If everyone played the same instrument, you could never have a symphony orchestra. And if a body consisted only of a tongue, it would be a monstrosity.

12:12. The human **body** is an illustration of unity and diversity. **The body is one**, yet **has many members**. Although all the believers are different and perform different functions, yet they all combine to make one functioning unit—the **body**.

So also is Christ is more precisely translated: "So also is *the* Christ." "The Christ" here refers not only to the glorified Lord Jesus Christ in heaven, but to the head in heaven and to His members here on earth. All believers are members of the body of Christ. Just as the human body is a vehicle by which a person expresses himself to others, so the body of Christ is the vehicle on earth by which He chooses to make Himself known to the world. It is an evidence of wonderful grace that the Lord allows the expression "the Christ" to be used to include those of us who are members of His body.

 For insight on Paul's comparison of the church to parts of the body, see "Lessons from the Human Body" on p. 199.

12:13. Paul goes on to explain how we became members of the body of Christ. **By** (or in) **one Spirit we were all baptized into one body**. The more literal translation here is "*in* one Spirit." This may mean that the Spirit is the element in which we were baptized, just as water is the element in which we are immersed in believer's baptism. Or it may mean that the Spirit is the agent who does the baptizing, thus **by one Spirit**. This is the more probable and understandable meaning.

The baptism of the Holy Spirit took place on the day of Pentecost. The church was born at that time. We partake of the benefits of that baptism when we are born again. We become members of the body of Christ.

Several important points should be noted here. First, the baptism of the Holy Spirit is that divine operation which places believers in the body of Christ. It is not the same as water baptism. This is clear from Matthew 3:11; John 1:33; Acts 1:5. It is not a work of grace subsequent to salvation whereby believers become more spiritual. **All** the Corinthians had been **baptized** in the Spirit, yet Paul rebukes them for being carnal—not spiritual (3:1). It is *not* true that speaking in tongues is the invariable sign of being baptized by the Spirit. **All** the Corinthians had been **baptized**, but not all spoke in tongues (12:30). There *are* crisis experiences of the Holy Spirit when a believer surrenders to the Spirit's control and is then empowered from on high. But such an experience is *not* the same as the baptism of the Spirit, and should not be confused with it.

The verse goes on to say that believers **have all been made to drink into one Spirit**. This means that they partake of the **Spirit** of God in the sense that they receive Him as an indwelling person and receive the benefits of His ministry in their lives.

12:14. Without a variety of members you could not have a human **body**. There must be **many** members, each one different from the others, working in obedience to the head and in cooperation with the others.

12:15. When we see that diversity is essential to a normal, healthy body, it will save us from two dangers—from belittling ourselves (vv. 15–20) and from belittling others (vv. 21–25). It would be absurd for **the foot** to feel unimportant because it can't do the work of **a hand**. After all, the foot can stand, walk, run, climb, dance—and kick, as well as a host of other things.

12:16. **The ear** shouldn't try to become a dropout because it is **not an eye**. We take our ears for granted until deafness overtakes us. Then we realize what a tremendously useful function they perform.

12:17. **If the whole body were an eye**, you would have a deaf oddity fit only for a circus sideshow. Or if the body had only ears, it wouldn't have a nose to detect when the gas was escaping and soon wouldn't even be able to hear because it would be unconscious or dead.

The point that Paul is driving at is that if the body were all tongue, it would be a freak and a monstrosity. And yet the Corinthians were so overemphasizing the gift of tongues that they were, in effect, creating a local fellowship that would be *all tongue*. It could talk, but that was all it could do!

12:18. **God** has not been guilty of such folly. In His matchless wisdom, He has arranged the different **members . . . in the body just as He pleased**. We should give Him credit for knowing what He is doing! We should be profoundly grateful for whatever gift He has given us and use it joyfully for His glory and for building up others. To be envious of someone else's gift is sin. It is rebellion against God's perfect plan for our lives.

12:19. It is impossible to think of a body with only **one member**. So the Corinthians should remember that if they all had the gift of tongues, then they would not have a functioning **body**. Other gifts, though less spectacular and less sensational, are nonetheless necessary.

12:20. As God has ordained, there are **many members, yet one body**. These facts are obvious to us in connection with the human body, and they should be equally obvious to us in connection with our service in the church.

12:21. Just as it is folly for one person to envy another's gift, so it is equally foolish for anyone to depreciate another's gift or feel that he doesn't need the others. **The eye cannot say to the hand, I have no need of you; nor again the head to the feet, I have no need of you.** The eye can see things to be done, but it can't do them. It depends on the hand for that. Again, the head might know that it is necessary to go to a certain place, but it depends on the feet to take it there.

12:22. Some **members of the body . . . seem to be weaker** than others. The kidneys, for instance, don't seem to be as strong as the arms. But the kidneys are indispensable whereas the arms are not. We can live without arms and legs, or even without a tongue, but we cannot live without heart, lungs, liver, or brain. Yet these vital organs never put themselves on public display. They just carry on their functions without fanfare.

12:23. Some **members** of the body are attractive while others are not so elegant. We compensate by putting clothes over those that are not so beautiful. Thus there is a certain mutual care among the members, minimizing the differences.

12:24. Those **parts** of the body that are **presentable** don't need extra attention. **But God** has combined all the differing members of **the body** into an organic structure. Some members are comely, some homely. Some do well in public, some not so well. Yet God has given us the instinct to appreciate all the members, to realize that they are all interdependent, and to counterbalance the deficiencies of those that are not so handsome.

12:25. The mutual care of the members prevents division or **schism in the body.** One gives to another what is needed, and receives in return the help which only that other member can give. This is the way it must be in the church. Overemphasis on any one gift of the Spirit will result in conflict and schism.

12:26. What affects **one member** affects **all**. This is a well-known fact in the human body. Fever, for instance, is not confined to one part of the body, but affects the whole system. So it is with other types of sickness and pain. An eye doctor often can detect brain tumor, kidney disease, or liver infection by looking into the eye. The reason is that, although all these members are distinct and separate, yet they all form part of the one body, and they are so vitally linked together that what affects one member affects all. Therefore, instead of being discontent with our lot, or, on the other hand, instead of feeling a sense of independence from others, we should have a real sense of solidarity in the body of Christ. Anything that hurts another Christian should cause us the keenest sorrow. Likewise, if we see another Christian **honored**, we should not feel jealous, but we should **rejoice with** him.

12:27. Paul reminds the Corinthians that they **are the body of Christ**. This cannot mean *the* body of Christ in its totality. Neither can it mean *a* body of Christ, since there is only one body. It can only mean that they collectively formed a microcosm or miniature of the body of Christ. **Individually** each one is a member of that great cooperative society. As such he should fulfill his function without any feeling of pride, independence, envy, or worthlessness.

 For insight on the importance of every member of the body of Christ, see "Are Some Jobs More Important Than Others?" on p. 199.

12:28. The apostle now gives us another list of gifts. None of these lists is to be considered as complete. **And God has appointed these in the church: first apostles.** The word **first** indicates that not all are apostles. The Twelve were men who had been commissioned by the Lord as His messengers. They were with Him during His earthly ministry (Acts 1:21, 22) and, with the exception of Judas, saw Him after His resurrection (Acts 1:2, 3, 22). But others besides the Twelve were apostles. The most notable was Paul. There were also Barnabas (Acts 14:4, 14); James, the Lord's brother (Gal. 1:19); and Silas and Timothy (1 Thess. 1:1; 2:6). Together with the New Testament prophets, the apostles laid the doctrinal foundation of the church in what they taught about the Lord Jesus Christ (Eph. 2:20).

In the strict meaning of the word, we no longer have apostles. In a wider sense, we still have messengers and church planters sent forth by the Lord. By calling them *missionaries* instead of apostles, we avoid creating the impression that they have the extraordinary authority and power of the early apostles.

Next are the **prophets**. We have already mentioned that prophets were spokesmen of God, men who uttered the very word of God in the day before it was given in complete written form. **Teachers** are those who take the word of God and explain it to the people in an understandable way. **Miracles** might refer to raising the dead, casting out demons, etc. **Healings** have to do with the instantaneous cure of bodily diseases. **Helps** are commonly associated with the work of deacons, those entrusted with the material affairs of the church. The gift of **administrations**, on the other hand, is usually applied to elders or bishops. These are the men who have the godly, spiritual care of the local church. Last is the gift of **tongues**. We believe that there is a significance in the order. Paul mentions apostles first and tongues last. The Corinthians were putting tongues *first* and disparaging the apostle!

12:29, 30. When the apostle asks if every believer has the same gift—whether apostle, prophet, teacher, miracles, healings, helps, governments, tongues, interpretations of tongues—the grammar in the original shows that he expects and requires a "No" answer. Therefore any suggestion, expressed or implied, that *everyone* should have the gift of tongues, is contrary to the Word of God and is foreign to the whole concept of the body with its many different members, each with its own function.

If, as stated here, not everyone has the gift of tongues, then it is wrong to teach that tongues are the sign of the baptism of the Spirit. For, in that case, not everyone could expect that baptism. But the truth is that *every* believer has already been baptized by the Spirit (v. 13).

12:31. When Paul says: **But earnestly desire the best gifts,** he is speaking to the Corinthians as a local church, not as individuals. We know this because the verb is plural in the original. He is saying that as an assembly they should desire to have in their midst a good selection of gifts that edify. The best gifts are those that are most useful rather than those that are spectacular. All gifts are given by the Holy Spirit and none should be despised. Yet the fact is that some are of greater benefit to the body than others. These are the ones that every local fellowship should ask the Lord to raise up in the assembly.

And yet I show you a more excellent way. With these words Paul introduces the love chapter (1 Cor. 13). What he is saying is that the possession of gifts is not as important as the exercise of these gifts in love. Love thinks of others, not of self. It is wonderful to see a person who is unusually gifted by the Holy Spirit, but it is still more wonderful when that person uses that gift to build up others in the faith rather than to attract attention to himself.

 See discussion questions on issues raised in chapter 12 of 1 Corinthians on p. 208.

CHAPTER 13

People tend to divorce chapter 13 from its context. They think it is a parenthesis, designed to relieve the tension over tongues in chapters 12 and 14. But that is not the case. It is a vital and continuing part of Paul's argument.

The abuse of tongues had apparently caused strife in the assembly. Using their gifts for self-display, self-edification, and self-gratification, the people with this spectacular gift were not acting in love. They received satisfaction out of speaking publicly in a language they had never learned, but it was a real hardship on others to have to sit and listen to something they did not understand. Paul insists that all gifts must be exercised in a spirit of love. The aim of love is to help others and not to please self.

And perhaps the other believers at Corinth had overreacted in acts which were not characterized by love. They might even have gone so far as to say that all tongues are of the devil. Their Greek tongues might have been worse than the "charismatic" tongues! Their lack of love might have been worse than the abuse of tongues itself.

So Paul wisely reminds all of them that love is needed on both sides. If they would act in love toward one another, the problem would be largely solved. It is not a problem that calls for excommunication or division; it calls for love.

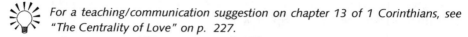 For a teaching/communication suggestion on chapter 13 of 1 Corinthians, see *"The Centrality of Love" on p. 227.*

13:1. Even if a person could **speak** in all languages, human and angelic, but didn't use this ability for the good of others, it would be no more profitable or pleasant than the **clanging**, jangling sound of metals crashing against each other. Where the spoken word is not understood, there is no profit. It is just a nerve-racking din contributing nothing to the common good. For tongues to be beneficial, they must be interpreted. Even then, what is said must be edifying. **The tongues of angels** may be figurative for exalted speech, but it does not mean an unknown language, because whenever angels spoke to men in the Bible, it was in the common speech, easily understood.

 For insight on the meaning of the phrase *"sounding brass or a clanging cymbal,"* see the article with this title on p.191.

13:2. Likewise one might receive marvelous revelations from God. He might **understand** the great **mysteries** of God, tremendous truths hitherto unrevealed but now made known to him. He might receive a great inflow of divine **knowledge**, supernaturally imparted. He might be given that heroic **faith** that is able to **remove mountains.** Yet if these wonderful gifts are used only for his own benefit and not for the edifying of other members of the body of Christ, they are of no value, and the holder is **nothing**, that is, he is of no help to others.

13:3. If the apostle gave all his **goods to feed the poor**, or even gave his **body to be burned**, these valiant acts would not profit him unless they were done in a spirit of **love**. If he were merely trying to attract attention to himself and seek a name for himself, then his display of virtue would be valueless.

13:4. Someone has said: "This did not start out to be a treatise on love, but like most literary gems of the New Testament, it was introduced in connection with some local situation." Hodge has pointed out that the Corinthians were impatient, discontented, envious, inflated, selfish, indecorous, unmindful of the feelings and interests of others, suspicious, resentful, and censorious.

And so the apostle now contrasts the characteristics of true love. First of all, **love suffers long and is kind**. Long-suffering is patient endurance under provocation. Kindness is active goodness, going forth in the interests of others. **Love does not envy** others; rather, it is pleased that others should be honored and exalted. **Love does not parade itself, is not puffed up**. It realizes that whatever it has is the gift of God, and that there is nothing in man of which to be proud. Even gifts of the Holy Spirit are sovereignly bestowed by God and should not make a person proud or haughty, no matter how spectacular the gift might be.

13:5. Love **does not behave rudely**. If a person is truly acting in love, he will be courteous and considerate. Love **does not** selfishly **seek its own**, but is interested in what will assist others. Love **is not provoked**, but is willing to endure slights and insults. Love **thinks no evil**, that is, it does not attribute bad motives to others. It does not suspect their actions. It is guileless.

 For insight on the nature of Christian love, see "The Meaning of Love" on p. 192.

13:6. Love **does not rejoice in iniquity, but rejoices in the truth**. There is a certain mean streak in human nature which takes pleasure in what is unrighteous, especially if an unrighteous act seems to benefit one's self. This is not the spirit of love. Love **rejoices** with every triumph of **the truth**.

13:7. The expression **bears all things** may mean that love patiently endures **all things**, or that it hides or conceals the faults of others. The word **bears** may also be translated "covers." Love does not needlessly publicize the failures of others, although it must be firm in giving godly discipline when necessary.

Love **believes all things**, that is, it tries to put the best possible construction on actions and events. Love **hopes all things** in the sense that it earnestly desires that all things work out for the best. Love **endures all things** in the way of persecution or ill treatment.

 For a teaching/communication suggestion on the traits of Christian love, see "Characteristics of Genuine Love" on p. 227.

13:8. Having described the qualities that characterize those who exercise their gift in love, the apostle now takes up the permanence of love, as contrasted with the temporary character of gifts. **Love never fails**. Throughout eternity, love will go on in the sense that we will still love the Lord and love one another. These gifts, on the other hand, are of temporary duration.

 For insight on the Greek word agape, *see "Agape: Self-Giving Love" on p. 200.*

There are two principal interpretations of verses 8–13. One traditional view is that the gifts of prophecy, tongues, and knowledge will cease when believers enter the eternal state. The other view is that these gifts have already ceased, and that this occurred when the canon of Scripture was completed. In order to present both views, we will paraphrase verses 8–12 under the labels ETERNAL STATE and COMPLETED CANON.

ETERNAL STATE	COMPLETED CANON
Love will never cease. In contrast, the prophecies which exist at the present time will be ended when God's people are home in heaven. While there is the gift of knowledge just now, this will be stopped when we reach the final consummation in glory. (When Paul says, knowledge . . . will vanish away, he cannot mean that there will be no knowledge in heaven. He must be referring to the gift of knowledge by which divine truth was supernaturally imparted.)	Love will never cease. While there are prophecies (at the time of Paul), the need for such direct revelations would end when the last book of the New Testament was completed. Tongues were still used in Paul's day, but they would cease in and of themselves when the sixty-six books of the Bible were finished, because they would no longer be necessary to confirm the preaching of the apostles and prophets (Heb. 2:3, 4). Knowledge of divine truth was being given by God to the apostles and prophets, but this would also stop when the complete body of Christian doctrine was once for all delivered.
13:9. In this life our knowledge is partial at best, and so are our prophecies. There are many things we do not understand in the Bible, and many mysteries in the providence of God.	We, i.e., the apostles, know in part (in the sense that we are still receiving inspired knowledge by direct revelation from God), and we prophesy in part (because we can only express the partial revelations we are receiving).

13:10. But when that which is perfect has come, i.e., when we reach the perfect state in the eternal world, then the gifts of partial knowledge and partial prophecy will be done away.	But when that which is perfect has come, i.e., when the canon is complete by the last book's being added to the New Testament, then periodic or piecemeal revelations of truth will be stopped, and the telling forth of this truth will be done away. There will be no more need for partial revelations since the complete word of God will be here.
13:11. This life may be compared to childhood, when our speech, understanding, and thoughts are very limited and immature. The heavenly state is comparable to full adulthood. Then our childish condition will be a thing of the past.	The sign gifts were connected with the childhood of the church. The gifts were not childish; they were necessary gifts of the Holy Spirit. But once the full revelation of God was available in the Bible, the miracle gifts were no longer needed and were put aside. The word *child* here means a baby without the full power of speech.
13:12. As long as we are on earth, we see things dimly and indistinctly, as if we were looking in a blurry mirror. Heaven, by contrast will be like seeing things face to face, i.e., without anything between to obscure the vision. Now our knowledge is partial, but then we shall know just as we also are known—which means more fully. We will never have perfect knowledge, even in heaven. Only God is omniscient. But our knowledge will be vastly greater than it is now.	Now (during the apostolic age) we see in a mirror, dimly. No single one of us (apostles) has received God's full revelation. It is being given to us in portions, like parts of a puzzle. When the canon of Scripture is complete, the obscurity will be removed and we will see the picture in its entirety. Our knowledge (as apostles and prophets) is partial at present. But when the last book has been added to the New Testament, we will know more fully and intimately than ever before.

13:13. Faith, hope, and **love** are what Kelly calls "the main moral principles characteristic of Christianity." These graces of the Spirit are superior to the gifts of the Spirit, and they are more lasting, too. In short, the *fruit* of the Spirit is more important than the *gifts* of the Spirit.

And **love** is **the greatest** of the graces because it is most useful to others. It is not self-centered but others-centered.

Now before leaving this chapter, there are a few observations to be made. As mentioned above, a widely accepted interpretation of verses 8–12 is that they contrast conditions in this life with those in the eternal state.

But many devout Christians hold to the completed canon view, believing that the purpose of the sign gifts was to confirm the preaching of the apostles before the word of God was given in final written form, and that the need for these miracle gifts passed when the New Testament was completed. While this second view merits serious consideration, it can hardly be proved decisively. Even if we believe that the sign gifts largely passed away at the end of the apostolic era, we cannot say with finality that God could not, if He wished, use these gifts today. Whichever view we hold, the abiding lesson is that while the gifts of the Spirit are partial and temporary, the fruit of the Spirit is eternal and is more excellent. If we practice love, it will save us from the misuse of gifts and from the strife and divisions that have arisen as a result of their abuse.

 See discussion questions on issues raised in chapter 13 of 1 Corinthians on p. 209.

CHAPTER 14

14:1. The connection with the previous chapter is apparent. Christians should **pursue love,** and this will mean that they will always be trying to serve others. They should also earnestly **desire spiritual gifts** for their assembly. While it is true that gifts are distributed by the Spirit as He wishes, it is also true that we can ask for gifts that will be of greatest value in the local fellowship. That is why Paul suggests that the gift of prophecy is eminently desirable. He goes on to explain why prophecy, for instance, is of greater benefit than tongues.

 For a teaching/communication suggestion on chapter 14 of 1 Corinthians, see "Why Go to Church?" on p. 229.

14:2. He who speaks in a tongue without interpretation is not speaking for the benefit of the congregation. **God** understands what he is saying but the people don't because it is a foreign language to them. He might be setting forth marvelous truths, hitherto unknown, but it does no good because it is all unintelligible.

14:3. The man **who prophesies**, on the other hand, builds people up, encourages them, and comforts them. The reason for this is that he is speaking in the language of the people; that is what makes the difference. When Paul says that the prophet builds up, stirs up, and binds up, he is not giving a definition. He is simply saying that these results follow when the message is given in a language the people know.

14:4. Verse 4 is commonly used to justify the private use of tongues for self-edification. But the fact that the word *church* is found nine times in this chapter (vv. 4, 5, 12, 19, 23, 28, 33, 34, 35) offers rather convincing evidence that Paul is not dealing with a believer's devotional life in the privacy of his room, but with the use of tongues in the local assembly. The context shows that, far from advocating the use of tongues for self-edification, the apostle is condemning any use of the gift in the church that does not result in helping *others*. Love thinks of others and not of self. If the gift of tongues is used in love, it will benefit others and not only oneself.

He who prophesies edifies the church. He is not parading his gift for personal advantage, but speaking constructively in a language the congregation can understand.

14:5. Paul does not despise the gift of tongues; he realizes that it is a gift of the Holy Spirit. He could not and would not despise anything that comes from the Spirit. When he says **I wish you all spoke with tongues,** he is renouncing any selfish desire to limit the gift to himself and a favored few. His desire is similar to one expressed by Moses: "O, that all the Lord's people were prophets, and that the Lord would put His Spirit upon them" (Num. 11:29b). But in saying this, Paul knew that it was not God's will that all believers should have any one gift (see 12:29, 30).

He would *rather* that the Corinthians **prophesied,** because in so doing they would be building up one another, whereas when they spoke in tongues without interpretation, their listeners would not understand and therefore would not be benefited. Paul preferred **edification** to display. "What astonishes is far less important for the spiritual mind than what edifies," as Kelly expresses it.

The expression **unless indeed he interprets** could mean "unless the one speaking in tongues interprets" or "unless someone interprets."

14:6. Even if Paul himself came to Corinth **speaking with tongues,** it would not **profit** them unless they could understand what he said. They would have to be able to recognize what he was saying as **revelation** and **knowledge,** or **prophesying** and **teaching.** Commentators agree that **revelation** and

knowledge have to do with inward reception, whereas **prophesying** and **teaching** have to do with the giving out of the same. Paul's point in this verse is that in order to profit the church, a message must be understood. He goes on to prove this in the following verses.

14:7. First of all, he uses the illustration of musical instruments. Unless a **flute or harp** makes a **distinction** in the notes, no one will know what is being **piped or played.** The very idea of enjoyable music includes the thought of distinction in notes, a definite rhythm, and a certain amount of clarity.

14:8. The same is true of a **trumpet.** The call to arms must be clear and distinct; otherwise, no one **will prepare for battle.** If the trumpeter merely stands up and blows one long blast in a monotone, no one will stir.

14:9. So it is with the human tongue. Unless the speech we utter is intelligible, no one will know what is being said. It would be as profitless as **speaking into the air.** (In verse 9, "tongue" means the organ of speech, not a foreign language.) There is a practical application in all of this—that ministry or teaching should be clear and simple. If it is "deep" and over the heads of the people, then it will not profit them. It might result in bringing a certain measure of gratification to the speaker, but it will not help the people of God.

14:10. Paul passes to another illustration of the truth he has been setting forth. He speaks of the **many** different **kinds of languages in the world.** Here the subject is broader than human languages; it includes the communications of other creatures. Perhaps Paul is thinking of the various birdcalls and the squeals and grunts used by animals. We know, for instance, that there are certain mating, migratory, and feeding calls used by birds. Also there are certain sounds used by animals to warn of danger. Paul is simply stating that all of these voices have a definite meaning. **None of them is without significance.** Each one is used to convey some definite message.

14:11. It is true also with human speech. Unless a person speaks with articulate sounds, no one can understand him. He might as well be repeating meaningless gibberish. Few experiences can be more trying than the attempt to communicate with one who does not understand your language.

14:12. In view of this, the Corinthians should mingle their zeal **for spiritual gifts** with the desire to edify **the church.** "Make the edification of the church your aim in this desire to excel," Moffatt translates it. Notice that Paul never discourages them in their zeal for spiritual gifts, but seeks to guide and instruct them so that in the use of these gifts they will reach the highest goal.

14:13. If a person **speaks in a tongue,** he should **pray that he may interpret.** Or the meaning might be to pray that *someone* may interpret. It is possible that a person who has the gift of tongues might also have the gift of interpretation, but that would be the exception rather than the rule. The analogy of the human body suggests different functions for different members.

14:14. If a person, for instance, prays **in a tongue** at a meeting of the church, his **spirit prays** in the sense that his feelings find utterance, though not in the commonly used language. But his **understanding is unfruitful** in the sense that it doesn't benefit anyone else. The congregation doesn't know what he is saying. As we will explain in the notes on 14:19, we take the phrase **my understanding** to mean "other people's understanding of me."

14:15. What is the conclusion then? It is simply this: Paul **will** not only **pray with the spirit, but** he **will also pray** in such a manner as to be understood. This is what is meant by the expression: **I will also pray with the understanding.** It does not mean that he will pray with his *own* understanding, but rather that he will pray in order to help others understand. Likewise, he **will sing with the spirit**, and **also sing** so as to be understood.

14:16. That this is the correct meaning of the passage is made clear by verse 16. If Paul gave thanks with his own spirit, but not in such a way as to be understood by others, how could one who did not understand the language he was using **say Amen** at the close?

He who occupies the place of the uninformed means a person who is sitting in the audience and does not know the language that is being used by the speaker. This verse incidentally authorizes the intelligent use of the **Amen** in public gatherings of the church.

14:17. Speaking in a foreign language, one might indeed be giving **thanks** to God, but others are **not edified** if they do not know what is being said.

14:18. The apostle apparently had the ability to speak **more** foreign languages than **all** of them. We know that Paul had learned some languages, but here the reference is undoubtedly to his gift of tongues.

14:19. In spite of this superior language ability, Paul says that he **would rather speak five words with** his **understanding**, that is, in order to be understood, **than ten thousand words in** a foreign **tongue**. He was not interested in using this gift for self-display. His chief aim was to help the people of God. Therefore, he determined that when he spoke he would do so in such a way that others would understand him.

The expression **my understanding** is what is known as an "objective genitive." It does not mean what I myself understand, but what others understand when I speak.

Hodge demonstrates that the context here has to do not with Paul's own understanding of what he spoke in tongues but of other people's understanding him:

That Paul should give thanks to God that he was more abundantly endowed with the gift of tongues, if that gift consisted in the ability to speak in languages which he himself did not understand, and the use of which, on that assumption, could according to his principle benefit neither himself nor others, is not to be believed. Equally clear is it from this verse that to speak with tongues was not to speak in a state of mental unconsciousness. The common doctrine about the nature of the gift is the only one consistent with this passage. Paul says that although he could speak in foreign languages more than the Corinthians, he would rather speak five words *with his understanding*, i.e., so as to be intelligible, than ten thousand words in an unknown tongue. *In the church*, that is, in the assembly, that I might teach others also (katēcheō) to instruct orally, Gal. 6:6. This shows what is meant by speaking *with the understanding*. It is speaking in such a way as to convey instruction.

14:20. Paul next exhorts the Corinthians against immaturity in their thinking. Children prefer amusement to usefulness, flashy things to stable ones. Paul is saying, "Don't take a childish delight in these spectacular gifts which you use for self-display. There is one sense in which you should be childlike, and that is in the matter of **malice** or evil. But in other matters, you should think with the maturity of men."

14:21. Next the apostle quotes from Isaiah to show that tongues are a sign to *unbelievers* rather than to believers. God said that because the children of Israel had rejected His message and had mocked it, He would speak to them through a foreign language (Is. 28:11). The fulfillment of this took place when the Assyrian invaders came into the land of Israel, and the Israelites heard the Assyrian language being spoken in their midst. This was a sign to them of their rejection of God's word.

14:22. The argument here is that since God intended **tongues** as **a sign** to **unbelievers**, the Corinthians should not insist on using them so freely in gatherings of believers. It would be better if they prophesied, since prophesying was a sign for believers and **not for unbelievers**.

14:23. If the whole church comes together in one place, and all the Christians **speak with tongues** without interpretation, what would strangers coming in think about it all? It would not be a testimony to them; rather, they would think that the saints were mental cases.

There is an *apparent* contradiction between verse 22 and verses 23–25. In verse 22, we are told that tongues are a sign to unbelievers whereas prophecy is for believers. But in verses 23–25, Paul says that tongues used in the church might only confuse and cause unbelievers to stumble whereas prophecy might help them.

The explanation of the seeming contradiction is this: The unbelievers in verse 22 are those who have rejected the Word of God and closed their hearts to the truth. Tongues are a sign of God's judgment on them, as they were on Israel in the Isaiah passage (v. 21). The unbelievers in verses 23–25 are those who are willing to be taught. They are open to hear the Word of God, as is evidenced by their presence in a Christian assembly. If they hear Christians speaking in foreign languages without interpretation, they will be hindered, not helped.

14:24. If strangers enter a meeting where the Christians are prophesying rather than speaking in tongues, the visitors hear and understand what is being said and they are **convinced by all** and **convicted by all**. What the apostle is emphasizing here is that no real conviction of sin is produced unless the listeners understand what is being said. When tongues are being used with no interpretation, then obviously visitors are not helped at all. Those who prophesy would, of course, do it in the language in current use in that area, and as a result listeners would be impressed by what they heard.

14:25. **The secrets of** a person's **heart are revealed** by prophecy. He feels that the speaker is addressing him directly. The Spirit of God works conviction in his soul. **And so, falling down on his face, he will worship God and report that God is truly among** these people.

And so Paul's point in verses 22–25 is that tongues without interpretation produce no conviction among unbelievers, whereas prophecy does.

14:26. Because of the abuses that had entered the church in connection with the gift of tongues, it was necessary for the Spirit of God to set forth certain regulations to control the use of this gift. In verses 26–28, we have such controls.

What happened when the early church came **together**? It appears from verse 26 that the meetings were very informal and free. There was liberty for the Spirit of God to use the various gifts which He had given to the church. One man, for instance, would read **a psalm**, and then another would set forth some **teaching**. Another would speak in **a** foreign **tongue**. Another would present **a revelation** which he had received directly from the Lord. Another would interpret the tongue that had already been given.

Paul gives tacit approval to this "open meeting" where there was liberty for the Spirit of God to speak through different brothers. But having stated this, he sets forth the first control in the exercise of these gifts. Everything must **be done** with a view to **edification**. Just because a thing is sensational or spectacular does not mean that it has any place in the church. In order to be acceptable, ministry must have the effect of building up the people of God. That is what is meant by **edification**—spiritual growth.

14:27. The second control is that in any one meeting no more than **three** may speak in tongues. **If anyone speaks in a tongue, let there be two or at the most three.** There was to be no such thing as a meeting where a multitude of people would arise to show their proficiency in foreign languages.

Next we learn that the two or three who were permitted to speak in tongues in any one meeting must do so **in turn.** That means that they must not speak at the same time, but one after the other. This would avoid the bedlam and disorder of several people speaking at once.

The fourth rule is that there must be an **interpreter. Let one interpret.** If a man got up to speak in a foreign language, he must first determine that there was someone present to interpret what he was about to say.

 For insight on the spiritual gift of speaking in tongues, see the word study on "Tongues" on p. 187.

14:28. **If there** was **no interpreter** present, then he must **keep silent in church.** He could sit there and **speak** inaudibly **to himself and to God** in this foreign language, but he was not permitted to do so publicly.

14:29. Rules for governing the prophetic gift are set forth in verses 29-33a. First of all, **two or three prophets** were to speak and **the others** were to **judge.** No more than **three** were to take part in any one meeting, and the Christians who listened were to determine whether this was truly a divine utterance or whether the man might be a false prophet.

14:30. As we have mentioned previously, a prophet received direct communications from the Lord and revealed them to the church. But it is possible that after giving this revelation, he might go on to preach to the people. So the apostle lays down the rule that if a prophet is speaking and **anything is revealed to another** prophet sitting in the audience, then **the first** is required to stop speaking to make way for the one who has received the latest revelation. The reason, as suggested, is that the longer the first man talks, the more apt he is to speak by his own power rather than by inspiration. In continued speech there is always the danger of shifting from God's words to one's own words. Revelation is superior to anything else.

14:31. The prophets should be given the opportunity to speak **one by one.** No one prophet should take all the time. In that way, the greatest benefit would result to the church—**all** would be able to **learn** and **all** would be exhorted or **encouraged.**

14:32. A very important principle is set forth in verse 32. Reading between the lines, we suspect that the Corinthians had the false idea that the more a person was possessed by the Spirit of God, the less self-control he had. They felt that he was carried away in a state of ecstasy and they contended, according to Godet, that the more spirit, the less intelligence or self-consciousness there would be. To them, a man under the control of the Spirit was in a state of passivity, and could not control his speech, the length of time he spoke, or his actions in general. Such an idea is thoroughly refuted by the passage of Scripture before us. **The spirits of the prophets are subject to the prophets.** That means that he is not carried away without his consent, or against his will. He cannot evade the instructions of this chapter on the pretense that he just couldn't help it. He himself can determine when or how long he should speak.

14:33. For God is not the author of confusion but of peace. In other words, if a meeting is the scene of pandemonium and disorder, then you can be *sure* that the Spirit of God is not in control!

14:34. As is well-known, the verse divisions and even the punctuation of the New Testament were added centuries after the original manuscripts were written. The last clause of verse 33 makes much greater sense modifying the church practice in verse 34 than a universal truth about the omnipresent God (some Greek Testaments and English translations use this punctuation). For instance, the ASV reads: "As in all the churches of the saints, let the women keep silent in the churches: for it is not permitted unto them to speak; but let them be in subjection, as also saith the law." The instructions that Paul is giving to the Corinthian saints do not apply to them alone. These are the same instructions that have been addressed to **all the churches of the saints.** The uniform testimony of the New Testament is that while women have many valuable ministries, it is not given to them to have a public ministry to the whole church. They are entrusted with the unspeakably important work of the home and of raising children. But they are not allowed to speak publicly in the assembly. Theirs is to be a place of submission to the man.

We believe that the expression **as the law also says** has reference to the woman's being submissive to the man. This is clearly taught in the law, which here probably means the Pentateuch primarily. Genesis 3:16, for instance, says, "Your desire shall be for your husband. And he shall rule over you."

It is often contended that what Paul is forbidding in this verse is for the women to chatter or gossip while the service is going on. However, such an interpretation is untenable. The word here translated speak (*laleō*) did not mean to chatter in Koinē Greek. The same word is used of God in verse 21 of this chapter, and in Hebrews 1:1. It means to speak authoritatively.

14:35. Indeed, women are not permitted to ask questions publicly in the church. **If they want to learn something,** they should **ask their own husbands at home.** Some women might try to evade the previous prohibition against speaking by asking questions. It is possible to teach by the simple act of questioning others. So this verse closes any such loophole or objection.

If it is asked how this applies to an unmarried woman or a widow, the answer is that the Scriptures do not try to take up each individual case, but merely set forth general principles. If a woman does not have a husband, she could ask her father, her brother, or one of the elders of the church. Actually, this may be translated, "Let them ask their men-folks at home." The basic rule to be remembered is that **it is shameful for women to speak in church.**

14:36. Apparently the apostle Paul realized that his teaching here would cause considerable contention. How right he was! To meet any arguments, he uses irony in verse 36 by asking: **Or did the word of God come originally from you? Or was it you only that it reached?** In other words, if the Corinthians professed to know more about these matters than the apostle, he would ask them if they, as a church, produced **the word of God,** or if they were the **only** ones who had received it. By their attitude they seemed to set themselves up as an official authority on these matters. But the facts are that no church originated the Word of God, and no church has exclusive rights to it.

14:37. In connection with all the foregoing instructions, the apostle here emphasizes that they are not his own ideas or interpretations, but that they **are the commandments of the Lord,** and any man who is **a prophet** of the Lord or who is truly **spiritual** will **acknowledge** that that is the case. This verse is a sufficient answer to those who insist that some of Paul's teachings, especially those concerning women, reflected his own prejudices. These matters are not Paul's private view; they are **the commandments of the Lord.**

14:38. Of course, some would not be willing to accept them as such, and so the apostle adds that **if anyone is ignorant, let him be ignorant.** If a person refuses to acknowledge the inspiration of these writings and to bow to them obediently, then there is no alternative but for him to continue in his ignorance.

14:39. To sum up the preceding instructions on the exercise of gifts, Paul now tells the **brethren** to **desire earnestly to prophesy,** but **not** to **forbid** men **to speak with tongues.** This verse shows the relative importance of these two gifts—one they were to **desire earnestly,** while the other they were **not** to ban. Prophecy was more valuable than tongues because sinners were convicted through it and saints edified. Tongues without interpretation served no other purpose than to speak to God and to one's self, and to display one's own proficiency with a foreign language, a proficiency that had been given to them by God.

14:40. Paul's final word of admonition is that **all things** must **be done decently and in order**. It is significant that this control should be placed in this chapter. Down through the years, those who have professed to have the ability to speak in tongues have not been noted for the orderliness of their meetings. Rather, many of their meetings have been scenes of uncontrolled emotion and general confusion.

To summarize, then, the apostle Paul sets forth the following controls for the use of tongues in the local church:

1. We must not forbid the use of tongues (v. 39).
2. If a person speaks in a tongue, there must be an interpreter (vv. 27c, 28).
3. Not more than three people may speak in tongues in any one meeting (v. 27a).
4. They must speak one at a time (v. 27b).
5. What they say must be edifying (v. 26b).
6. The women must be silent (v. 34).
7. Everything must **be done decently and in order** (v. 40).

These are the abiding controls that apply to the church in our day.

 See discussion questions on issues raised in chapter 14 of 1 Corinthians on p. 209.

CHAPTER 15

Chapter 15 of 1 Corinthians is the great resurrection chapter. Some teachers had entered the church at Corinth, and they were denying the possibility of bodily resurrection. They did not deny the fact of life after death, but probably suggested that we would simply be spirit beings and not have literal bodies. The apostle here gives his classic answer to these denials.

 For insight on and a handy review of the central truths of the resurrection presented in chapter 15 of 1 Corinthians, see "Facts About the Resurrection" on p. 200.

15:1, 2. Paul reminds them of the good news that he had **preached** to them, which they had **received**, and **in which** they now stood. This was not a new doctrine for the Corinthians, but it was necessary that they should be reminded of it at this critical time. It was this **gospel** by which the Corinthians had been **saved**. Then Paul adds the words **if you hold fast that word which I preached to you—unless you believed in vain**. It was by the gospel of the resurrection that they had been saved—unless, of course, there was no such thing as resurrection, in which case they could not have been saved at all.

For a teaching/communication suggestion on chapter 15 of 1 Corinthians, see "Three Great Possessions of Believers" on p. 230.

The **if** in this passage does not express any doubt about their salvation, nor does it teach that they were saved by holding fast. Rather, Paul is simply stating that if there is no such thing as resurrection, then they weren't saved at all. In other words, those who denied bodily resurrection were launching a frontal attack on the whole truth of the gospel. To Paul, the resurrection was fundamental. Without it there was no Christianity. Thus this verse is a challenge to the Corinthians to hold fast the gospel which they had received in the face of the attacks which were currently being made against it.

15:3. Paul had **delivered to** the Corinthians the message that he had **also received** by divine revelation. The first cardinal doctrine of that message was **that Christ died for our sins according to the Scriptures**. This emphasizes the substitutionary character of the death of Christ. He did not die for His own sins, or as a martyr; He **died for our sins**. He **died** to pay the penalty that **our sins** deserved. This was all **according to the Scriptures**. **The Scriptures** here refer to the Old Testament Scriptures, since the New Testament was not yet in written form. Did the Old Testament Scriptures actually predict that Christ would die for the sins of the people? The answer is an emphatic "Yes!" Isaiah 53:5, 6 is sufficient proof of this.

15:4. The burial of Christ was prophesied in Isaiah 53:9, and His resurrection in Psalm 16:9, 10. It is important to notice how Paul emphasizes the testimony of **the Scriptures**. This should always be the test in all matters relating to our faith: "What do the Scriptures say?"

15:5. In verses 5–7, we have a list of those who were eyewitnesses of the resurrection. First of all, the Lord appeared to **Cephas** (Peter). This is very touching indeed. The same faithless disciple who had denied his Lord three times is graciously privileged to have a private appearance of that same Lord in resurrection. Truly, how great is the grace of the Lord Jesus Christ! **Then** the Lord also appeared to **the twelve** disciples. Actually, the Twelve were not all together at this time, but the expression **the twelve** was used to denote the body of disciples, even though not complete at any one particular moment. It should be stated that not all the appearances that are recorded in the Gospels are mentioned in this list. The Spirit of God selects those resurrection appearances of Christ which are most pertinent for His use.

15:6. The Lord's appearance to **over five hundred brethren** is commonly believed to have taken place in Galilee. At the time Paul wrote, most of these brethren were still living, although some had gone home to be with the Lord. In other words, should anyone wish to contest the truthfulness of what Paul was saying, the witnesses were still alive and could be questioned.

15:7. There is no way of knowing which **James** is referred to here, although most commentators assume him to be the Lord's half-brother. Verse 7 also tells us that the Lord appeared to **all the apostles.**

15:8. Paul next speaks of his own personal acquaintance with the risen Christ. This took place on the road to Damascus, when he saw a great light from heaven and met the glorified Christ face to face. **One born out of due time** means an abortion or an untimely birth. Vine explains it as meaning that in point of time, Paul speaks of himself as inferior to the rest of the apostles, just as an immature birth comes short of a mature one. He uses it as a term of self-reproach in view of his past life as a persecutor of the church.

15:9. As the apostle thinks of the privilege he had of meeting the Savior face to face, he is filled with a spirit of unworthiness. He thinks of how he **persecuted the church of God** and how, in spite of that, the Lord called him to be an apostle. Therefore he bows himself in the dust as **the least of the apostles,** and **not worthy to be called an apostle.**

15:10. He hastens to acknowledge that whatever he now is, he is **by the grace of God.** And he did not accept this grace as a matter of fact. Rather, it put him under the deepest obligation, and he labored tirelessly to serve the Christ who saved him. Yet in a very real sense it was not Paul himself, **but the grace of God** which was working with him.

15:11. Now Paul joins himself with the other apostles and states that no matter which of them it was who preached, they were all united in their testimony about the gospel, and particularly about the resurrection of Christ.

15:12. In verses 12–19, Paul lists the consequences of the denial of bodily resurrection. First of all, it would mean that Christ Himself has not risen. Paul's logic here is unanswerable. Some were saying that there is no such thing as bodily resurrection. All right, Paul says, if that is the case, then Christ has not risen. Are you Corinthians willing to admit this? Of course, they were not. In order to prove the possibility of any fact, all you have to do is to demonstrate that it has already taken place once. To prove the fact of bodily resurrection, Paul is willing to base his case upon the simple fact that **Christ** has already **been raised from the dead.**

15:13. **But if there is no resurrection of the dead,** then obviously **Christ is not risen.** Such a conclusion would involve the Corinthians in hopeless gloom and despair.

15:14. **If Christ is not risen,** then the **preaching** of the apostles was **empty,** or having no substance. Why was it empty? First of all, because the Lord Jesus had promised that He would rise from the dead on the third day. If He did *not* rise at that time, then He was either an imposter or mistaken. In either case, He would not be worthy of trust. Secondly, apart from the resurrection of Christ, there could be no salvation. If the Lord Jesus did not rise from the dead, then there would be no way of knowing that His death had been of any greater value than any other person's. But in raising Him from the dead, God testified to the fact that He was completely satisfied with the redemptive work of Christ.

Obviously, if the apostolic message was false, then **faith** would be **empty** too. There would be no value in trusting a message that was false or empty.

15:15. It would not simply be a matter that the apostles were preaching a false message; actually it would mean that they had been testifying against **God.** They **testified of God that He raised up Christ** from the dead. If God didn't do this, then the apostles had been bringing **false** witness against Him.

15:16. If resurrection is an utter impossibility, then there can be no exception to it. On the other hand, if resurrection had taken place once, for instance in the case of Christ, then it can no longer be thought of as an impossibility.

15:17. **If Christ** has not been raised, the **faith** of believers **is futile** and devoid of power. And there is no forgiveness of **sins.** Thus, to reject the resurrection is to reject the value of the work of Christ.

15:18. As for those who had died believing **in Christ,** their case would be absolutely hopeless. If Christ did not rise, then their faith was just a worthless thing. The expression **fallen asleep** refers to the bodies of believers. Sleep is never used of the soul in the New Testament. The soul of the believer departs to be with Christ at the time of death, while the body is spoken of as sleeping in the grave.

We should also say a word concerning the word **perished.** This word *never* means annihilation or cessation of being. As Vine has pointed out, it is not loss of *being,* but rather loss of *well-being.* It speaks of ruin as far as the purpose for which a person or thing was created.

15:19. If Christ is not risen, then living believers are in a condition just as wretched as those who have died. They, too, have been deceived. They **are of all men the most pitiable.** Paul is here doubtless thinking of the sorrows, sufferings, trials, and persecutions to which Christians are exposed. To undergo such afflictions for a false cause would be pathetic indeed.

15:20. The tension is relieved as Paul triumphantly announces the fact of the resurrection of Christ and of the blessed consequences that follow. **But now Christ is risen from the dead . . . the firstfruits of those who have fallen asleep.** There is a difference in the Scripture between the resurrection *of* the dead and the resurrection *from* the dead. The previous verses have been dealing with the resurrection of the dead. In other words, Paul has been arguing in a general way that the dead do indeed rise. But Christ rose *from* the dead. This means that when He rose, not all the dead rose. In this sense it was a limited resurrection. Every resurrection is a resurrection of the dead, but only that of Christ and of believers is a resurrection *from among* dead people.

15:21. It was **by man** that **death** first **came** into the world. That **man** was Adam. Through his sin, death came upon all men. God sent His Son into the world as a **Man** in order to undo the work of the first man and to raise believers to a state of blessedness such as they could never have known in Adam. Thus it was by the **Man** Christ Jesus that there **came the resurrection of the dead.**

15:22. **Adam** and **Christ** are presented as federal heads. This means that they acted for other people. And all who are related to them are affected by their actions. **All** who are descended from **Adam die. So in Christ all shall be made alive.** This verse has sometimes been taken to teach universal salvation. It is argued that the same ones who die in Adam will be made alive in Christ, and that all will eventually be saved. But that is not what the verse says. The key expressions are **in Adam** and **in Christ. All** who are **in Adam die. All** who are **in Christ shall be made alive**—that is, only believers in the Lord Jesus Christ will be raised from the dead to dwell eternally with Him. The **all** who **shall be made alive** is defined in verse 23 as those who are Christ's at His Coming. It does not include Christ's enemies, because they shall be put under His feet (v. 25), which, as someone has said, is a strange name for heaven.

15:23. Next we have the groups or classes involved in the first resurrection. First is the resurrection of **Christ** Himself. He is spoken of here as **the firstfruits.** Firstfruits were a handful of ripened grain from the harvest field before the actual harvest started. They were a pledge, a guarantee, a foretaste of what was to follow. The expression does not necessarily mean that Christ was the first one to rise. We have instances of resurrection in the Old Testament, and the cases of Lazarus, the widow's son, and Jairus's daughter in the New Testament. But Christ's Resurrection was different from all of these in that, whereas they rose to die again, Christ rose to die no more. He rose to live in the power of an endless life. He rose with a glorified body.

The second class in the first resurrection is described as **those who are Christ's at His Coming.** This includes those who will be raised at the time of the rapture, and also those believers who will die during the tribulation and will be raised at the end of that time of trouble, when Christ comes back to reign. Just as there are stages in the coming of Christ, so there will be stages in the resurrection of His saints. The first resurrection does not include all who have ever died, but only those who have died with faith in Christ.

Some teach that only those Christians who have been faithful to Christ, or who have been overcomers will be raised at this time, but the Scriptures are very clear in refuting this. All **who are Christ's** will be raised at His coming.

For insight and information on the resurrection of Christ and believers, see the word study on "Resurrection" on p. 187.

15:24. The expression **then comes the end** refers, we believe, to **the end** *of the resurrection.* At the close of Christ's millennial reign, when He shall have put down all His enemies, there will be the resurrection of the wicked dead. This is the last resurrection ever to take place. All who have ever died in unbelief will stand before the judgment of the Great White Throne to hear their doom.

After the millennium and the destruction of Satan (Rev. 20:7–10), the Lord Jesus will deliver **the kingdom to God the Father.** By that time He will have abolished **all rule and all authority and power.** Up to this time the Lord Jesus Christ has been reigning *as the Son of Man,* serving as God's mediator. At the end of the thousand-year reign, God's purposes on earth will have been perfectly accomplished. All opposition will have been put down and all enemies destroyed. The reign of Christ *as Son of Man* will then give way to the eternal kingdom in heaven. His reign *as Son of God* in heaven will continue forever.

15:25. Verse 25 emphasizes what has just been said—that Christ's reign will continue until every trace of rebellion and enmity has been put down.

15:26. Even during Christ's millennial reign, people will continue to die, especially those who openly rebel against the Lord. But at the judgment of the Great White Throne, **death** and hades will be cast into the lake of fire.

15:27. God has decreed that **all things** shall be **put** under the **feet** of the Lord Jesus. Of course, in putting **all things under Him,** God necessarily excepted Himself. Verse 27 is rather hard to follow because it is not clear to whom each pronoun is referring. We might paraphrase it as follows: "For God has put all things under Christ's feet. But when God says, all things are put under Christ, it is obvious that God is excluded, who put all things under Christ."

15:28. Even after **all things** have been put in subjection to the Son, He Himself will continue to be **subject** to **God** forever.

God has made Christ ruler, administrator of all His plans and counsels. All authority and power is put in His hands. There is a time coming when He will render His account of the administration committed to Him. After He has brought everything into subjection, He will hand the kingdom back to the Father. Creation will be brought back to God in a perfect condition. Having accomplished the work of redemption and restoration for which He became Man, He will retain the subordinate place that He took in Incarnation. If He should cease to be man after having brought to pass all that God purposed and designated, the very link that brings God and man together would be gone.

15:29. Verse 29 is perhaps one of the most difficult and obscure verses in all the Bible. Many explanations have been offered about its meaning. For instance, it is contended by some that living believers may be baptized for those who have died without having undergone this rite. Such a meaning is quite foreign to the Scriptures. It is based on a single verse and must be rejected, not having the collective support of other Scripture. Others believe that baptism for the dead means that in baptism we reckon ourselves to have died. This is a possible meaning, but it does not fit in well with the context.

The interpretation that seems to suit the context best is this: At the time Paul wrote, there was fierce persecution against those who took a public stand for Christ. This persecution was especially vicious at the time of their baptism. It often happened that those who publicly proclaimed their faith in Christ in the waters of baptism were martyred shortly thereafter. But did this stop others from being saved and from taking their place in baptism? Not at all. It seemed as though there were always new replacements coming along to fill up the ranks of those who had been martyred. As they stepped into the waters of baptism, in a very real sense **they** were being **baptized for,** or *in the place of* (Gk., *huper*) the dead. Hence **the dead** here refers to those who died as a result of their bold witness for Christ. Now the apostle's argument here is that it would be foolish to be thus baptized to fill up the ranks of those who had died if there is no such thing as resurrection from the dead. It would be like sending replacement troops to fill up the ranks of an army that is fighting a lost cause. It would be like fighting on in a hopeless situation. **If the dead do not rise at all, why then are they baptized for the dead?**

15:30. And why do we stand in jeopardy every hour? The apostle Paul was constantly exposed to danger. Because of his fearlessness in preaching Christ, he made enemies wherever he went. Secret plots were hatched against him in an effort to take his life. He could have avoided all this by abandoning his profession of Christ. In fact, it would have been wise for him to abandon it if there was no such thing as resurrection from the dead.

15:31. I affirm, by the boasting in you which I have in Christ Jesus our Lord, I die daily might be paraphrased: "As surely as I rejoice over you as my children in Christ Jesus, every day of my life I am exposed to death."

15:32. The apostle now recalls the fierce persecution that he encountered **at Ephesus.** We do not believe that he was actually thrown into the arena with wild beasts, but rather that he is speaking here of wicked men as wild **beasts**. Actually, as a Roman citizen, Paul could not have been forced to fight with wild animals. We do not know to what incident he refers. However, the argument is clear that the apostle would have been foolish to engage in such dangerous warfare as he had if he were not assured of resurrection from the dead. Indeed it would have been much wiser for him to adopt the philosophy: **If the dead do not rise, Let us eat and drink, for tomorrow we die!**

We sometimes hear Christians say that if this life were the end of existence, they would still rather be Christians. But Paul disagrees with such an idea. If there were no resurrection, we would be better off to make the most of *this* life. We would live for food, clothing, and pleasure. This would be the only heaven we could look forward to. But since there *is* a resurrection, we dare not spend our lives for these things of passing interest. We must live for "then" and not for "now."

15:33. The Corinthians should **not be deceived** on this score. **Evil company corrupts good habits.** Paul is referring to the false teachers who had come into the church at Corinth, denying the resurrection. The Christians should realize that it is impossible to associate with **evil** people or evil teachings without being corrupted by them. Evil doctrine inevitably has an effect on one's life. False teachings do not lead to holiness.

15:34. The Corinthians should **awake to righteousness** and **not sin.** They should not be deluded by these evil teachings. **Some do not have the knowledge of God. I speak this to your shame.** This verse is commonly interpreted to mean that there are still men and women who have never heard the gospel story, and that Christians should be ashamed of their failure to evangelize the world. However, while this may be true, we believe that the primary meaning of the passage is that there were people in the fellowship at Corinth who did **not have the knowledge of God.** They were not true believers, but wolves in sheep's clothing, false teachers who had crept in unawares. It was to the **shame** of the Corinthians that these men were allowed to take their place with the Christians and to teach these wicked doctrines. The carelessness which let ungodly people enter the assembly resulted in lowering the congregation's whole moral tone, thus preparing an opening for the intrusion of all kinds of error.

15:35. In verses 35–49, the apostle goes into greater detail concerning the actual mode of the resurrection. He anticipates two questions that would arise inevitably in the minds of those who questioned the fact of bodily resurrection. The first is: **How are the dead raised up?** The second is: **And with what body do they come?**

15:36. The first question is answered in verse 36. A common illustration from nature is used to illustrate the possibility of resurrection. A seed must fall into the ground and die before the plant can come forth. It is wonderful indeed to think of the mystery of life that is hidden in every tiny seed. We may dissect the seed and study it under the microscope, but the secret of the life principle remains an unfathomable mystery. All we know is that the seed falls into the ground and from that unlikely beginning there springs forth life from the dead.

15:37. The second question is taken up next. Paul explains that when you **sow** a seed, **you do not sow** the plant that shall eventually result, but you sow a bare **grain—perhaps wheat or some other grain.** What do we conclude from this? Is the plant the same as the seed? No, the plant is not the same as the seed; however, there is a vital connection between the two. Without the seed there would have been no plant. Also, the plant derives its features from the seed. So it is in resurrection. The resurrection body has identity of kind and continuity of substance with that which is sown, but it is purified from corruption, dishonor, and weakness, and made incorrupt, glorious, powerful, and spiritual. It is the same body, but it is sown in one form and raised in another.

15:38. God produces **a body** according to the seed that was sown, and **each seed** has its own type of plant as a result. All the factors that determine the size, color, leaf, and flower of the plant are somehow contained in the seed that is sown.

15:39. To illustrate the fact that the glory of the resurrection body will be different from the glory of our present bodies, the apostle Paul points out that **all flesh is not the same** kind. For instance, there is human **flesh, flesh of animals,** flesh **of fish,** and flesh **of birds.** These are distinctly different, and yet they are all flesh. There is similarity without exact duplication.

15:40. And just as there is a difference between the splendor of heavenly **bodies** (the stars, etc.) and bodies which are associated with this earth, so there is a difference between the body of the believer now and the one which he will have after death.

15:41. Even among the celestial bodies themselves, there is a difference of **glory.** For instance, **the sun** is brighter than **the moon, and one star differs from another in** brightness.

Most commentators agree that Paul is still emphasizing that the glory of the resurrection body will be different from the glory of the body which we have on earth at the present time. They do not think that verse 41, for instance, indicates that in heaven there will be differences of glory among believers themselves. However, we tend to agree with Holsten that "the way in which Paul emphasizes the diversities of the heavenly bodies implies the supposition of an analogous difference of glory between the risen." It is clear from other passages of Scripture that we shall not all be identical in heaven. Although all will resemble the Lord Jesus morally, that is, in freedom from sin, it does not follow that we shall all *look* like the Lord Jesus physically. He will be distinctly recognizable as such throughout all eternity.

Likewise, we believe that each individual Christian will be a distinct personality recognizable as such. But there will be differences of reward granted at the judgment seat of Christ according to one's faithfulness in service. While all will be supremely happy in heaven, some will have greater *capacity* for enjoying heaven. Just as there will be differences of suffering in hell, according to the sins that a person has committed, so there will be differences of enjoyment in heaven, according to what we have done as believers.

15:42. Verses 42–49 show the contrast between what the believer's body is now and what it will be in its eternal state. **The body is sown in corruption, it is raised in incorruption.** At the present time, our bodies are subject to disease and death. When they are placed in the grave, they decompose and return to dust. But it will not be so with the resurrection body. It will no longer be subject to sickness or decay.

15:43. The present body **is sown in dishonor.** There is nothing very majestic or glorious about a dead body. However, this same body will be **raised in glory.** It will be free from wrinkles, scars, the marks of age, overweight, and the traces of sin.

It is sown in weakness, it is raised in power. With the coming of old age, **weakness** increases until death itself strips a person of all strength. In eternity, the body will not be subject to these limitations, but will be possessed of powers that it does not have at the present time. For instance, the Lord Jesus Christ in resurrection was able to enter a room where the doors were locked.

15:44. It is sown a natural body, it is raised a spiritual body. Here we must be very careful to emphasize that spiritual does *not* mean nonmaterial. Some people have the idea that in resurrection we will be disembodied spirits. That is not the meaning of this passage, nor is it true. We know that the resurrection body of the Lord Jesus was composed of flesh and bones because He said, "A spirit does not have flesh and bones as you see I have" (Luke 24:39). The difference between **a natural body** and **a spiritual body** is that the former is suited to life here on earth whereas the latter will be suited to life in heaven. The former is usually soul-controlled whereas the latter is spirit-controlled. **A spiritual body** is one that will be truly the servant of the spirit.

God created man as spirit, soul, and body. He always mentions the spirit first, because His intention was that the spirit should be in the place of preeminence or dominance. With the entrance of sin, something strange happened.

God's order seems to have been upset, and the result is that man always says "body, soul, and spirit." He has given the body the place that the spirit should have had. In resurrection it will not be so; the spirit will be in the place of control that God originally intended.

15:45. And so it is written, The first man Adam became a living being. The last Adam became a life-giving spirit. Here again **the first man Adam** is contrasted with the Lord Jesus Christ. God breathed into Adam's nostrils the breath of life and he became a living being (Gen. 2:7). All who are descended from him bear his characteristics. **The last Adam**, the Savior, **became a life-giving spirit** (John 5:21, 26). The difference is that in the first case, Adam *was given* physical life, whereas in the second case Christ *gives* eternal life to others. Erdman explains: "As the descendants of Adam, we are made like him, living souls inhabiting mortal bodies, and bearing the image of an earthly parent. But as the followers of Christ, we are yet to be clothed with immortal bodies and to bear the image of our heavenly Lord."

 For insight on the new bodies that believers will receive at the resurrection, see the word study on "Life-Giving Spirit" on p. 188.

15:46. The apostle now sets forth a fundamental law in God's universe— **the spiritual is not first, but the natural, and afterward the spiritual.** This can be understood in several ways. Adam, **the natural** man, came first on the stage of human history; then Jesus, **the spiritual** Man. Second, we are born into the world as **natural** beings; then when we are born again, we become **spiritual** beings. Finally, we first receive **natural** bodies, then in resurrection we will receive **spiritual** bodies.

15:47. The first man was of the earth, made of dust. This means that his origin was **of the earth** and that his characteristics were earthly. He was **made of the dust** of the ground in the first place, and in his life he seemed in a very real sense to be earth-bound. **The second Man is the Lord from heaven.**

15:48. Of the two men mentioned in verse 45, Jesus was the second. He existed from all eternity, but as Man, he came after Adam. He came from heaven, and everything He did and said was **heavenly** and spiritual rather than earthly and soulish.

As it is with these two federal heads, so it is with their followers. Those who are born of Adam inherit his characteristics. Also those who are born of Christ are a **heavenly** people.

15:49. As we have borne the characteristics of Adam in our natural birth, **we shall also bear the image of** Christ in our resurrection bodies.

15:50. Now the apostle turns to the subject of the transformation that will take place in the bodies of believers, both living and dead, at the time of the Lord's return. He prefaces his remarks with the statement **that flesh and blood cannot inherit the kingdom of God**. By this he means that the present body which we have is not suited to **the kingdom of God** in its eternal aspect, that is, our heavenly home. It is also true that **corruption** cannot **inherit incorruption**. In other words, our present bodies which are subject to disease, decay, and decomposition, would not be suited for life in a state where there is no corruption. This raises the problem, then, of how the bodies of living believers can be suited for life in heaven.

15:51. The answer is in the form of **a mystery**. As previously stated, a **mystery** is a truth previously unknown, but now revealed by God to the apostles and made known through them to us.

We shall not all sleep, that is, not all believers will experience death. Some will be alive when the Lord returns. But whether we have died or are still alive, **we shall all be changed.** The truth of resurrection itself is not a mystery, since it appears in the Old Testament, but the fact that not all will die and also the change of living saints at the Lord's return is something that had never been known before.

15:52. The change will take place instantly, **in the twinkling of an eye, at the last trumpet. The last trumpet** here does not mean the end of the world, or even the last trumpet mentioned in Revelation. Rather, it refers to the **trumpet** of God which will sound when Christ comes into the air for His saints (1 Thess. 4:16). When the **trumpet** sounds, **the dead will be raised incorruptible, and we shall be changed.** What a tremendous moment that will be, when the earth and the sea will yield up the dust of all those who have died trusting in Christ down through the centuries! It is almost impossible for the human mind to take in the magnitude of such an event; yet the humble believer can accept it by faith.

15:53. We believe that verse 53 refers to the two classes of believers at the time of Christ's return. **This corruptible** refers to those whose bodies have returned to the dust. They will **put on incorruption. This mortal,** on the other hand, refers to those who are still alive in body but are subject to death. Such bodies will **put on immortality.**

15:54. When the dead in Christ are raised and the living changed with them, **then shall be brought to pass the saying that is written, Death is swallowed up in victory** (Is. 25:8). How magnificent! C. H. Mackintosh exclaims: "What are death, the grave, and decomposition in the presence of such power as this? Talk of being dead four days as a difficulty! Millions that have been mouldering in the dust for thousands of years shall spring up in a moment into life, immortality and eternal glory, at the voice of that blessed One."

15:55. This verse may well be a taunt song that believers sing as they rise to meet the Lord in the air. It is as if they mock **Death** because for them it has lost its **sting**. They also mock **Hades** because for them *it* has lost the battle to keep them as its own. Death holds no terror for them because they know their sins have been forgiven and they stand before God in all the acceptability of His beloved Son.

15:56. Death would have no **sting** for anyone if it were not for **sin**. It is the consciousness of sins unconfessed and unforgiven that makes men afraid to die. If we know our sins are forgiven, we can face death with confidence. If, on the other hand, sin is on the conscience, death is terrible—the beginning of eternal punishment.

The strength of sin is the law, that is, **the law** condemns the sinner. It pronounces the doom of all who have failed to obey God's holy precepts. It has been well said that if there were no sin, there would be no death. And if there were no law, there would be no condemnation. The throne of death rests on two bases: sin, which calls for condemnation, and the law that pronounces it. Consequently, it is on these two powers that the work of the deliverer bore.

15:57. Through faith in Him, we have **victory** over death and the grave. Death is robbed of its sting. It is a known fact that when certain insects sting a person, they leave their stinger imbedded in the person's flesh, and being thus robbed of their "sting," they die. In a very real sense death stung itself to death at the cross of **our Lord Jesus Christ**, and now the king of terrors is robbed of his terror as far as the believer is concerned.

15:58. In view, then, of the certainty of the resurrection and the fact that faith in Christ is not in vain, the apostle Paul exhorts his **beloved brethren to be steadfast, immovable, always abounding in the work of the Lord, knowing that** their **labor is not in vain in the Lord.** The truth of resurrection changes everything. It provides hope and steadfastness, and enables us to go on in the face of overwhelming and difficult circumstances.

See discussion questions on issues raised in chapter 15 of 1 Corinthians on p. 210.

CHAPTER 16

16:1. The first verse of chapter 16 concerns a **collection** that was to be taken up by the church in Corinth and sent to needy **saints** in Jerusalem. The exact cause of their poverty is not known. Some have suggested that it was a result of famine (Acts 11:28–30). Possibly another reason is that those Jews who professed faith in Christ were ostracized and boycotted by their unbelieving relatives, friends, and fellow countrymen. They doubtlessly lost their jobs and in countless ways were subjected to economic pressures designed to force them to give up their profession of faith in Christ. Paul had already **given orders to the churches of Galatia** in connection with this very matter, and he now instructs the Corinthians to respond in the same manner that the Galatian saints had been exhorted to do.

 For a teaching/communication suggestion on chapter 16 of 1 Corinthians, see "Expressions of Christian Love" on p. 230.

16:2. Although the instructions given in verse 2 were for a specific collection, the principles involved are of abiding value. First of all, the laying by of funds was to be done **on the first day of the week**. Here we have a strong indication that the early Christians no longer regarded the Sabbath or seventh day as an obligatory observance. The Lord had risen on the first day of the week, the day of Pentecost was on the first day of the week, and the disciples gathered together on the first day of the week to break bread (Acts 20:7). Now they are to **lay something aside** for the saints **on the first day of the week**.

The second important principle is that the instructions concerning the collections were for **each one**. Rich and poor, slave and free—all were to have a part in the sacrifice of giving of their possessions.

Further, this was to be done systematically. **On the first day of the week** they were to **lay something aside, storing up**. It was not to be haphazard, or reserved for special occasions. The gift was to be set aside from other money and devoted to special use as occasion demanded. Their giving was also to be proportionate. This is indicated by the expression **as he may prosper**.

That there be no collections when I come. The apostle Paul did not want this to be a matter of last-minute arrangement. He realized the serious possibility of giving without due preparation of heart or pocketbook.

16:3. Verses 3 and 4 give us very valuable insight into the care that should be taken with funds that are gathered in a Christian assembly. It is noticeable, first, that the funds were not to be entrusted to any one person. Even Paul himself was not to be the sole recipient. Secondly, we notice that the arrangements about who would carry the money were not made arbitrarily by the apostle Paul. Rather, this decision was left to the local assembly. When they selected the messengers, Paul would **send** them **to Jerusalem**.

 For a teaching/communication suggestion on Christian giving, see "Putting Money to Work" on p. 231.

16:4. If it was decided that it would be well for the apostle to **go** to Jerusalem **also**, then the local brethren would accompany him there. Notice that he says **they will go with me** rather than "I will go with them." Perhaps this is an allusion to Paul's authority as an apostle. Some commentators suggest that the factor that would determine whether or not Paul went would be the size of the gift, but we hardly believe that the great apostle would be guided by such a principle.

16:5. Paul discusses his personal plans in verses 5–9. From Ephesus, where he wrote this letter, he planned to **pass through Macedonia**. Then he hoped to move south to Corinth.

16:6–8. Possibly Paul would **spend the winter** with the saints in Corinth and then they would speed him on his way, wherever he would go from there. For the present, then, he would not see them en route to Macedonia, but he did look forward to staying with them later for a while, **if the Lord** would so permit. Before leaving Macedonia, Paul expected to **tarry in Ephesus until Pentecost.** It is from verse 8 that we learn that the epistle was written from Ephesus.

16:9. Paul realized there was a golden opportunity for serving Christ at that time at Ephesus. At the same time he realized there were **many adversaries.** What an unchanging picture this verse gives us of Christian service: On the one hand, there are the fields white already to harvest; on the other, there is a sleepless foe who seeks to obstruct, divide, and oppose in every conceivable way!

16:10. The apostle adds a word concerning **Timothy.** If this devoted young servant of the Lord came to Corinth, they should receive him **without fear.** Perhaps this means that Timothy was naturally of a timid disposition, and that they should not do anything to intensify this tendency. Perhaps, on the other hand, it means that he should be able to come to them **without** any **fear** of not being accepted as a servant of the Lord. That the latter is probably the proper meaning is indicated by Paul's words: **For he does the work of the Lord, as I also do.**

 For insight on Paul's relationship to Timothy, see "Who Was Timothy?" on p. 192.

16:11. Because of Timothy's faithful service for Christ, **no one** should **despise him.** Instead, an earnest effort should be made to **send him on his journey in peace,** that he might return to Paul in due time. The apostle was looking forward to a reunion with Timothy and **with the brethren.**

16:12. Now **concerning . . . brother Apollos,** Paul had **strongly urged him**

to visit Corinth **with the brethren.** Apollos did not feel that this was God's will for him at the time, but he indicated that he would go to Corinth when he had the opportunity. Verse 12 is valuable to us in showing the loving spirit that prevailed among the servants of the Lord. Someone has called it a beautiful picture of "unjealous love and respect." It also shows the liberty that prevailed for each servant of the Lord to be guided by the Lord without dictation from any other source. Even the apostle Paul himself was not authorized to tell Apollos what to do. In this connection Ironside commented: "I would not like to tear this chapter out of my Bible. It helps me to understand God's way of guiding His servants in their ministry for Him."

16:13, 14. Now Paul delivers some pithy exhortations to the saints. They are to **watch** constantly, to **stand fast in the faith,** to **be brave** and to **be strong.** Perhaps Paul is thinking again of the danger of false teachers. The saints are to be on guard all the time. They are not to give up an inch of vital territory. They are to behave with true courage. Finally, they are to **be strong** in the Lord. In **all that** they **do,** they are to manifest **love.** This will mean lives of devotion to God and to others. It will mean a giving of themselves.

16:15. Next follows an exhortation concerning **the household of Stephanas.** These dear Christians were **the firstfruits of Achaia,** that is, the earliest converts in **Achaia.** Apparently from the time of their conversion, they had addicted **themselves to the ministry** (service) **of the saints.** They set themselves to serve the people of God. The household of Stephanas was mentioned previously in 1:16. There Paul states that he baptized that household. Many have insisted that the household of Stephanas included infants, and have sought thereby to justify the baptism of babies. However, it seems clear from this verse that there were no infants in this household, since it is distinctly stated that they **devoted themselves to the ministry of the saints.**

 For a teaching/communication suggestion on Paul and Christian friendship, see "From Enemies to Family and Friends" on p. 231.

16:16. The apostle exhorts the Christians to **submit to such, and to everyone who** helps in the work **and labors.** We learn from the general teaching of the New Testament that those who set themselves apart for the service of Christ should be shown the loving respect of all the people of God. If this were done more generally, it would prevent a great deal of division and jealousy.

16:17. **The coming of Stephanas, Fortunatus, and Achaicus** had brought joy to Paul's heart. They **supplied what was lacking** on the part of the Corinthians. This may mean that they showed kindness to the apostle which the Corinthians had neglected to do. Or more probably it means that what the

Corinthians were *unable* to do because of their distance from Paul, these men had accomplished.

16:18. They brought news from Corinth to Paul, and conversely they brought back news from the apostle to their home assembly. Again Paul commends them to the loving respect of the local church.

16:19. The churches of Asia refers to the congregations in the *province* of Asia (*Asia Minor* today), of which Ephesus was the capital. **Aquila and Priscilla** were apparently living in Ephesus at this time. At one time they had lived in Corinth, and thus were known to the saints there. **Aquila** was a tent-maker by trade, and had worked with Paul in this occupation. The expression **the church that is in their house** gives us a view of the simplicity of assembly life at that time. Christians would gather together in their homes for worship, prayer, and fellowship. Then they would go out to preach the gospel at their work, in the marketplace, in the local prison, and wherever their lot was cast.

 For insight on Paul's relationship to Aquila and Priscilla, see "Who Were Aquila and Priscilla?" on p. 192.

16:20. All the brethren in the assembly join in sending their loving greet-ings to their fellow believers in Corinth. The apostle enjoins his readers to **greet one another with a holy kiss.** At that time, the **kiss** was a common mode of greeting, even among men. **A holy kiss** means a greeting without shame or impurity. In our sex-obsessed society, where perversion is so prevalent, the widespread use of the kiss as a mode of greeting might present serious temp-tations and lead to gross moral failures. For that reason, the handshake has largely taken the place of the kiss among Christians in English-speaking cultures. Ordinarily we should not allow cultural considerations to excuse us from strict adherence to the words of Scripture. But in a case like this, where literal obedience might lead to sin or even the appearance of evil because of local cultural conditions, we are probably justified in substituting the hand-shake for the kiss.

16:21. Paul's usual habit was to dictate his letters to one of his coworkers. However, at the end he would take pen in hand, add a few words in his own writing, and then give his characteristic **salutation.** That is what he does at this point.

16:22. Accursed translates the Greek word *anathema.* Those who do **not love the Lord Jesus** are condemned already, but their doom will be manifest at the coming of the Lord Jesus Christ. A Christian is one who loves the Savior. He loves the Lord Jesus more than anyone or anything in the world. Failure to love God's Son is a crime against God Himself. Ryle comments: "St. Paul allows no way of escape to the man who does not love Christ. He leaves no loophole or excuse. A man may lack clear head-knowledge and yet be saved. He may fail in courage, and be overcome by the fear of man, like Peter. He may fall tremendously, like David, and yet rise again. But if a person does not love Christ he is not in the way of life. The curse is yet upon him. He is on the broad road that leadeth to destruction."

O Lord, come! translates *maranatha,* an Aramaic expression used by the early Christians. If spaced "maran atha" it means "Our Lord has come," and if spaced "marana tha" it means Our **Lord, come!**

16:23. Grace was Paul's favorite theme. He loved to open and end his letters on this exalted note. It is one of the true marks of his authorship.

16:24. Throughout all of 1 Corinthians we have listened to the heartbeat of this devoted apostle of Christ. We have listened to him as he sought to edify, comfort, exhort, and admonish his children in the faith. There was no doubt of his **love** for them. When they read these closing words, perhaps they would feel ashamed that they had allowed false teachers to come in, questioned Paul's apostleship, and turned away from their original love for him.

 See discussion questions on issues raised in chapter 16 of 1 Corinthians on p. 211.

6
Background Studies for Deeper Understanding

BIBLICAL WORD STUDIES

"Fellowship" (1 Cor. 1:9)

(Gk., *koinonia;* see also Acts 2:42; Phil. 2:1; 1 John 1:3, 6, 7). The Greek term means "that which is shared in common." In the New Testament the word was used to denote the believers' common participation in the triune God—the Father, the Son, and the Holy Spirit. The Father and Son have enjoyed communion with each other before the creation of the world. When the Son entered into time, His fellowship with the Father also entered into time. During the days of His ministry, Jesus was introducing the Father to the disciples and initiating them into this fellowship. Then once the disciples were regenerated unto eternal life, they actually entered into fellowship with the Father and the Son. Thus, the unique fellowship between the Father and the Son begun in eternity was manifested in time through the incarnation of the Son, was introduced to the apostles, and then through the apostles was extended to each and every believer through the indwelling of the Holy Spirit (2 Cor. 13:14; Phil. 2:1).

—from *Nelson's New Illustrated Bible Commentary*

"Temple" (1 Cor. 3:16; 6:19)

(Gk., *naos;* see also 2 Cor. 6:16; Eph. 2:21; Rev. 21:22). This Greek word for *temple* refers more to the building itself than *hieron,* which was used to indicate the entire temple complex. Paul told the believers that each one of their bodies was a *naos,* a sanctuary for God (6:19). Paul also said that the church, as Christ's body, is a spiritual *temple* for God (3:16, 17; 2 Cor. 6:16; Eph. 2:21). What a special privilege it is to be God's spiritual dwelling place, both individually and corporately. The glory of God filled the tabernacle (Ex. 40:34) and the temple

(1 Kin. 8:10, 11). Now the glory of God in the person of the Holy Spirit dwells within every believer (John 14:16, 17) and thus inhabits the entire church. In the New Jerusalem, there will be no need for a physical temple because God and the Lamb will be the eternal temple (Rev. 21:22).

—from *Nelson's New Illustrated Bible Commentary*

"Futile" (1 Cor. 3:20; 15:17)

(Gk., *mataios;* see also Titus 3:9; James 1:26). This word means "pointless" and "purposeless." The New Testament writers, especially Paul, used it to portray the meaninglessness that pervades the thought life of fallen human beings. Paul characterizes the "thoughts of the wise" as being futile (1 Cor. 3:20), and he describes the Gentiles as living "in the futility of their minds, having their understanding darkened" because they are "alienated from the life of God" (Eph. 4:17, 18). The ideas of the unregenerate are futile and aimless because they lack divine insight; they produce a life of purposelessness and ineffectiveness. Salvation from such futility comes from the indwelling Spirit of Christ in believers (Rom. 8:10, 11, 26, 27).

—from *Nelson's New Illustrated Bible Commentary*

"Liberty" (1 Cor. 7:37; 8:9; 9:18)

(Gk., *exousia;* see also Matt. 7:29; Rom. 9:21). The Greek term usually denotes "right," "authority," or even "privilege." In certain contexts, such as these in 1 Corinthians, it connotes the freedom to exercise one's right. Specifically, Paul was addressing the Corinthians' right to eat meat that may have come from pagan temples. To be clear, the eating of sacrificial food—the cultic meals in pagan temples—was censured by Paul because it was understood that the participants in those meals were uniting themselves to demons (10:19–21). However, Paul had no problem with those who purchased food that had been left over from these events and that was later sold in the marketplace. In his judgment if they ate it at home, they were not participating in idolatry. They had the liberty—or right—to eat this food in good conscience. The exception was if they would be destroying a weaker believer by doing so. For the sake of such believers, one should abstain.

—from *Nelson's New Illustrated Bible Commentary*

"Idolatry" (1 Cor. 10:14)

(Gk., *eidololatreia;* see also Gal. 3:20; Col. 3:5). This word refers to the practice of worshiping idols. Related Greek words are translated "idolater" in 5:10, 11; 6:9; 10:7; "idol" in 8:4, 7; 10:19; 12:2; and "things offered to idols" in 8:1, 4, 7;

10:19, 28. The fullest discussion in the New Testament concerning idolatry is found in First Corinthians. Paul had told the Corinthians not to associate with those who called themselves believers but were still idolaters (5:9–11). The Corinthians must have asked Paul for clarification on this matter, for in First Corinthians Paul warns the believers to refrain from all forms of idol worship.

—from *Nelson's New Illustrated Bible Commentary*

"Tongues" (1 Cor. 12:10; 14:2, 4–6, 9, 13, 14, 18, 27)

(Gk., *glossa;* see also Acts 2:4; 10:46; 19:6). The Greek term *glossa* means "tongue" or "language." When the early believers were empowered by the Holy Spirit on the day of Pentecost, they were given the ability to speak in many different languages, so that people visiting from all around the Roman world could hear the glories of God being uttered in their native tongue (Acts 2:4–11). The household of Cornelius also spoke in different languages when they were baptized in the Holy Spirit (Acts 10:46). And the same thing happened with the new disciples from Ephesus (Acts 19:6). Other than these instances, priority mention of tongue speaking is at Corinth, where they spoke in different languages as a way of praying to God. When these languages were spoken outside the corporate worship setting, interpretation was not needed; when they were spoken in the meetings, Paul required interpretation so that others could understand and be edified (14:2–27).

—from *Nelson's New Illustrated Bible Commentary*

"Resurrection" (1 Cor. 15:12, 13, 21, 42)

(Gk., *anastasis;* see also Acts 17:32; Rom. 1:4; 1 Pet. 1:3). The Scriptures often speak of Christ's Resurrection with the phrase that is literally "resurrection out from among dead ones." This is the wording in the first half of 1 Corinthians 15:12 and in other verses (Acts 17:31; 1 Pet. 1:3). When Scripture speaks of the resurrection in general, commonly the phrase is "a resurrection of dead ones." This is the wording in the second half of 1 Corinthians 15:12 (15:13, 42). In Romans 1:4, Christ's Resurrection is spoken of as "a resurrection of dead ones." The same terminology is used in 1 Corinthians 15:21, where the Greek text literally reads: "For since through a man death came, so also through a Man came a resurrection of dead persons."

This shows that Christ's Resurrection included the resurrection of believers to eternal life. When He arose, many arose with Him, for they were united with Him in His Resurrection (Rom. 6:4, 5; Eph. 2:6; Col. 3:1).

—from *Nelson's New Illustrated Bible Commentary*

"Life-Giving Spirit" (1 Cor. 15:45)

(Gk., *pneuma zoopoioun;* see also 2 Cor. 3:6; 1 Pet. 3:18). The Greek expression denotes "the spirit that gives life" or "the spirit that makes alive." The Lord Jesus entered into a new kind of existence when He was raised from the dead because He was glorified and simultaneously became life-giving spirit. The verse does not say Jesus became "the Spirit," since the Second Person of the Trinity did not become the Third Person. Rather, Jesus became spirit in the sense that His mortal existence and form were changed into that which is spiritual. As One now united with the Spirit in a glorified body, Jesus is no longer bound by His mortal body. He is alive in the Spirit (1 Pet. 3:18), to give life to all who believe. This is why Paul speaks of the Spirit of life in Christ Jesus (Rom. 8:2).

—from *Nelson's New Illustrated Bible Commentary*

HISTORICAL AND CULTURAL INFORMATION

The Peloponnesus, Achaea, and the Isthmus of Corinth (1 Cor. 1:2)

The city of Corinth was located in a section of ancient Greece known as the Peloponnesus. This peninsula, shaped like a mulberry leaf, has actually been an island since the Corinth Canal was finished in A.D. 1893. Slightly smaller than New Hampshire, the Peloponnesus had several important districts. The Peloponnesus formed the larger part of the Roman province of Achaea.

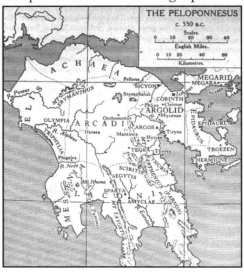

Occupying the northeast corner of the Peloponnesus was the city state of Corinth, which controlled only about 330 square miles, a third of the size of Rhode Island. Blessed with considerable deposits of white and cream-colored clay, Corinth developed the most prolific ceramic industry of early Greece, but after about 550–525 B.C. lost out to Athenian competition.

More important to the development of Corinth, however, was her geographical position. Located a mile and a half south of the Isthmus

Map of Peloponnesus

of Corinth, she commanded this four-mile-wide neck of land, as well as its eastern port of Cenchreae (Cenchrea, Acts 18:18) and its western port of Lechaeum. In New Testament as well as classical times, a large amount of shipping passed through Greek waters, and the trip around the southern tip of Greece was not only long but extremely dangerous. Therefore it became customary to transport goods across the Isthmus of Corinth, a saving of more than 150 miles. Teams pulled smaller ships across the isthmus on a tramway; they unloaded larger ones and reloaded their cargoes on the other side. Short stretches of this tramway

The *diolkos* or tramway on which ships and goods were moved across the Isthmus of Corinth in ancient times.
(Photo by Howard Vos)

can still be seen. Corinth served as the capital of the Roman province of Achaea.

—from *Nelson's New Illustrated Bible Manners & Customs*

Who Was Apollos? (1 Cor. 1:12)

The name Apollos means "destroyer," but Apollos probably wouldn't have wanted the destructive factions that afflicted the church at Corinth. He was a learned and eloquent Jew from Alexandria in Egypt who first comes to our attention in the church at Ephesus. Well-versed in the Old Testament, Apollos was a disciple of John the Baptist and "taught accurately the things of the Lord" (Acts 18:25). However, while Apollos knew some of Jesus' teachings, "he knew only the baptism of John" (Acts 18:25). When Priscilla and Aquila, two other leaders in the early church, arrived in Ephesus, they instructed Apollos more accurately in the way of God (Acts 18:26).

Apollos was known to be eloquent and extremely popular, and the Corinthians set up a faction around him. Perhaps to avoid causing any further controversy or fuel any party spirit, he did not return to Corinth, despite Paul's request (1 Cor. 16:12).

—from *Word in Life Study Bible*

Women and Work in the Ancient World (1 Cor. 7:32–35)

Paul's observation that a married woman must care about "the things of the world" (1 Cor. 7:34) hints at the busy lives that first-century women lived, especially in the large cities of the Roman Empire.

The New Testament shows that women carried out a wide range of tasks: for example, drawing water, grinding grain, manufacturing tents, hosting guests, governing and influencing civic affairs, making clothes, teaching, prophesying and filling other spiritual functions, burying the dead, and doing the work of slaves, to name but a few. Additional evidence from the period reveals that women also served as wool workers, midwives, hairdressers, nurses, vendors, entertainers, political leaders, and even construction workers, among many other occupations.

If a woman was among the upper classes, she enjoyed relative economic security and social privileges. According to the Roman ideal, her role in society was to marry a citizen, produce legitimate heirs for him, and manage the household according to his orders. However, by the first century few families attained that ideal.

Wealthy women used slaves to perform such household tasks as cooking, making clothes, washing laundry, and caring for children. Slaves also functioned as nurses, midwives, hairdressers, stenographers, and secretaries, and it was common for a high-ranking slave to be designated the household manager.

Female slaves were not only considered to be household property, but sexual property as well. The master of the house could legally force a slave to have sex with him, or with anyone he chose. Any children that she bore became his property. In this way a citizen could increase his number of slaves.

Women who were former slaves, or freeborn, lacked the economic security of either the citizen or the slave. Nevertheless, many women sought to buy their way out of slavery. Some of these working-class women earned their living as vendors, selling fish, grain, vegetables, clothing, or perfume. Others became wet nurses, and some chose to become entertainers or prostitutes, occupations that were considered beneath the dignity of respectable women.

—from *Word in Life Study Bible*

Paul and the Greek Games (1 Cor. 9:24–27)

Paul's use of running, boxing, and other athletic feats as metaphors for spiritual discipline was suited perfectly to the Corinthian culture. Corinth hosted numerous athletic events, including the prestigious Isthmian Games, one of four major athletic festivals of the Greeks.

The Isthmian Games were held every other year, and they attracted athletes from all over Greece. The competitions were between individuals, not teams, who vied more for glory than for tangible prizes. At the Corinthian games, victors were crowned with pine needle garlands, the "perishable crown" to which Paul referred (9:25).

One of the important institutions associated with these athletic contests was the gymnasium, where young men were educated by the philosophers and trained in various physical routines. The name derived from the fact that the athletes trained and performed naked (*gumnos,* "naked"). That and the fact that gymnastic activities were closely tied to Greek culture made the institution repulsive to most Jewish people. But Paul's Corinthian readers were no doubt well acquainted with this prominent part of Greek life.

—from *Word in Life Study Bible*

Head Coverings (1 Cor. 11:2–16)

Head coverings were an important part of first-century wardrobes. Outdoors they provided both men and women protection from the intense sun and heat as well as rain. In addition, a woman's head covering was a sign of modesty and commitment to her husband. Jewish and other women of the Near East wore veils in public, but Roman women never wore veils, and among the Greeks, some did and some did not. In some cultures, a woman without a veil was assumed to have loose morals.

These cultural issues came to bear on the women believers at Corinth. Controversy arose over whether they were required to keep their heads covered during worship or not. Paul wrote that the churches had no universal policy on the matter (11:16), indicating that the women had some freedom to choose how they would handle the issue.

Observing the custom to wear a covering may have been especially important in Corinth, where a favorite slogan was, "Everything is permissible" (cf. 1 Cor. 6:12; 10:23). Paul was eager for Christians to maintain a good reputation and give no cause for offense so that people hearing the gospel would have no barriers to becoming followers of Christ.

—from *Word in Life Study Bible*

"Sounding Brass or a Clanging Cymbal" (1 Cor 13:1)

The deficiency of exercising the gift of tongues without love reduced its benefit to little more than pagan worship. Kenneth Chafin explains the background to this interesting reference in his commentary on 1 and 2 Corinthians: "In many of the temples there was hanging at the entrance a large cymbal. Often, as the would-be worshipers entered the temple, they struck it, causing a loud noise. Some said the noise was for the purpose of rousing the gods. By the time Paul wrote this letter, the loud 'gong' which was made from striking the cymbal had become the symbol for superficial oratory. With this picture in the background, Paul is saying that without love, the finest oratory is nothing more than an empty pagan rite."

—from *Pathways to Pure Power*

The Meaning of Love (1 Cor. 13)

More songs have been written about love than about any other topic. It has inspired some of the world's best, and worst, poetry. It has set on fire, and broken, countless hearts throughout human history. Many things are said about love. Yet for the final word on the topic, we must turn to the Bible. In 1 Corinthians 13, the apostle Paul, under the inspiration of the Holy Spirit, provides the world's most beautiful ode to love.

One common word for love in the Greek language was *eros*, which suggested physical sexual desire and not much else. Another word *(philos)* suggested the esteem and affection found in a casual friendship. Because neither of these words came close to describing the kind of love he wanted to communicate, Paul chose a relatively rare Greek word for his definitive passage on love. This word, *agapē*, describes a love that is based on the deliberate choice of the one who loves rather than the worthiness of the one who is loved. This kind of love goes against natural human inclination. It is a giving, selfless, expect-nothing-in-return kind of love. Paul's description of love is short but full of power.

Love accepts any hardship or rejection, and continues unabated to build up and encourage. The love described by Paul in this "love chapter" means determining what is best for another person and then doing it. This is the kind of love that God shows to us.

—from *Nelson Study Bible*

Who Was Timothy? (1 Cor. 16:10)

Timothy, whose name means "honored of God," first appears in Paul's second missionary journey when the apostle revisited Lystra (Acts 16:1–3). Timothy was the son of a Gentile father and a Jewish-Christian mother named Eunice, and the grandson of Lois (Acts 16:1; 2 Tim. 1:5). Timothy may have been converted under Paul's ministry, because the apostle refers to him as his "beloved and faithful son in the Lord" (1 Cor. 4:17). He traveled with Paul on the remainder of his second missionary journey. Timothy may have been closer to the apostle than any other associate, since Paul refers to him as his "true son in the faith" (1 Tim. 1:2).

During Paul's third missionary journey, Timothy is listed as one of the group that accompanied the apostle along the coast of Asia Minor on his way to Jerusalem (Acts 20:4–5). Timothy also appears as a companion of Paul during his imprisonment in Rome (Col. 1:1; Phil. 1:1). Tradition holds that he eventually became bishop of Ephesus. Timothy also helped in the sending of the epistles of 2 Corinthians, Philippians, Colossians, 1 and 2 Thessalonians, and Philemon.

—from *Word in Life Study Bible*

Who Were Aquila and Priscilla? (1 Cor. 16:19)

Aquila and Priscilla were old friends of Paul and the Corinthians. In fact, they had been instrumental in starting the church at Corinth (Acts 18:1–11). Aquila was originally from Pontus in Asia Minor, bordering the Black Sea. They lived in Rome before Claudius forced all Jews to leave Rome. They then relocated to Corinth, and later to Ephesus. Eventually they returned to Rome. They are best known today for taking Apollos the speaker aside and explaining to him the way of God more accurately (Acts 18:26); also helping to start at least three churches—at Rome, Corinth, and Ephesus.

—from *Word in Life Study Bible*

CONTEXT AND APPLICATION ARTICLES

The Problem with Cover-Ups (1 Cor. 5:1–13)

Evil can never be remedied by ignoring or hiding it. In fact, covering it up is the worst that can happen, for like yeast, evil does its terrible work from within (1 Cor. 5:6–8).

The same is true of believers who live in consistent disobedience to God's expressed will. Their behavior will badly infect the larger groups of which they are a part. It can even lead to a distorted perception of sin in which the group tolerates or even approves of disobedience among its own members yet condemns outsiders for the very same activity (Rom. 1:32; 1 Cor. 5:9–10).

Paul challenged the Corinthians to confront the subtle deterioration they had allowed within their congregation (1 Cor. 5:5). However, once the perpetrator had repented, they were then to seek his restoration. Even though corrective activity among believers may be severe, confrontation should always be to promote healing rather than to expel wrongdoers (compare Matt. 18:15–22; 2 Cor. 10:8). There are no throwaway people in the kingdom of God.

—from *Word in Life Study Bible*

Lawsuits Among Believers (1 Cor. 6:1–11)

Scripture is explicit: for a Christian to take another Christian to court is "an utter failure" (1 Cor. 6:7). What, then, should we as believers do when we have disputes that normally call for litigation? Paul recommends that we take the matter before wise believers who can make a judgment (vv. 4–5). But suppose we can't arrange that? Then Paul says it would be better to "accept wrong" than to go before unbelievers for judgment.

Does that categorically rule out lawsuits between Christians today? Not necessarily. Modern Christians disagree over how to apply this passage. Our society is very different from the first-century Roman Empire. But we know that early churches took Paul's instructions literally. They forbade their members to resort to the pagan courts of the day. Instead, they appointed their own elders to judge civil disputes between members.

Those courts gained such a reputation for justice that they even attracted non-Christians, who found them preferable to the notoriously corrupt imperial courts.

—from *Word in Life Study Bible*

Practical Lessons on Marriage (1 Cor. 7:1)

Have you ever listened in on half of a telephone conversation, trying to figure out what the whole conversation is about? That's what we have in 1 Corinthians 7—half of a very important conversation on marriage between Paul and the Corinthian believers. But we can glean many practical lessons from this passage, because marriage was undergoing profound changes then just as it is today.

Some of the believers in the early church had married before they became Christians. They wondered whether they should divorce their unbelieving spouses in order to remarry Christians and live more wholeheartedly for Christ.

An argument could be made for that. After all, if people's primary loyalty were now to Jesus, shouldn't that invalidate their pre-conversion marriage vows? (Of course, it would also provide them with a convenient excuse to escape bad marriages.)

But Paul didn't recommend that. He viewed the abandonment of one's family as a very serious matter (1 Cor. 7:10–11), arguing that the believer should stay in the marriage as long as possible (7:12–13). However, God desires peace in relationships (7:15), and that may not be possible in a family where Christian values are not shared. If the unbeliever wants to leave, he or she should be allowed to do so (7:15).

Paul made it clear that it is possible for one believer to "sanctify" a family—to be an agent of God's love and grace, and perhaps to eventually bring other family members into the faith. No matter how unconventional the situation might be, Scripture doesn't counsel sudden changes. God may have work left to do in that family, and He may use the believer to do it—if he or she stays.

—from *Word in Life Study Bible*

A New View of Sexuality (1 Cor. 7:3–6)

In an era when Greek women were often deprived both emotionally and sexually, Paul insisted that the Christian husband should recognize and fulfill the needs of his wife. He declared that marriage partners have authority over each other. That means that both husband and wife were forbidden from using sex as a means of control, but were to enjoy mutuality in that aspect of their marriage.

The gospel required a different understanding of sex and marriage than the surrounding culture's. Two thousand years later, it still does.

—from *Word in Life Study Bible*

Paul's Marital Status (1 Cor. 7:8)

Paul's own marital state has been a matter of considerable speculation. It is clear from 1 Corinthians 7:8 that Paul was not married. However, some interpreters have suggested that he may have been a widower who lost his wife while young. There are perhaps three reasons for this speculation.

First, in Paul's defense before Agrippa (Acts 26) he told of his role in persecuting the believers in Jerusalem. He readily admitted a zeal and madness that resulted in many Christians being imprisoned, persecuted, and even killed. He did this under the authority of the chief priests, "and when they were put to death, I cast my vote against *them*" (v. 10). The fact that he voted in the Sanhedrin indicates to some interpreters that he was married, since this was a prerequisite for that position.

Second, 1 Corinthians 7 seems to be subjective, that is, it seems to have been written by one who knew something of the intimacies and demands of married life (see vv. 3–5, 9, 32, 33).

Third, the context of 1 Corinthians 7:8 is Paul's counsel on the purity of marriage. The "unmarried" who are paired in this verse with the widows, may, in fact, be "widowers" in modern language. It has been observed that there is no word for "widower" in the Greek language. A "widow" *(chera)* was a person "without" or "left without." While a woman might be "left without" a husband and have to await the social functioning of her kinsmen or the affection of a new man, a man could quite easily take steps to obtain a new spouse. A Greek woman left without a spouse was left a "widow," a person without a source of support. A man in a comparable state was simply a man who chose not to remain "unmarried." Paul's "as I am" in 1 Corinthians 7:8 may indicate that he had also lost his spouse to death.

—from *Pathways to Pure Power*

Living Out God's Call Where We Are (1 Cor. 7:17–24)

Most people place a high value on mobility and freedom of choice. So how should Christians in our culture deal with Paul's admonition to remain in the situation where God has called us? This sounds antiquated in a society where the average person changes careers at least four times in life. In the ancient world, people normally worked for a lifetime at the same job.

Paul wrote that becoming a believer doesn't necessarily mean a career change. Wherever God has assigned us, that is our calling and we should pursue it to God's glory. On the other hand, there is nothing in the faith that locks a person into a work situation, any more than an unmarried woman must remain single all her life (7:8–9).

Paul's teaching about vocation parallels what he wrote about pre-conversion marriage (7:10–16). A believer is not compelled to leave his or her unbelieving spouse. On the other hand, the marriage may be dissolved if necessary to maintain peace. In the same way, believers should not use conversion as an excuse to leave their jobs.

This is an important point because Christianity introduces new values into our lives that may make us anxious to escape our work environment. The atmosphere of language and jokes, competition and politics, quotas and numbers may begin to feel uncomfortable. Wouldn't it be easier to quit one's job and go to work for a Christian employer—or better yet, pursue a career in a church or ministry? But Paul didn't encourage that choice as the normal path. A job change may be a possibility, as Jesus' disciples found out. But it is not necessarily virtuous to leave our "nets," especially if our only reason is to escape the realities of the work world.

—from *Word in Life Study Bible*

Dealing with Gray Areas (1 Cor. 8:1–13)

In first-century Corinth, meat sacrificed to idols (1 Cor. 8:1) proved to be an issue on which believers vehemently disagreed. It was a "gray" area of life, a matter for which there seemed to be no clear-cut instruction. How should

Christians settle such disputes? Through a predetermined set of dos and don'ts? No, Paul offered a different perspective, one that appeals to conscience.

Paul argued that food and drink do not determine our relationship to God (8:8). Meat offered to idols is inconsequential because, ultimately, there is no such thing as an idol (8:4–6). An idol is not God, so the fact that a priest blesses meat and offers it to an idol means nothing. From that point of view, Christians should be able to enjoy whatever food they want.

However, questionable practices may affect one's relationships with fellow believers or unbelievers (8:9). As members of Christ's family we are obligated not to be a "stumbling block," but a loving neighbor. Our faith is not merely private, but has a corporate ethic and public responsibility as well.

So we live in a tension: God's grace frees us to choose as we please, but God's love requires us to ask questions of conscience about our choices. From what we eat, to whom we live and work with, to where we live, to what we do with our money and time—almost everything we do affects our neighbors (8:10–13). So we need to ask, Are we treating them with love?

We need not allow others to manipulate us through legalistic criticism. But we do need discretion about how our choices affect those around us. It's not enough to follow Christ just in our hearts; we also need to follow Him in our consciences.

—from *Word in Life Study Bible*

Paying Vocational Christian Workers (1 Cor. 9:1–23)

How much should pastors, missionaries, and others who work in churches and ministries be paid? Or should they be paid at all? Paul's example with the Corinthians offers some insight.

In Paul's day, philosophers traveled from city to city, teaching publicly for a fee. The more prestigious the teacher, the larger the fee. However, Paul charged the Corinthians nothing when he came and delivered the gospel message. As a result, some people were criticizing him, asserting that he must not be an authentic leader of the church if he was rendering his services for free.

In reply, Paul explained himself. First, he insisted that those who labor spiritually should be supported materially by those with whom they work. He pointed to five familiar examples to support his position:

1. Roman soldiers drew pay for their service (9:7).
2. Vintners enjoyed the fruits of their vineyards (9:7).
3. Shepherds received food from their flocks (9:7).

4. The Old Testament law affirmed the right of laborers to receive fair compensation (9:8–10).
5. The law also allowed temple priests and attendants to live off the sacrifices that the people brought (9:13).

Paul also explained that the Lord Himself allowed those who preach the gospel to make their living from that occupation (9:14). Elsewhere the apostle wrote that church elders who rule well are worthy of "double honor" (1 Tim. 5:17–18). The context shows that Paul had payment in mind. In short, effective vocational Christian workers should be paid fairly for their labor.

Yet Paul refused payment in Corinth. Why? Because he felt that he owed it to God to communicate the gospel for free. When he considered his past and how God had saved him, the "chief of sinners" (1 Tim. 1:15), it was payment enough to be able to tell people about Jesus (1 Cor. 9:18).

Should workers in churches and ministries be paid? This passage insists that they have a right to a fair wage, and Christians today do well to pay attention to Paul's words here in light of the many workers who are leaving the ministry because of inadequate support. On the other hand, Paul's example opens the door to an alternative—the idea of carrying out ministry for free while supporting oneself through other means. That is also a model worth considering in a day when, for a variety of reasons, an increasing number of churches and ministries are strapped for funds.

—from *Word in Life Study Bible*

What Is Headship? (1 Cor. 11:3)

What exactly did Paul mean when he used the word *head* (1 Cor. 11:3)? Some believe that the term by definition implies subordination of one person to another. Others disagree. For example, John Chrysostom, an early church leader, declared that only a heretic would understand "head" as chief or authority over. Rather, he understood the word as meaning absolute oneness, cause, or primal source.

Either way, it's important to note that while "the head of Christ is God" (11:3), Christ is elsewhere shown to be equal with God (for example, John 1:1–3; 10:30; Col. 1:15). So the term *head* need not exclude the idea of equality. At the same time, even though Christ is the equal of God, He became obedient to the point of death (Phil. 2:5–8), demonstrating that equality need not rule out submission.

—from *Word in Life Study Bible*

Lessons from the Human Body (1 Cor. 12:14–26)

The human body is an exquisite organism. Scientists cannot duplicate it or even fully understand it. It is a synthesis of many parts, all working together in comprehensive unity. What affects one part of the body affects the whole. Each member of the body relates to and depends upon other parts of the body. Each contributes to the welfare of the entire body. So are all believers as members of the body of Christ. We should function in Christ's body as the parts of the human body function in it. The amputation of a limb handicaps the entire body. There is no Christian brother whom we do not need.

The word *body* (Gk., *soma*) is related to *soza,* meaning "to heal, preserve, be made whole." This clearly shows how our lives are inextricably woven together within the body of Christ, and how well-being depends upon the well-being of others (Rom. 14:7). Paul's point is that no matter how different we may be as individual parts in the body (vv. 15, 16), we desperately need one another in order to function effectively as the whole (vv. 19, 21). Each member—without exception—is essential to the other (vv. 22, 24). None is unimportant nor more important than another.

—from *Pathways to Pure Power*

Are Some Jobs More Important Than Others? (1 Cor. 12:28–31)

Does a hierarchy of gifts mean God values some jobs more than others? Judging by popular opinion, one might conclude that He does. In fact, for centuries Christians have subscribed to a subtle yet powerful hierarchy of vocations.

In our culture, that hierarchy tends to position clergy (missionaries and evangelists, pastors and priests) at the top, members of the "helping professions" (doctors and nurses, teachers and educators, social workers) next, and "secular" workers (business executives, salespeople, factory laborers, and farmers) at the bottom.

So what determines the spiritual value of a job? How does God assign significance? The hierarchy assumes sacred and secular distinctions, and assigns priority to the sacred. But God does not view vocations that way. All legitimate work matters to God. He Himself is a worker. In fact, human occupations find their origin in His work to create the world (Ps. 8:6–8). Work is a gift from Him to meet the needs of people and the creation.

God creates people to carry out specific kinds of work. God uniquely designs each of us, fitting us for certain kinds of tasks. He distributes skills, abilities, interests, and personalities among us so we can carry out His work in the world. That work includes "spiritual" tasks, but also extends to health, education, agriculture, business, law, communication, the arts, and so on.

God cares more about character and conduct than occupational status. Paul's teaching in this passage is about gifts, not vocations. At the time Paul wrote it, there were few if any "professional" clergy in the church. Paul himself was a tentmaker by occupation, along with his friends, Aquila and Priscilla (1 Cor. 16:19; see Rom. 16:3–5). Other church leaders practiced a wide variety of professions and trades. God may assign rank among the spiritual gifts, but there's no indication that He looks at vocations that way.

Furthermore, Scripture says there is something more important than gifts, "a more excellent way" (1 Cor. 12:31). Chapter 13 of 1 Corinthians reveals it to be the way of Christlike love and character. Implication: If you want status in God's economy, excel at love, no matter what you do for work. Love has the greatest value to God (1 Cor. 13:13; Matt. 22:35–40).

—from *Word in Life Study Bible*

Agape: Self-Giving Love (1 Cor. 13:1–13)

Many different words for love are found in the Greek language, while in English we have just one. *Eros* was the word the Greeks used for romantic or sensual love. They also had a word for the mutual affection of friends and family that was used in the Bible a number of times. That word, *philos*, describes more of a "brotherly love." It is where we get the word *Philadelphia*, the "city of brotherly love."

But the word that Paul used in 1 Corinthians 13 to describe the basis of all ethical behavior was *agape*. This word denotes an undefeatable benevolence and unconquerable goodwill that always seeks the highest good of the other person. It is self-giving love that gives freely without asking anything in return and does not consider the worth of its object. Agape is more a love by choice than *philos*, which is love by chance; and it refers to the will rather than the emotions. *Agape* describes the unconditional love that God has for the world, and the love that believers are to have for others.

—from *Pathways to Pure Power*

Facts About the Resurrection (1 Cor. 15)

The resurrection of Christ was proclaimed eagerly by the early church. This miracle was considered an essential part of the gospel message. Surely Christ had died, but more importantly, He had been raised. More than just a suffering Savior, Jesus is our living Lord.

Christ's resurrection was prophesied in the Old Testament Scriptures (Ps. 16:10).	15:4
The risen Christ appeared to more than five hundred witnesses, including Paul.	15:5–8
If Jesus did not rise from the dead, the gospel message is pointless, empty, and dishonest. Jesus Christ would not be alive, interceding for us, and we would not be able to place our hope in a glorious future with Him. The resurrection is central to the gospel.	15:14, 15
According to Paul, "If Christ is not risen, your faith is futile; you are still in your sins" (15:17; see Rom. 4:25). Christ's resurrection, not merely His death on the cross, secured our justification. His resurrection was a sign of God's approval of Christ's sacrifice for our sins. In short, no Resurrection equals no forgiveness of sin.	15:17–19
The resurrection of Christ was designed to reveal what lies ahead for those who put their trust in Jesus (15:20–57). Paul called Christ "the firstfruits of those who have fallen asleep" (15:20). This Old Testament image (see Ex. 23:16–19) means that Christ serves as both an example and a guarantee of what we can expect. Because He has conquered death (15:26, 27, 54–57), we need not fear death. Because He now enjoys a glorified body, we also can expect to inherit a "spiritual body" (15:44–46) after this mortal one wears out.	15:20–26
Our dead, physical body will one day be resurrected.	15:42
We will once again be both material and immaterial beings, our soul being reunited with our resurrected body.	15:43, 44

(Table continued on next page)

The power behind this marvelous, yet mysterious event is Jesus, the self-declared "resurrection and the life" (John 11:25).	15:45
Our physical body will be altered and changed to prepareus for the life to come. If Jesus is the prototype, we will still be recognizable, but our new body will be capable of supernatural activities (see Luke 24:31, 36, 51).	15:51–54
Our resurrection will take place when Jesus returns (see 1 Thess. 4:13–18).	15:53

—From *Nelson Study Bible*

7
Questions for Personal Reflection and Group Discussion

CHAPTER 1

1. What kind of people were in the church at Corinth? (1 Cor. 1:2)
2. How did Paul describe them in his greeting? (1 Cor. 1:2, 3)
3. What did Paul thank God for in the lives and experiences of the Corinthian believers? (1 Cor. 1:4)
4. In what ways had the believers at Corinth been "enriched"? (1 Cor. 1:5–7)
5. Paul's confidence that the Corinthians would be declared "blameless in the day of our Lord Jesus Christ" was based on what? (1 Cor. 1:8, 9)
6. In your opinion, what kind of issues threaten unity in the body of Christ today? (1 Cor. 1:10–17)
7. Do you feel Paul's remarks in 1 Corinthians 1:14–17 minimize the doctrine of water baptism? Why or why not?
8. Was water baptism practiced during Paul's pastorate in Corinth? Use Acts 18:8 and 1 Corinthians 1:14–17 to explain your answer.
9. Why do you think Paul's call was to "preach the gospel," and why did he say, "For Christ did not send me to baptize"? (1 Cor. 1:17)

CHAPTER 2

1. Why do you think Paul emphasized he did not come to the Corinthians with "excellency of speech or of wisdom"? (1 Cor. 2:1)
2. Describe the contrast that Paul makes between the "natural man" and the "spiritual man" in 1 Corinthians 2:11–15.
3. What does it mean for a believer to have "the mind of Christ"? (1 Cor. 2:16)

CHAPTER 3

1. What building materials are described in 1 Corinthians 3:5–17?
2. What do you think these materials represent in a believer's life? (1 Cor. 3:5–17)
3. How do these materials relate to one another? (1 Cor. 3:5–17)
4. What will the burning of fire test or reveal? (1 Cor. 3:13)
5. What will determine if an individual will receive a reward? (1 Cor. 3:13, 14)
6. How should the fact that God's Spirit lives in every Christian affect the way we live? (1 Cor. 3:16)
7. In what ways have you been able to plant and water God's Word in other people this week?
8. What could you do in your church this month to help build up other Christians?

CHAPTER 4

1. How should we treat people who are in positions of ministry leadership? (1 Cor. 4:1–21)
2. How can congregations show honor and respect without putting church leaders on a pedestal? (1 Cor. 4:1–21)
3. Who has been a "father in the faith" to you? (1 Cor. 4:17)
4. What are the characteristics of this kind of person? (1 Cor. 4:17)
5. Have you told them "thank you" recently? When? How? (1 Cor. 4:17)
6. Who would consider *you* a "spiritual parent"? Why? (1 Cor. 4:17)

CHAPTER 5

1. What would be the impact if all local churches were committed to the practice of church discipline? What if none practiced it? (1 Cor. 5)
2. How secret was the scandal in the Corinthian church? (1 Cor. 5:1–8)
3. What exactly was the sin in the Corinthian church? (1 Cor. 5:1–8)
4. What was the reaction of the godless Gentiles in the community to this open sin? (1 Cor. 5:1–8)
5. Why do you think the Corinthian congregation tolerated this immorality in their midst? (1 Cor. 5:1–8)
6. How did Paul suggest the Corinthians should have responded? (1 Cor. 5:2)
7. How do you view blatant sin among believers? Like the Corinthians, do you shrug it off? Why? (1 Cor. 5:1–8)
8. What special circumstances were to accompany the expulsion of the immoral member? Why? (1 Cor. 5:4, 5)

9. Why was it necessary for the Corinthian church to expel the man who was living in sin from their congregation? (1 Cor. 5:5)

10. Do you find it easy to be full of indignation at sin and yet full of compassion for the sinner? (1 Cor. 5:5)

11. Is it loving or cruel to allow our brothers and sisters to be broad-minded and permit sin to reign in their lives? Why? (1 Cor. 5:5)

12. Do you have friends or family members who need to discern right from wrong before such a drastic discipline would need to be taken in their lives? Explain. (1 Cor. 5:5)

13. Why is church discipline practiced so infrequently in congregations today? (1 Cor. 5:9–13)

14. Is it possible that one of the reasons for the lack of spiritual power in many contemporary churches is failure to follow this biblical principle of corporate discipline? Explain. (1 Cor. 5:9–13)

15. Is God's condemnation of these practices a judging of the sin or the sinner? (1 Cor. 5:9–13)

16. How have you prayed for any person who is a bad influence on you? (1 Cor. 5:9–13)

17. At what point would you stop associating with a professing believer who continued in gross sin? (1 Cor. 5:9–13)

18. To what extent should those who desire to become members of a local church body be living in moral and spiritual purity and be willing to submit to the demands of discipleship? (1 Cor. 5:9–13)

19. What is the difference regarding moral and spiritual accountability between a member of a local body or a supposedly mature Christian and a new convert who has just accepted Jesus Christ? (1 Cor. 5:9–13)

CHAPTER 6

1. What bearing do Paul's words to the Corinthian believers have on Christians today? (1 Cor. 6:1–11)

2. Are we under the same prohibition regarding bringing lawsuits against our fellow believers as the Corinthians were? Why? (1 Cor. 6:1–11)

3. Have courts of law improved since Paul's day? Does that make any difference on whether Christians should bring lawsuits against fellow believers? (1 Cor. 6:1–11)

4. What if we are not sure if the other disputant is truly a believer? Would this make a difference in our actions? (1 Cor. 6:1–11)

5. What if a lawsuit is not personal but between your respective insurance companies? (1 Cor. 6:1–11)

6. Who will judge the world? (1 Cor. 6:2)
7. Who will judge angels? (1 Cor. 6:3)
8. Who is qualified to serve as a judge between believers? (1 Cor. 6:4)
9. How can we avoid being absorbed by secular thinking on "gray areas" of ethical or moral issues? (1 Cor. 6:12–20; see also Col. 3:3–7; 1 Thess. 4:1–8)
10. What makes our bodies special? (1 Cor. 6:15)
11. How should this affect how we use our bodies and what we put in them? (1 Cor. 6:15)
12. When evaluating ethical decisions, how would thinking of yourself as "God's property" affect your actions? Explain. (1 Cor. 6:15)
13. Paul says sexual immorality is sin against our own bodies. What do you think he meant by that? (1 Cor. 6:18)
14. How could promiscuous premarital activity become a "habit" (or an appetite, a "felt need") that marriage doesn't break? (1 Cor. 6:18)

CHAPTER 7

1. Why should "each man have his own wife"? (1 Cor. 7:2)
2. What obligations does a Christian wife have toward her husband? (1 Cor. 7:4)
3. To whom does a Christian's body belong if he or she is married? (1 Cor. 7:4)
4. What are some advantages of being single? (1 Cor. 7:25–40)
5. What are some advantages of being married? (1 Cor. 7:25–40)
6. What opportunities do married people have that single people do not have? (1 Cor. 7:25–40)
7. How can you use your unique experiences as a married or single person in service to God? (1 Cor. 7:25–40)
8. What is the one essential requirement Paul gives for a Christian in marriage? (1 Cor. 7:39)

CHAPTER 8

Consider the following principles and questions to help in developing your own personal convictions. Objectively apply *all* the following "guidelines for gray areas" to a given issue before deciding if the matter in question is right or wrong for you.

1. *Profit.* Ask: "Is it good for me?" "Will it add a plus quality to my life?" (1 Cor. 6:12)

2. *Control.* Ask: "Will it get control of me, or will it lessen Christ's control of me?" (1 Cor. 6:12)
3. *Ownership.* Ask: "As God's property, can I justify this activity? Is this activity suitable for an ambassador of Jesus Christ?" (1 Cor. 6:19, 20)
4. *Influence.* Ask: "Could this action negatively influence any of my friends or cause them to stumble?" (1 Cor. 8:9, 12, 13)

CHAPTER 9

1. What is appealing to you about Paul's freedom? (1 Cor. 9:1–27)
2. Have you ever tried to exert your freedom by rebelling against authority? If so, how did God deal with you about it? (1 Cor. 9:1–27)
3. Do others find grace and freedom in your attitudes and actions? (1 Cor. 9:1–27)
4. Is there anything in your life that might hinder the spread of the gospel? Talk to God about this. (1 Cor. 9:1–27)
5. Is there a liberty you are holding onto that is causing this hindrance? (1 Cor. 9:1–27)
6. If so, what steps can you take to remove this hindrance? (1 Cor. 9:1–27)

CHAPTER 10

1. What were the five prohibitions that Paul gave to the Corinthians? (1 Cor. 10:6–10)
2. What truths about temptation did Paul state in 1 Corinthians 10:13?
3. What did Paul mean by his statement that "all things are lawful for me, but not all things are expedient"? (1 Cor. 10:23)
4. Under what circumstances, according to Paul, should the Corinthian believers abstain from eating meat that had been offered to idols? (1 Cor. 10:25–33)

CHAPTER 11

1. Do you think that Christians and our churches give true recognition to the worth and value of women? (1 Cor. 11:2–16)
2. What did Paul mean by saying that a woman should not pray with her head uncovered? (1 Cor. 11:5)
3. What does this mean to modern believers? (1 Cor. 11:5)
4. Does Paul seem to acknowledge women praying and prophesying in the Corinthian congregation? Is this significant? (1 Cor. 11:5–6)
5. What are some ways that women today struggle to symbolize their equality with men? (1 Cor. 11:1–16)

6. Which, if any, of these issues involve a denial of the identity and value of women? (1 Cor. 11:1–16)
7. What differences between men and women should be acknowledged? (1 Cor. 11:1–16)
8. Do these differences make one sex of lesser or greater importance? Why or why not? (1 Cor. 11:1–16)
9. Do you think that we Christians and our churches as a rule give true recognition to the worth and value of women? Why or why not? (1 Cor. 11:1–16)
10. Why did God establish man as the family head? (1 Cor. 11:3)
11. What does this say about the relative intelligence or wisdom of women? (1 Cor. 11:3)
12. Who is the head of Jesus? (1 Cor. 11:3b)
13. Who is the head of man, and who is the head of woman? (1 Cor. 11:3)
14. How did some believers at Corinth abuse the wine intended for the Holy Communion? (1 Cor. 11:21)
15. How did Paul respond to these practices? (1 Cor. 11:17–34)
16. Could this kind of thing happen in today's church? (1 Cor. 11:17–34)
17. What should be done to prevent it? (1 Cor. 11:17–34)
18. How does your church observe the Lord's Supper? How often? (1 Cor. 11:17–34)
19. What did each of the elements of the Lord's Supper (or Communion or Eucharist) represent? (1 Cor. 11: 23–25)
20. Why is self-judgment important before participating in the Lord's Supper? (1 Cor. 11:31, 32)
21. Why had judgment already come upon some of the Corinthian believers? (1 Cor. 11:30)
22. What should we do to be "acceptable" at the Lord's Table? (1 Cor. 11:28–34)
23. How often are we to partake of the Lord's Supper? (1 Cor. 11:26)
24. Can the Lord's Supper be received by individuals or families in their homes? (1 Cor. 11:25)

CHAPTER 12

1. What was Paul's purpose in giving the Corinthians instructions about spiritual gifts? (1 Cor. 12:1)
2. How is ignorance about spiritual gifts demonstrated in the lives of some Christians today? (1 Cor. 12:1–11)

3. What spiritual gifts have you seen used in your local church? (1 Cor. 12:1–11)

4. How is the Holy Spirit different from the "dumb idols" the Corinthians worshiped as pagans? (1 Cor. 12:2)

5. Would God ever motivate someone to call "Jesus accursed"? (1 Cor. 12:3)

6. What role does the Holy Spirit play in believers' affirmation of the lordship of Jesus Christ? (1 Cor. 12:3)

7. How would you compare your place in the body of Christ to a part of the human body? (1 Cor. 12:12–24)

8. In what circumstances have you felt like an important or insignificant part of the body of Christ? (1 Cor. 12:12–24)

9. Do you find it difficult to share with others the needs or deficiencies in your own life? Why? (1 Cor. 12:12–24)

10. Do you find it difficult to give others compliments or to tell them you appreciate them? Why? (1 Cor. 12:12–24)

CHAPTER 13

1. Does 1 Corinthians 13:2 actually say that love is superior to the gifts of prophecy, word of wisdom, word of knowledge, or miracle-working faith?

2. According to 1 Corinthians 13:3, who is not profited by philanthropy and martyrdom?

3. According to 1 Corinthians 13:3, is love superior to philanthropy and martyrdom, or is it the only proper motivation that makes it profitable to the philanthropist and martyr? Explain your answer.

4. Does the absence of love negate the potential benefit of the exercise of spiritual gifts, which are given "for the profit *of all*"? (1 Cor. 13:1–13)

5. Can other people be blessed, edified, and comforted by the exercise of spiritual gifts, while the person who passes on these gifts is not "profited"? (1 Cor. 13:2, 3)

6. Why is love so enduring that it can be said to "never fail" or end? (1 Cor. 13:8; see also 1 John 4:16)

7. Why do you feel that spiritual gifts (like prophecy, tongues, and knowledge) will not be necessary in heaven? (1 Cor. 13:1–13)

CHAPTER 14

1. Compare 1 Corinthians 14 with Acts 2. Do you notice anything different about the "tongues" these two passages seem to be describing? (1 Cor. 14)

2. Does 1 Corinthians 14:26 describe a typical worship service in your local church? Why or why not?

3. Did the apostle Paul teach that speaking in tongues was a valid spiritual gift for public ministry? Why? (1 Cor. 14:5, 26)

4. Which gift was preferred in public over speaking in tongues? Why? (1 Cor. 14:5)

5. What is the benefit to the church if speaking in tongues is accompanied with the gift of interpretation? (1 Cor. 14:5)

6. The exercise of the gift of tongues, with interpretation, in a public meeting was the equivalent of what gift? (1 Cor. 14:3–5)

7. Why do you think limitations were placed on tongues (and interpretation) in a public meeting? (1 Cor. 14:26–28)

8. Were tongues to be forbidden in a gathering of believers? (1 Cor. 14:39)

9. What place did tongues have in the private prayer life of the apostle Paul? (1 Cor. 14:15)

10. How did Paul underscore the value of tongues in his personal devotions? (1 Cor. 14:18)

11. Did Paul prefer to speak in a spiritual language or a known tongue while in church? Why? (1 Cor. 14:19)

CHAPTER 15

1. The resurrection of Jesus was authenticated by His appearing to hundreds of witnesses. Who were they? (1 Cor. 15:5–8)

2. Which witness is not mentioned by Paul? Why? (See John 20:11–18)

3. What does the term *sleep* or *fallen asleep* frequently mean when applied to Christians? Why? (1 Cor. 15:6; see also 1 Thess. 4:14)

4. It is unclear if some of the Corinthians actually questioned Christ's resurrection, or whether or not Christians who died would be resurrected also. In challenging their doubt on this matter, Paul bluntly pointed out the consequences of their denial of either. If Christ is not risen, what four negative factors must be faced? (1 Cor. 15:13–17)

5. What does Paul mean in 1 Corinthians 15:20 when he says that Christ "has become the firstfruits of those who have fallen asleep"?

6. Why does Paul compare Christ with Adam? What is represented by each? (1 Cor. 15:22)

7. Christ's resurrected body reveals something of the kind of bodies resurrected believers will have in heaven. Review John 20 and Luke 24, then compare and contrast characteristics of the spiritual body with the natural body. (1 Cor. 15:44)

8. In 1 Corinthians 15:39–41 Paul suggests that the new spiritual body is superior to the old natural body. What three comparisons does he make?

9. Paul then presents four attributes of the old sinful body. Read 1 Corinthians 15:42–44 and list the four attributes, clarifying their meanings in that context.

10. Finally, Paul shares four attributes of the new sinless body. Read 1 Corinthians 15:42–44 in several translations or versions of the Bible, and then list and amplify the meaning of each attribute.

CHAPTER 16

1. Paul had already presented this "fund-raising" opportunity to the churches in what other regions? (1 Cor. 16:1; see also Rom. 15:25–27)

2. Do you believe the old adage, "God's work, done in God's way, will always have God's supply"? Why or why not? (1 Cor. 16:1–3)

3. Do you believe a lack of finances for a ministry may be a part of God's plan, or is it always an attack of Satan? Why? (1 Cor. 16:1–3)

4. May a lack of finances for a ministry occur because God's people are just not aware of the need? Why? (1 Cor. 16:1–3)

5. How can ministries share that need and encourage believers to give without seeming to be manipulative? (1 Cor. 16:1–3)

6. Who have been the people in your life who have "paved the way" for you by exhibiting personal loyalty to you and helping you make the right "contacts"? (1 Cor. 16:5–12)

7. Who should you be personally discipling or helping to find acceptance and ministry opportunities? Why? (1 Cor. 16:5–12)

8. Are you content to make plans and have God change them by circumstances or revelation? (1 Cor. 16:5–12)

9. When was the last time God intervened in your life and changed your plans? (1 Cor. 16:5–12)

10. What would you do if a mature spiritual leader "strongly urged" you to go somewhere or assume a ministry assignment that you didn't feel comfortable with? (1 Cor. 16:5–12)

11. If Paul were describing your life and ministry, what would he say about you? (1 Cor. 16:13–24)

Appendix: Illustrations, Outlines, and Sermon Starters

CHAPTER 1

Divisions in the Church (1 Cor. 1)

Even though believers are "all one in Christ Jesus" (Gal. 3:28), the local church often suffers from division. Why?

For one thing, we forget the calling we have in Christ (1 Cor. 1:2, 9, 24–29). It is only by God's grace that we have been called, and this fact should humble us and encourage us to love one another (John 15:17).

Another factor is our tendency to follow human leaders and develop a fan-club mentality. Christ died for us and lives to bless us, and He must have the preeminence.

A third factor is dependence on human wisdom and philosophies, of which there were many in Corinth. The world's wisdom had crept into the church, and it did not mix with the wisdom of God (Is. 8:20). Various theologies are the attempts of scholars to interpret the Word of God, but they are not the Word. Never allow them to be a cause of division.

—from Wiersbe, *With the Word*

CHAPTER 2

Wisdom and Power Go Together (1 Cor. 2)

Power (vv. 1–5). Paul did not imitate the itinerant teachers in Corinth who depended on their eloquence and intellectual brilliance. Paul's faith was in God, not in himself (Zech. 4:6). He wanted sinners to trust in Christ's power. You may think you lack ability to serve God, but God can turn your weakness into strength. The gospel still works (Rom. 1:16).

Wisdom (vv. 6–16). The Jews asked for demonstrations of power, and the

Greeks looked for wisdom, both of which are available in Jesus Christ (1 Cor. 1:24). A deeper wisdom of God is available for those who are mature (Heb. 5:12–14). Allow the Spirit of God to teach you about the Son of God from the Word of God, and grow up in Him.

Wisdom and power go together. They need each other, and they keep the Christian life balanced.

—from Wiersbe, *With the Word*

What About Judging All Things? (1 Cor. 2:15)

Paul's claim about judging all things (1 Cor. 2:15) sounds rather presumptuous. Is he urging believers to become moral policemen, passing judgment on everyone and everything around us?

Yes and no. Paul was challenging the spiritually immature believers at Corinth to grow up by applying spiritual discernment to the world around them. In this passage he mentions three categories of people:

1. *Natural* (2:14), those without Christ, still living in the lost condition in which they were born;
2. *Spiritual* (2:15), believers in Christ who have been born of the Spirit and in whom the Spirit of God lives and is producing growth; and
3. *Carnal* (3:1), believers who remain immature in the faith because they don't allow the Spirit to work in their lives.

Spiritual people "judge" all things that come their way (2:15) in the sense of scrutinizing, examining, and investigating spiritual value and implications. This is not something that we should do merely as individuals, but also corporately with other believers. For example, in the workplace Christians in various occupations need to band together to explore how the faith applies to particular vocations. By analyzing work situations in light of Scripture, we can discern what the issues are and how we might respond with Christlikeness.

"Judging all things" has nothing to do with damning others, but with recognizing and doing what God would want. Instead of pride, it calls for humility, since God will be the final Judge of everything we do (2 Cor. 5:10).

—from *Word in Life Study Bible*

CHAPTER 3

Maturing, Harvesting, Building, and Glorifying (1 Cor. 3)

Maturing (vv. 1–4). We never outgrow the nourishing milk of the Word (1 Pet. 2:2), but we cannot grow strong unless we also have the "solid food" (Heb.

5:12–14; Matt. 4:4). You grow by eating and exercising (1 Tim. 4:6–8), and it takes both. Age is no guarantee of spiritual maturity.

Harvesting (vv. 5–9). Everybody has a place in the Lord's harvest, and all are doing His work (John 4:34–38). There must be no competing or comparing, because the Lord alone recognizes the work and gives the reward. It makes no difference who the servant is as long as Jesus Christ is Lord of the harvest.

Building (vv. 10–17). Paul writes about the local church and the materials we put into it as we minister (Prov. 2:1–5; 3:13–15). Substituting human wisdom for God's Word means building with perishable materials that will burn up at the judgment seat of Christ.

Glorifying God (vv. 18–23). Because the Corinthian believers gloried in human teachers (1:12) and human wisdom, they robbed God of the glory that belonged to Him. "Let no one boast in men" is a command, not a suggestion.

—from Wiersbe, *With the Word*

How to Cure Divisions in the Church (1 Cor. 3:1–11)

The divisions in the church at Corinth had been caused by giving more devotion to the servants than to the Lord. This particular Corinthian problem continues to plague the church today. In every community there are Christians who are divided because of those who have a greater loyalty to one of God's servants than to that servant's Lord. The divided church is created by our forgetting that we are all servants and ministers of the one Lord and that both the field and the harvest are His.

When Paul's word is applied to us, it means that we are not only partners with everyone else who is at work in the church today but also with those who have gone before and those who will come after. Just as there ought not to be any sense of competition between fellow pastors, the same spirit ought to prevail with predecessors and successors. Churches are often hurt by leaders who are so anxious to make a name for themselves that they cannot appreciate and applaud the work that was done by those who preceded them. I was the seventh pastor of the church where I was serving as I began the writing of this commentary. My immediate predecessor was there for thirty-three years before retirement. His predecessor was the pastor for almost twenty years. God used those two men to buy land, build buildings, win people and develop them in service, and to create in the church a sense of mission.

Paul describes quite accurately the relationship when he says that different servants at different times do their particular task, but that the God who is their Lord continues to give the increase. The source of real unity among

Christian workers is that we are all servants of the same Master, and the source of unity in the whole church is that we are all products of God's grace. Since it is God who convicts of sin, convinces us of the truth of the gospel, and calls us to faith, then our greatest loyalty ought to be to Him and not to one of His servants, no matter how important a role that person may have played in the work of the church and in our lives.

Paul considered himself the wise master builder of the Corinthian church by virtue of his having begun the work there and having nurtured it during its first one and one-half years. He was there in advance of the first convert and had laid the very foundation of the church. But even as he began to write about the great care that needed to be exercised in building upon that foundation, he felt the need to remind the church what the foundation was Jesus Christ. The gospel that Paul had received and had preached to them was of Christ's death, burial, and resurrection (1 Cor. 15:1–5). And while the church might have a variety of builders and different materials, it had only one foundation and that was Jesus Christ. This was the church's real basis of unity then, and it remains so today.

—from Chafin, *1 & 2 Corinthians*

Who Gets the Credit? (1 Cor. 3:5–8)

Paul pointed out that the work of planting the church at Corinth was a joint venture between himself, Apollos, and the Lord (1 Cor. 3:5–8). Actually, many others were involved as well. But the point was that cooperation, not competition, is what God desires.

Paul was speaking about the start-up of a church, but the principles apply in the workplace as well. An attitude of competition worries about who gets the credit for success, which is really a selfish concern. By contrast, cooperative efforts over time generally result in achievements far greater than what any individual could do in isolation. That's because the skill, insight, and energy in an organization's work force have enormous potential. But that potential will never be realized if everyone's chief objective is to take credit for results.

Who gets the credit where you work? Do you promote cooperation toward mutual goals rather than competition between individual agendas?

—from *Word in Life Study Bible*

The Ultimate Performance Review (1 Cor. 3:9–15)

People often joke about standing before God and having their lives examined. But the picture Paul paints in 1 Corinthians 3:9–15 is anything but funny. He is dead serious about a day of accountability for believers. Most of us are familiar with performance reviews on the job. Paul describes the ultimate performance review—the moment when we stand before God and He evaluates the worth of our lives on the earth, not for salvation but for reward or loss.

Paul uses the image of metal being purified in a refining fire (1 Cor. 3:13–15). The fire burns away the worthless impurities, leaving only what is valuable. Based on the values set forth in many passages of Scripture, we can imagine the kinds of things that constitute "gold, silver, [and] precious stones": acts of charity and kindness; ethical decision-making; the pursuit of justice and fair play; keeping our word; courage and perseverance in the face of opposition and persecution; humility; communicating the message of Christ to coworkers; honoring our marriage vows; working diligently at the work God gives us; trusting God to keep His promises. Whatever is left when the fire burns down, Paul says, God will reward us for it (3:14).

Conversely, we can envision what sorts of "wood, hay, [and] straw" will burn up: the lies we've told; ways we may have cheated customers; abuse heaped on family and relatives; manipulation of situations to our advantage; selfishness of all kinds; the squandering of income on trivial luxuries; turning a deaf ear to the poor; damage allowed to our environment; the systems created to lock ourselves into power and lock others out; the arrogance of self-sufficiency; lack of faith.

When the smoke clears, what will be left of your life?

—from *Word in Life Study Bible*

CHAPTER 4

The Dimensions of Life (1 Cor. 4)

Life is *a stewardship*, so be faithful (vv. 1–5). We judge ourselves, and others judge us; but the final judge is the Lord. Live to please Him alone.

Life is *a gift*, so be humble (vv. 6–9). Your abilities and blessings came from God; you cannot take credit for them. They are God's gift to you, and your use of them is your gift to God. It is sinful to contrast various Christian workers (1 Cor. 1:12) because only God knows their hearts.

Life is *a battle*, so be courageous (vv. 9–13). If the apostles were the greatest Christians who ever lived, and they were filth and the scum of the earth, where did that leave the boasting Corinthians?

Life is *a school*, so be teachable (vv. 14–21). Paul saw himself as a father in the Lord who had to instruct and discipline his children. Our Father in heaven uses many hands and voices to teach us, and we must be willing pupils as we go through life.

—from *With the Word*

CHAPTER 5

Separation, Celebration, and Isolation (1 Cor. 5)

Separation (vv. 1–7). The background of the chapter is the Passover Feast (Ex. 12). The presence of the immoral man should have turned the feast into a funeral (v. 2), but the church was boasting about the sinner instead of weeping over him. Tolerating known sin in the church is like putting leaven into the Passover Feast: it does not belong.

Celebration (v. 8). Paul saw the Christian life as "keeping the feast" (v. 8), that is, feeding on Christ, being ready to move, and being sure we are not defiled by sin (leaven, yeast). The Lamb has set us free, and we are on our way to our promised inheritance.

Isolation (vv. 9–13). Sin in the life of the believer is far worse than sin in the life of an unbeliever. We cannot isolate ourselves from the world, but we can separate ourselves from disobedient believers so God can discipline them.

—from Wiersbe, *With the Word*

Guidelines for Redemptive Church Discipline (1 Cor. 5:1–13)

The contemporary church needs to salvage from this difficult experience of immorality within the Corinthian church some guidelines for a redemptive approach to church discipline. Three questions need to be raised.

First: *Does the action calling for discipline threaten the life and existence of the church itself?* Depending on the particular church, I can see where the answer could be "yes" in one situation and "no" in another. For example, in a small and new congregation that is trying to witness for Christ in a hostile environment, if one of its members is involved in immoral activities, the congregation may decide that a failure to take quick, decisive, and public action might cause the fragile organization to collapse if the offending member is not expelled from the church. On the other hand and under the same circumstances, an old and well-established church might choose first to have the minister or one of the lay officers of the church visit with the offending member and try to "redeem" him or her.

The second question: *Is there danger that the sinful act will infect the whole church?* This will always be a judgment call, but it is a good question and must be wrestled with. And it is a question a church must answer when it seeks to minister to persons who have experienced failure in some area of their lives. For example, when our church began to minister to people who had been in prison, I sensed there were those in the congregation who were fearful that it might look as if we condoned the actions of those who had broken the law. And when we started a special ministry to the formerly married, there were those who were concerned that we might be weakening our stand on marriage.

While such questions may have been born of fear, they are important as we also ask ourselves whether or not a particular activity would be harmful for the church as a whole. We decided that in these instances there was such a strong commitment to the Christian lifestyle in the congregation that our involvement in such ministries would not water down the church's witness. But we readily acknowledge that other churches might not be in a position to answer the way we did.

Third question: *Will allowing a specific activity to go on lessen the distinction between the church and the world?* This is a most difficult question because the very existence of the church in the world creates a climate for compromise. In the last verses of 1 Corinthians 5, Paul deals with a misunderstanding in the church on this particular point. Evidently he had written a letter on this issue which preceded 1 Corinthians because he clearly states, "I wrote to you in my epistle not to keep company with sexually immoral people" (v. 9). He made it clear that he was referring to immoral people within the church, not to nonbelievers in the world (v. 10).

On the surface, Paul's standard seems to suggest that we treat immoral lost people better than we treat immoral church members. But his point is consistent with the idea that we are not to judge the world, but we are responsible for the life of the church. We are to move about in the world without a judgmental or censorious attitude as stewards of the gospel. But in the church we are to impose upon ourselves a stern discipline so that our lives will not contradict the gospel we share.

—from Chafin, *1 & 2 Corinthians*

CHAPTER 6

Basic Truths of the Christian Life (1 Cor. 6)

Not only were the Corinthian believers compromising with the world, but they were also losing their testimony before the world by taking one another to court before pagan judges. Paul repeatedly asked, "Do you not know?" (vv. 2, 3, 15, 16, 19). They were ignorant of some basic truths of the Christian life.

We will judge angels (vv. 1–8). If God entrusts such a great a responsibility to His people, can't He help us with our petty decisions today?

We have been changed (vv. 9–12). We are not what we once were, so why should we live as we once lived? It is a matter not of "What is lawful?" but of "What is helpful?"

We belong to the Lord (vv. 13–20). He made the human body, He dwells in believers by His Spirit, and He purchased us at the Cross. The believer's body belongs to God and must be used to glorify Him.

-from Wiersbe, *With the Word*

What Controls You? (1 Cor. 6:12)

As Christians we live under grace, not law. We enjoy a certain freedom of choice and commitment. But Paul reminds us that our choices and commitments, while freely made, do not always bring freedom. Often they overpower us: we no longer possess our possessions—they possess us. We can be consumed by our jobs, our wealth, our houses, our hobbies, even our churches.

Are there any ways to manage this problem? Here are a few suggestions:
1. Determine your limits. What can you actually handle? What is realistic?
2. Let time go by before making decisions and commitments. Sooner or later you need to decide, but very few choices are better made sooner than later.
3. Pay attention to agreement or disagreement with your spouse and/or a close friend or associate. There is wisdom in mutual decision-making.
4. To manage the commitment you are taking on, what are you willing to give up? Taking on new responsibilities means trading one set of problems for another. Are you prepared for that?
5. Commit to giving away as well as taking on. That declares your freedom from the tyranny of things and responsibilities.

—from *Word in Life Study Bible*

CHAPTER 7

The Meanings of Marriage (1 Cor. 7)

Marriage is *a gift* (vv. 1–9), and not everybody has the same gift. Some people have more self-control than others. People remain unmarried for different reasons (Matt. 19:11–12), and each one must know the will of God.

Marriage is *a ministry* (vv. 10–16). Paul addressed people who had been converted after marriage and who wondered if they should remain with their unsaved spouses. "Yes," said Paul, "because you might win them to Christ." But even Christian spouses can have a wonderful ministry to each other as they grow in the Lord and love each other (Eph. 5:22ff.).

Marriage is *a calling* (vv. 17–24). When you become a Christian, that does not annul what you were before you trusted Christ. Jews are still Jews, slaves are still slaves, and married people are still married. But now, with the Lord's help, you can fulfill that calling in a greater way.

Marriage is *a challenge* (vv. 25–40). Paul does not deny the blessings of marriage, but he does remind us of the burdens that marriage brings, especially when the times are tough. Building a Christian home is a great ministry, but nobody should enter into it lightly or carelessly.

—from Wiersbe, *With the Word*

CHAPTER 8

Life, Conscience, and Knowledge (1 Cor. 8)

Life is controlled by conscience. Conscience is the judge within that commends us for doing right and condemns us for doing wrong (Rom. 2:14–15). If we sin against conscience, we do terrible damage to the inner person.

Conscience is strengthened by knowledge. As we grow in spiritual understanding, a weak conscience becomes stronger, and we appreciate our freedom in Christ more and more. The weak believer must not run ahead of his conscience, and the strong believer must never force him to do so.

Knowledge must be balanced by love. Your spiritual knowledge can be either a weapon to hurt people or a tool to build people. If your knowledge puffs you up, it will tear others down. Love knows when and how to yield to others without compromising the truth (review Rom. 14–15).

—from Wiersbe, *With the Word*

CHAPTER 9

Giving Up Our Rights (1 Cor. 9)

We do not have the right to give up our freedom, because that was purchased by Christ (Gal. 5:1); *but we do have the freedom to give up our rights.* For the sake of winning the lost (v. 12), Paul gave up his right to receive financial support, and he begged the Corinthians to give up their rights for the sake of the saved.

Christian ministry is like fighting a war, caring for a vineyard, tending a flock, and cultivating a field (vv. 7–11). Meditate on these images, and see what they teach you about serving the Lord.

Ministry is a stewardship (v. 17), and the servant must be faithful (1 Cor. 4:2). Ministers of Christ are also like runners who must keep the rules or be disqualified (vv. 24–27).

Verses 19–23 call for courtesy and wisdom in witness, not for compromise. "I have become all things to all men" does not mean Paul had no personal convictions. It means he used his convictions to build bridges, not walls. If he seemed inconsistent, it was only because people did not look deep enough. His one great desire was to win the lost, and that governed his every decision.

—from Wiersbe, *With the Word*

CHAPTER 10

How to Face Difficult Decisions (1 Cor. 10)

If you insist on using your rights, you may cause a weaker believer to stumble; and you may also bring trouble on yourself. When you face difficult decisions, take these elements into consideration.

God's blessing (vv. 1–5). The parallel to God's people today is obvious. We have been redeemed from the world, identified with Jesus Christ, and nourished by spiritual food and drink. But these blessings are no guarantee that we will be successful.

God's judgment (vv. 6–12). When Israel sinned, God disciplined them; and He will do the same to His people today. Do you practice and tolerate in your life any of the sins named here? God gives His children freedom, but the freedom to sin is not included.

God's promise (vv. 13–22). God knows how much we can take and always provides the way of escape. Sometimes the smartest thing to do is to flee (v. 14; 1 Cor. 6:18). Always look for the open door and the blessing on the other side.

God's glory (vv. 23–33). Two extremes must be avoided: practicing license in the name of Christian freedom, and being so fussy that we cannot live in a real world and make rational decisions. When you seek to edify others and glorify the Lord, you will know what to do.

—from Wiersbe, *With the Word*

Dealing with Trials and Temptations (1 Cor. 10:9–13)

1. *We need to be realistic both about the trials we must face and our own strength to resist.* "Let [the man] who thinks he stands take heed lest he fall" (v. 12) is a warning against unfounded pride and a call to be humble about our own spiritual strength. It is such an easy thing for Christians to make the enemies that we face seem like "straw men" who can be pushed aside easily with a verse of Scripture or a religious platitude, when actually they are powerful, persuasive, persistent opponents who often invade our minds and hearts and take us captive before we even know they are anywhere near.

The evil we face in life is a master at disguise and frequently changes the labels on things to confuse us. I've heard what God calls fornication redefined and referred to as being "sexually liberated," and I've watched Christians be seduced by a materialism so subtle that they had a religious feeling about it. One of the best defenses we have is to become realistic about the temptations of the world in which we live and to be honest about our own limited spiritual resources to resist.

2. *We need to realize that we are not exempt from trials.* Paul assured the Corinthians that "no temptation has overtaken you except such as is common to men" (v. 12). These words have assurance for two different groups. Those who feel that because they are Christians they will not have to face certain temptations are reminded that there are trials that are common to everyone. Paul alludes to this truth later when writing to the church at Philippi and says that he had been "thoroughly initiated into the human lot with all its ups and downs, fullness and hunger, plenty and want" (Phil. 4:12). This statement comes as a shock to all those who have felt that they had in their relationship with Christ an exemption to problems.

On the other hand, to people who are going through difficult times this passage is a source of assurance that they are not alone. Sometimes we are a bit paranoid about the suffering we go through, and we look around and get the feeling that everyone else is having it easy while we, alone, are having a hard time. This word is a reminder of the common lot we all share as human beings.

3. *We have two great words of assurance about our trials and temptations.* First, Paul told the Corinthians that God would set some limits on what He would allow to happen to them: God "will not allow you to be tempted beyond what you are able" (v. 13). There is in this statement the idea that is found in other places in the Bible that God knows us, our strengths and our weaknesses. This doesn't mean that we will never be overcome by evil but that our failures will not be the result of having more than we can handle. The great promise of this passage is that there is nothing any of us will face in life that will be so overwhelming but that if we turn to God He will help.

Second, Paul assures us that "with the temptation [He] will also make the way of escape, that you may be able to bear it" (v. 13). This promise is one that I have tested over and over and have found to be true. There have been times when I tried in my own strength to deal with problems and they became worse, but on every occasion that I have asked God for help He has given it.

—from Chafin, *1 & 2 Corinthians*

How to Deal with Temptation (1 Cor. 10:12–13)

Paul's warning to "take heed lest [you] fall" (1 Cor. 10:12) is as necessary today as it has ever been. For we, like all who have gone before us, are fallen, temptable, and subject to thinking and doing what is wrong. Few teachings of Scripture have more practical implications for day-to-day living.

Opportunities for temptation are almost endless. And since human nature is not getting any better, nor is any of us immune to the corrupted appetites of the flesh, we need to take Paul's warning seriously and watch out for temptation, or we will surely fall. Yet Scripture offers several alternatives for dealing with temptation as we find it:

1. We should *avoid* temptation whenever possible. Proverbs 4:14–15 urges us, "Do not enter the path of the wicked, and do not walk in the way of evil. Avoid it, do not travel on it." Often we know beforehand whether a certain set of circumstances is likely to lead to sin. Therefore, the obvious way to avoid sin is to avoid those circumstances. Paul described a "way of escape" from temptation (1 Cor. 10:13). Often the escape is to stay away from the place or the people where temptation lurks.

As believers, we can help others in this regard. We can avoid setting up situations that encourage people to do wrong. Teachers, for example, can help students avoid cheating by making assignments, giving tests, and communicating expectations in ways that reduce the need or incentive to cheat. Likewise, business owners and managers can devise procedures that don't needlessly place employees in a position where they might be tempted to steal cash, inventory, or equipment. It's not that a teacher or employer can't trust students or employees, but that no one can trust human nature to be immune from temptation.

2. We should *flee* from powerful temptations. Earlier in this letter, Paul warned the Corinthians to flee sexual immorality (6:18). Here he warned them to flee idolatry (10:14). Elsewhere he warned Timothy to flee the lust for material possessions and wealth (1 Tim. 6:9–11), as well as youthful lusts (2 Tim. 2:22). The message is clear: don't toy with temptation. Flee from it.

3. Chronic temptation is something we need to *confess* and offer to Christ, and ask for His cleansing work. Some temptations are powerful inner struggles, with thoughts and attitudes that graphically remind us of how fallen we really are. What should we do with that kind of temptation? Rather than deny it or try to repress it, we should bring it to Christ. He alone is capable of cleaning up the insides of our minds.

4. Finally, we must *resist* temptation until it leaves us. When Christ was tempted by the devil, He resisted until the devil went away (Matt. 4:1–11). James encouraged us to do the same (James 4:7). Resistance begins by bathing our minds with the Word of God and standing our ground. We have the promise, after all, that the temptations we experience will never go beyond the

common experiences of others, or beyond our ability to deal with them (1 Cor. 10:13). That is great news.

—from *Word in Life Study Bible*

CHAPTER 11

Questions to Ask About Worship (1 Cor. 11)

When it comes to sharing in public worship, we must ask ourselves some serious questions.

Do I dishonor authority (vv. 1–16)? We must be careful not to dishonor the Lord, no matter what the cultural standards may be. God has established headship in creation and in the church, and we must respect it.

Do I despise the church (vv. 17–22)? We are one in Christ and in love must honor one another. By the way they ate their love feast, the rich embarrassed the poor and brought shame on the church.

Do I discern the body (vv. 23–34)? When we meet to celebrate the Communion service, we must examine ourselves and not one another; and we must be honest with the Lord as we confess our sins. We discern His body in the bread, but we also discern it in the members of the church who eat with us. The Lord's Supper is a family feast. While it must be personal, it must not become so individual that it becomes selfish. It should be a means of promoting the unity of the church.

—from Wiersbe, *With the Word*

The Meaning of the Lord's Supper (1 Cor. 11:23–26)

1. *The Lord's Supper is rooted in history.* It was a certain man, the Lord Jesus, and it was a certain night, "the same night in which He was betrayed" (1 Cor. 11:23), and it was a certain event in which He took real bread and wine and instituted the sacred rite. The Passover meal that had preceded the Lord's Supper looked back in Israel's history to the event by which God delivered Israel out of the bondage of Egypt. The Lord's Supper at the time of its beginning looked forward to an event of deliverance for all mankind, Christ's death on the Cross and His Resurrection. At the Feast of the Passover it was traditional for a child to ask of his father, "Why is this night different from other nights?" and this would be the clue for the father to recount how God delivered Israel. Paul's explanation is an effort to remind the Corinthians of the historical roots of the sacred rite they were abusing.

2. *The Lord's Supper is about God's gift.* We catch the work of sacrifice in Christ's words, "This is My body which is broken for you." In this statement

He is identifying Himself with the Paschal Lamb, the lamb that was sacrificed in connection with the Passover. But we make a mistake if we interpret the admonition to "do this in remembrance of Me" (v. 24) as a call to remember only His death. We are to remember that His death brings life. But we are to remember His life and His teaching, His resurrection and the hope that it brings, and we are to remember His purpose in the world.

For many years I found participating in the Lord's Supper to be depressing. I never told anyone about it for fear that they would misunderstand me, but I never looked forward to the services in which we observed communion. I had the same feeling about some of the Holy Week services. There seemed to be almost a morbid preoccupation with man's sinfulness and Christ's death. I just couldn't understand why Christ wanted me to do something as a part of my worship that left me so glum. Then I realized that in the observance Christ wanted me to remember everything about Him—His love for me, His forgiveness, His purpose, His hope, His presence, and His power. It was only when my thoughts and my prayers connected with communion began to reach out to remember *everything* that I began to find myself cleansed and renewed by my participation.

3. *The Lord's Supper celebrates a new covenant.* The history of Israel was the story of a covenant that God initiated with them. It was a relationship in which He acted on their behalf and asked obedience from them in return. When Christ said, "This cup is the new covenant" (v. 25), He was announcing that He was entering into a relationship with those for whom He was to die upon the cross. We are more familiar in modern times with contracts than we are with covenants. Often when we buy a house or sell a house, borrow money, or take a job, we are asked to sign a contract. This means that we enter into an agreement according to the terms of the contract. Paul's reminder to his readers was that they had entered into a relationship with God through Jesus Christ that had demands connected with it.

4. *There is in the observing of the Lord's Supper a proclamation.* Christ had said to them that every time they took communion they "proclaim the Lord's death till He comes" (v. 26). This is a word of evangelism and also a word of hope. In this Supper, Christ gave the church another way of preaching the gospel, a way for the eyes to see as well as for the ears to hear.

One Sunday night I looked to the back of the sanctuary and saw a very large group of visitors who had come to the service from the International Seamen's Center located on the ship channel. Ships from all over the world docked there, and I realized that those who were visiting came from many different countries and in all probability were very limited in their understanding of English. To make matters even worse, it was the night on which a large part of the service was devoted to observing the Lord's Supper. Consequently, I was very surprised later when I received a letter from the chaplain who had brought them telling me how very meaningful the service had been to them. In the letter he told how their limited English had made it hard for them to understand my sermon, but that they were able to grasp clearly the symbolism of the Lord's Supper. As Christ had anticipated, they had followed the sermon with their eyes.

—from Chafin, *1 & 2 Corinthians*

CHAPTER 12

Some Truths About Spiritual Gifts (1 Cor. 12)
The Corinthian believers were especially gifted by God (1 Cor. 1:4–7), but some of them were creating problems by using their spiritual gifts in unspiritual ways. Paul reminded those people of three basic truths.

1. *There is one Lord* (vv. 1–11). The Spirit glorifies Christ (John 16:14), not Himself. The Spirit gives us gifts so we can serve Christ and His church "for the profit of all" (v. 7) and not for our own selfish enjoyment. Have you discovered what the Spirit has given you? Have you thanked God for it, and are you using your gift(s) under Christ's lordship?

2. *There is one body* (vv. 12–31). As members of the same body, we belong to one another, and we need one another. The believers you think you can do without may be the ones you need the most. We must minister to one another and care for one another as one body.

3. *There is one danger* (vv. 25). When a part of your physical body declares independence from the other parts, it starts to die and you have to visit the doctor. Division in the local church brings weakness and pain (1 Cor. 1:10–17) because no Christian can go it alone and be successful. Do you thank God for fellow Christians and seek to care for them?

—from Wiersbe, *With the Word*

CHAPTER 13

The Centrality of Love (1 Cor. 13)
This "hymn to love" was Paul's prescription for solving the sickness in the church body in Corinth. The believers had spiritual gifts, but they lacked spiritual graces and needed to be reminded why love is so important in the Christian life.

Love puts *quality into service* (vv. 1–3). When you have love, your words and actions amount to something and help other people.

Love also puts *maturity into character* (vv. 4–7). The Corinthians were impatient with one another, suing one another, tolerating sin in the church, and creating problems because they did not have love. Whatever qualities you may have, they are nothing without love.

Love puts *eternity into life* (vv. 8–13). Love lasts, and what love does will last. Love is the greatest and does the greatest because "God is love" (1 John 4:8).

—from Wiersbe, *With the Word*

Characteristics of Genuine Love (1 Cor. 13:1–13)

It is easy to recognize love by the way it acts. In several succinct phrases Paul defines this principle for relating to others that will transform all human life. He is not describing a natural human kind of love but that love which was defined by God's gift of Himself in Jesus Christ. As we look at each of the phrases, it becomes obvious that we are defining a style of life that is beyond our reach at a human level—something absolutely impossible unless God's Spirit dwells within us and helps us.

It will help in looking at each of these characteristics of love to recognize that they were being described to some Christians who were fighting among themselves. Paul was making an effort to show them a better way. These same enriching characteristics apply to our lives today.

To all those who are impatient with others Paul wrote, "Love suffers long" (v. 4). It doesn't give way to bitterness and wrath when evil is done but is very slow to anger. The emphasis is not so much a call to patience with circumstances as to *patience with people.* The positive side is that love "is kind" (v. 4). It's not merely passive; it is actively engaged in doing good to others. It's the picture of a person who spontaneously seeks the good for others and shows it with friendly acts.

Love is the best antidote there is for jealousy in that it "does not envy" (v. 4). People who have learned to love don't begrudge others their earthly goods, their positions, or their spiritual gifts.

Love does not "parade itself" nor is it "puffed up" (v. 4). That is, love creates a self-effacing stance rather than giving in to the temptation to assume an air of superiority. It protects us from having an inflated view of our own importance.

Love creates that kind of charm and winsomeness that keeps persons from behaving "rudely" (v. 5). Instead of practicing self-assertiveness, love makes us more tactful and polite. Love has a way of making us more concerned for the real needs of others and less preoccupied with our own rights. Not to be "provoked" means that when we love people we are good-natured and don't have temper tantrums or "fly off the handle." This makes us easier to live with.

When we are able to love, we don't store up or keep a record of the wrongs that have been done to us. One of the most destructive things couples do to each other is to keep track of the injuries or supposed injuries. I met a couple who had been married almost forty years who destroyed their relationship by writing down every wrong with the pencil of memory but never taking any off with the eraser of forgiveness and love.

To "think no evil" does not mean that no mean thought will ever come into your mind, but that you will learn to forgive and to forget the slights or imagined slights. There are many of us who would be much happier if we were able to close out some of the accounts of wrongs we have been keeping for too long. Love has a way of keeping us from enjoying it when bad things happen to others. Something perverse in human nature seems to make many people more anxious to hear the bad news than the good news. But those who really love do not "rejoice in iniquity" (v. 6). Rather, they are happy when the truth is known and acted upon and they have no desire to veil the truth, cover it up, or to edit it. They honestly "rejoice in the truth" (v. 6). Rather than being glad about the bad, those who love have a way of excusing the faults of others.

To say that love "believes all things" (v. 7) does not mean that it is gullible or unrealistic. But it does call for us to ascribe the best of motives to others and create a spirit of trust. Even when things are not looking good, love has a way of looking to God's future and seeing a better day. True love keeps us from being discouraged. The picture of "endures all things" (v. 7) is much more than passive endurance. Love allows us to remain true in the most adverse circumstances and even to transform the situation by the enduring.

When I hold this list of the characteristics of love up before my life like a mirror, I am immediately shaken by the many ways in which I fall short of the perfect love that Christ modeled for me. But I also know that nothing will be more important to my life than letting God perfect the gift of love in me, not in some abstract theological way but by helping me learn to truly love every person as God loves me.

—from Chafin, *1 & 2 Corinthians*

CHAPTER 14

Why Go to Church? (1 Cor. 14)

God's people assemble for one purpose: to worship God. They worship Him by their praying and singing (v. 15), teaching and preaching (v. 3). Worship should result in glory to God, blessing for God's people (v. 3), and fear and conviction for sinners (vv. 23–25).

But for these things to happen, Jesus Christ must be Lord of our lives, and we must yield to the Holy Spirit. If we come to church to display our spirituality, we will not only miss the blessing ourselves but also cause other people to miss the blessing. We come to honor Him.

A key word in this chapter is *edification* (vv. 3–5, 12, 17, 26), which means "building up." A worship service should lift up the Lord and build up the saints, not puff up the participants.

—from Wiersbe, *With the Word*

CHAPTER 15

Three Great Possessions of Believers (1 Cor. 15)

1. *We have a living Lord* (vv. 1–19). Jesus is alive, and the gospel message is true. Witnesses who saw Him have passed along their testimony to us. When you trust Him, you receive resurrection life, eternal life (John 5:24); death can hold you no more.

2. *We have a living hope* (vv. 20–49). Jesus Christ will come again, and the dead in Christ will be raised. We will have glorified bodies like Christ's body (1 John 3:1–3). Keep in mind that resurrection is not reconstruction. God does not reassemble the original body that has turned to dust. Like flowers and fruit from the planted seed, the glorified body is related to the "planted" body but different from it.

3. *We have a living dynamic* (vv. 50–58). We have no reason to give up because Jesus has conquered sin and death. If you really believe in the resurrection and return of Jesus, 1 Corinthians 15:58 will characterize your life. The best is yet to come, so let us give Him our best now.

—from Wiersbe, *With the Word*

CHAPTER 16

Expressions of Christian Love (1 Cor. 16)

Love for the needy (vv. 1–4). These instructions were about the offering Paul was taking up from the churches to help the needy believers in Judea (Rom. 15:25–27). The principles involved may be applied to Christian giving in general: our giving should be voluntary, in proportion to God's blessing, systematic, and handled honestly.

Love for leaders (vv. 5–12). We have the privilege of encouraging God's work as we pray for His servants. Even leaders like Paul, Timothy, and Apollos needed the help and encouragement of God's people. Are you praying for leaders?

Love for the church (vv. 13–18). Love, steadfastness, and submission make for a strong church. When you have people who are devoted to the work of the Lord, people who refresh you in the Lord, God will bless. What a joy to be a part of a church family that ministers in love.

Love for Christ (vv. 19–24). "O Lord, come!" is a prayer that reveals Paul's daily anticipation of the return of the Lord. When he made his plans (vv. 5–8), he included the blessed hope. Do you love Him and love His appearing (2 Tim. 4:8)?

—from Wiersbe, *With the Word*

Putting Money to Work (1 Cor. 16:1–4)

Money is powerful. It can bring out the best or the worst in a person. In our drive to gain lots of it or use it for personal comfort and convenience, we can become very cold and manipulative (1 Tim. 6:10). But that ought not to be the way for God's followers.

In 1 Corinthians 16, we see that Paul was coordinating a fund-raising drive to help some needy believers. He could have focused on the plight of the recipients. They were Christians in Jerusalem, perhaps suffering from persecution or famine. But instead he concentrated on how the Corinthians should initiate a regular pattern of giving to meet the need (1 Cor. 16:2). Their participation would be an act of loving worship as they met together on the first day of the week.

Paul also pointed out that the transfer of the funds would be carried out by responsible people chosen by the Corinthians themselves (16:3). That guaranteed accountability and integrity. Apparently Paul was quite realistic about the human tendency toward manipulation and greed.

How are you using your money to alleviate suffering and meet the needs of others?

—from *Word in Life Study Bible*

From Enemies to Family and Friends (1 Cor. 16:9–20)

Paul had once been a dangerous enemy to the followers of Christ. But his dramatic encounter with the Savior and subsequent change of heart brought him into the family of God (Acts 9:1–30). Courageous Christians such as Ananias (see Acts 9:10) and Barnabas (see Acts 4:36–37) began to nurture and aid the new believer. He had become a brother.

In the same way, Christ makes believers today into a new family. Having experienced the same gift from God—forgiveness and hope—we are now brothers and sisters in Christ.

Paul acknowledged several of his family of faith as he closed 1 Corinthians:

- *Young Timothy* (1 Cor. 16:10–11), who needed acceptance and affirmation.
- *Gifted Apollos* (16:12), one of the Corinthians' former leaders (1:12) who was unable to go to them at that time.
- *Stephanas* (16:15–16), baptized by Paul in the early days of the Corinthian church; the Corinthians needed to respect him.
- *Fortunatus and Achaicus* (16:17–18), encouragers of Paul who may have delivered to him the letter from the Corinthians that he was answering with 1 Corinthians; like Stephanas, they too needed recognition.
- *Priscilla and Aquila* (16:19), cofounders of the Corinthian work and business partners with Paul (Acts 18:1–4); they now were leading a similar work at Ephesus and sent warm greetings to their brothers and sisters across the "wine dark" Aegean Sea.

Once an enemy, Paul became a true friend, partner, and advocate of other believers. Just as others had once cared for him and his needs, he wrote to the Corinthians of the needs and concerns of his brothers and sisters in Christ.

Who are some of your friends in the faith? Who among them needs support or advocacy right now? To whom can you appeal on their behalf?

—from *Word in Life Study Bible*